EDITH WHARTON AND THE POLITICS OF RACE

Edith Wharton feared that the "ill-bred," foreign and poor would overwhelm what was known as the American native elite. Drawing on a range of turn-of-the-century social documents, unpublished archival material and Wharton's major novels, Jennie Kassanoff argues that a fuller appreciation of American culture and democracy becomes available through a sustained engagement with these controversial views. She pursues her theme through Wharton's spirited participation in a variety of turn-of-the-century discourses – from euthanasia and tourism to pragmatism and Native Americans – to produce a truly interdisciplinary study of this major American writer. Kassanoff locates Wharton squarely in the middle of the debates on race, class and democratic pluralism at the turn of the twentieth century. Drawing on diverse cultural materials, she offers close readings that will be of interest to scholars of American literature and culture.

JENNIE A. KASSANOFF is Associate Professor of English at Barnard College in New York. Her articles have appeared in *Arizona Quarterly* and *PMLA*.

T0381816

CAMBRIDGE STUDIES IN AMERICAN LITERATURE AND CULTURE

Recent books in this series

EDITH WHARTON AND THE POLITICS OF RACE

JENNIE A. KASSANOFF

CAMBRIDGE
UNIVERSITY PRESS

CAMBRIDGE UNIVERSITY PRESS
Cambridge, New York, Melbourne, Madrid, Cape Town, Singapore, São Paulo

Cambridge University Press
The Edinburgh Building, Cambridge CB2 8RU, UK

Published in the United States of America by Cambridge University Press, New York

www.cambridge.org
Information on this title: www.cambridge.org/9780521830898

First published 2004
Reprinted 2005, 2006
This digitally printed version 2008

A catalogue record for this publication is available from the British Library

ISBN 978-0-521-83089-8 hardback
ISBN 978-0-521-05103-3 paperback

For my parents
Dorothy Jane Spitzberg Kassanoff
and
Arnold Howard Kassanoff

and for
Dan

Contents

Acknowledgements

I felt that I was in great company and was glad.

Edith Wharton, 1934

This book focuses on one author, but it is not the study of one woman alone. Instead, it is an inquiry into the constellation of people, places, ideas and events that intersected to create the powerful writings of Edith Wharton. I find this approach eminently suited to my own situation, for in writing this book I have not been a single author. Rather, I have been at the crossroads of a dynamic group of teachers, friends, institutions and experiences that have alternately inspired, challenged, amused and enlightened me.

I have been the fortunate student of many extraordinary teachers. In my home town of Dallas, Texas, Christine Eastus and Ray Buchanan at the Greenhill School first introduced me to the pleasures and possibilities of literary and historical study. As an undergraduate at Harvard, I was privileged to work with Joseph A. Boone, Mary Carpentar, Sonya Michel and Henry Moses, each of whom instilled in me an enthusiasm for letters and learning. At Oxford, Kate Flint and John Bayley shared my interests in Edith Wharton, and encouraged me to "do New York." Their exemplary generosity of mind was pivotal to my own growth as scholar.

As a doctoral candidate at Princeton, I had the great good fortune to work with Maria Di Battista, Cathy N. Davidson, Diana Fuss, William Howarth, Michael McKeon, Earl Miner, Lee Mitchell, Andrew Ross, Brenda Silver and the late Lora Romero, each of whom modeled that important balance between innovative scholarship and caring pedagogy. I owe a particularly vibrant debt of thanks to Elaine Showalter, who has been an exemplary teacher, mentor and friend. Not only is Elaine a ground-breaking critic, a dynamic professor and a committed public intellectual, but she is also a superb matchmaker.

At Barnard and Columbia, I have found a dynamic and supportive group of friends and colleagues. I want to thank Rachel Adams, Jim Basker,

Elizabeth Dalton, Pat Denison, Peggy Ellsberg, Gretchen Gertzina, Mary Gordon, Maire Jaanus, Paula Loscocco, Monica Miller, Remington Patterson, Caryl Phillips, Cary Plotkin, Quandra Prettyman, Maura Spiegel, Timea Szell and Liz Weinstock for their companionship, encouragement and good humor. I am particularly indebted to my colleagues Christopher Baswell, Lisa Gordis, Ross Hamilton, Peter Platt, Anne Lake Prescott, Bill Sharpe, Herb Sloane, Margaret Vandenburg, and the members of the 1998 Willen Seminar in American Studies for their willingness to read portions of this book and for their many thoughtful and detailed suggestions along the way. My conversations with a number of colleagues and friends have considerably enriched my thinking about this project. Thanks to John Gruesser, Martha Hodes, Alan Price, Augusta Rohrbach, Carol Schaffer-Koros and Martin White for their interest and support. Finally, I would like to thank my students at Barnard and Columbia for perpetually keeping me on my toes. I am especially grateful to Rachel Abramowitz, Alice Boone, Emily McKenna and Taranee Wangsatorntanakhun for their expert research assistance.

Several institutions have provided crucial financial and scholarly support for this project. I wish to thank the Rotary Foundation of America, the English Department of Princeton University, Radcliffe College (now the Radcliffe Institute for Advanced Study at Harvard University), the American Philosophical Society, Barnard College, the Lilly Library of Indiana University, and the Gilder Lehrman Foundation for their generous funding. I would also like to thank the helpful archivists and librarians at the Beinecke Rare Book and Manuscript Library at Yale University, the Bodleian Library at Oxford University, the Butler Library at Columbia University, the Firestone Library at Princeton University, the Lilly Library at Indiana University, the Villa I Tatti of Harvard University and the Barnard College Library. Portions of this book have appeared elsewhere in earlier forms. Chapter 2 is reprinted by permission of the Regents of The University of Arizona from *Arizona Quarterly* 53.1 (1997). An earlier version of Chapter 1 appeared in *PMLA* 115 (Jan. 2000). Edith Wharton's unpublished letters and writings are reprinted here by permission of the Estate of Edith Wharton and the Watkins/Loomis Agency. I am grateful to the Yale Collection of American Literature, Beinecke Rare Book and Manuscript Library, Yale University, for permission to use their photograph of Edith Wharton for the cover of this book.

The readers and editors at Cambridge University Press have taken this project from mere manuscript to book. I have profited immensely from their suggestions, and I appreciate not only their keen eye for detail, but also their commitment to the broader outlines of this project. I wish, in particular, to thank Frances Brown for her meticulous and witty copy-editing, Jackie Warren for her care in shepherding a rookie through the process, Ray Ryan for his encouragement and ready support and Ross Posnock for his early interest in my work.

To Rita Bowen, John Lloyd Brown, Jonathan Cordell, Laura Fenster, Lola Mae Fields, Christine Fry, Patricia Krantz, Joyce MacDuff, Lynn McLanahan, Kevin O'Hare and Kyra Terrano I owe a profound and ongoing debt of thanks that they alone can fully appreciate. My friends Jessika Hegewisch Auerbach, Jonathan Auerbach, Dana Becker-Dunn, Brian Dunn and Astrid Guttmann have consistently made sure that I never lacked for a pinch-hitter research assistant, a well-timed glass of wine, a riotous onslaught of small children or a thoughtful friend. Thanks, you guys.

Finally, I would like to thank my family for the love, encouragement, patience and enthusiasm that have been my mainstay over the years. I am grateful to all of the Browns, Kassanoffs, Peretzs, Schulmans, Spitzbergs, Stones, Weinfelds, Wolfs and Woodcocks who have cheered me on, and who have even secretly read a Wharton novel or two – just to see what I was up to. Special thanks goes to my inner circle – Jim and Stephanie Kassanoff, Ben and Sharon Kassanoff, Jordan and Marla Kassanoff, Joel and Nancy Schulman, Logan Schulman and Ruth and Mel Schulman – whose love, wit and support have grounded me over the years. My grandmother, Florence Wolf Spitzberg Leonard has not only supported my love of learning, but has also made sure that the hair was always out of my eyes, and that my more controversial decisions were received with love – even when it meant opting for a Macintosh computer over a debut at the Tyler Texas Rose Festival. Above all, I want to thank my parents for their love and encouragement. They have been my proofreaders, cheerleaders, traveling companions, advisors and friends. I am more grateful to them than they will ever know.

Although this book is sorely lacking in the way of broom-flying wizards and underpant-clad superheroes, my children Molly Schulman and Jake Schulman have been my own sources of magic and courage. Their curiosity, energy and enthusiasm inform every page of this enterprise.

Finally, my deepest thanks go to Dan Schulman – my confidante, soulmate, jester and best friend. He alone knows the full measure of my love.

Introduction

The study of Edith Wharton's politics raises a number of challenges for the feminist scholar. Unlike Ezra Pound, whose conservatism has, in recent years, stimulated a wealth of critical controversy, Wharton's pedigree – her upbringing in a fashionable New York family of Dutch and English origin – has given many license to see her conservatism as a birthright, and her politics as less a site of deliberate forethought than a consequence of elite inheritance. Although Pound's dramatic espousal of "a virulently anti-democratic and elite egoism" has, in the words of Cary Wolfe, forced contemporary critics "*either* to bury *or* to praise" him, Wharton's conservatism, until now, has stimulated little critical attention (Wolfe 26). Indeed, many critics have taken a don't-ask-don't-tell approach to Wharton's conservatism. Even when her politics are faintly acknowledged, Frederick Wegener remarks, they tend to be "either neutrally presented and illustrated, or awkwardly defused, or reconceived on some more agreeable basis" ("Form" 134). In consequence, Wharton has become the May Welland of American letters. Like the genteel but underrated bride in *The Age of Innocence* (1920), she has been mistaken for a naïve and cosseted socialite, "so incapable of growth, that the world of her youth had fallen into pieces and rebuilt itself without her ever being conscious of the change" (Wharton, *The Age of Innocence* 290).

In a 1989 interview, R. W. B. and Nancy Lewis, the editors of Wharton's collected letters, were asked whether their editorial choices had been influenced by a desire "to protect Wharton in any way." The Lewises conceded that yes, on some level, their selections had been influenced by such factors. Recalling their publisher's warning that a letter with racist or anti-Semitic content "would over-shadow all the others in the media," they concluded that "it would be wrong to include an atypical letter that could distort the public view of Wharton" (Bendixen 1). However well intentioned, this protective impulse highlights a central and longstanding problem in Wharton criticism. Since 1921, when Vernon L. Parrington dismissed Wharton as a "literary aristocrat" who was preoccupied with "rich nobodies," Wharton's conservative politics have been treated as an obstacle to literary analysis (Parrington 153). According to Robert Morss Lovett, an early critic, Wharton's "conception of class [was] limited"; she was a writer for whom "The background of the human mass is barely perceptible through the high windows, and the immense rumor of the collective human voice is muffled by thick curtains" (Lovett 76). The complexities of American democratic politics had no place in such mannered settings. In the words of Irving Howe, "Mrs. Wharton had not a gift for the large and 'open' narrative forms . . . which in modern fiction have been employed to depict large areas of national experience" (4).

These assumptions bear witness to a widespread tendency in American criticism to oversimplify and patronize conservative politics. Among progressive literary critics in our own period, conservatism has been the straw man of choice, a flimsy opponent easily dismantled by the sophisticated instruments of liberal democratic thought. While recent scholars have readily probed the restive impulses that animate the socially oppositional writings of Mark Twain, W. E. B. DuBois, Stephen Crane and Nella Larsen, they have been less willing to acknowledge political and expressive complexity in the work of those whose ideas they do not share.

Edith Wharton forces us to confront a number of basic blind spots in American criticism. Her work calls into question some of our least contested assumptions about the relationship between social class, literary production and gender identity. If Wharton's politics have been understood as so innate that they do not warrant critical analysis, it is because this premise itself is grounded in a limited conception of gender and class. Such assumptions imply not only that the principles of American conservatism are always already self-evident, but also that a patrician woman would have no reason to mobilize her conservative ideology with the same deliberate forethought that we have come to expect from writers like Wyndham Lewis, George Santayana or Henry James. And the circumstances surrounding Wharton's re-entry into the American literary canon since the 1970s have only reinforced these impulses. Because renewed interest in Wharton criticism coincided with the ground-breaking impact of feminist scholarship, critics have been loathe to scrutinize her politics too closely. While Amy Kaplan and Nancy Bentley have discerningly acknowledged the role of class in such novels as *The House of Mirth* (1905) and *The Custom of the Country* (1913), other historically minded critics have all but ignored the cultural content of Wharton's major writings. Dale Bauer, for example, has argued that Wharton's early writings have "a strict preoccupation with form" – this despite Bauer's own richly interdisciplinary readings of Wharton's later fictions (xiii). Novels like *Ethan Frome* (1911) and *The Reef* (1912), Bauer insists, are best served by a "way of reading . . . first developed out of the New Critical model" (xii). In relegating Wharton's most widely read texts to the margins of cultural analysis, Bauer concurs with Walter Benn Michaels, who sweepingly claims in *Our Country* that "The major writers of the Progressive period – London, Dreiser, Wharton – were comparatively indifferent to questions of both racial and national identity."[1]

For her part, Wharton would have balked at the suggestion that her writings were immune to the dissonance of modern experience. Repeatedly rejecting the "kind of innocence . . . that seals the mind against imagination and the heart against experience," she condemned the impulse to police "the public view" of an artist as noxious (*Age of Innocence* 123). Early stories like "The Muse's Tragedy," "The Portrait" and "The Angel at the Grave" all register her cynical opinion of the reverential votary who scrupulously patrols the factitious image of some late great creative genius. From Wharton's standpoint, more interesting material lay in "regions perilous, dark and yet lit with mysterious fires, just outside the world of copy-book axioms, and the old obediences that were in my blood" (*A Backward Glance* 25).

Blood, I will show, is a central and complex Kate Chopin signifier in Wharton's work, as it is in the work of Pauline Hopkins, and William Faulkner. Profoundly invested in the interconnected logic of race, class and national identity, Wharton's early fiction articulates a host of early twentieth-century white patrician anxieties: that the ill-bred, the foreign and the poor would overwhelm the native elite; that American culture would fall victim to the "vulgar" tastes of the masses; and that the country's oligarchy would fail to reproduce itself and thereby commit "race suicide." In this regard, Wharton shared the turn of the century's expansive conception of race. Unlike today's observers, who often narrowly construe race as an exclusive matter of skin color, Wharton's generation applied the term liberally to a diverse array of possible identifications. Henry James, for example, noted in 1879 that Nathaniel Hawthorne was "by race of the clearest Puritan strain," while Thorstein Veblen, the sociologist and economist, confidently declared in 1899 that "canons of taste are race habits" (H. James, *Hawthorne* 12; Veblen 240). The settlement house pioneer Jane Addams embraced general humanity when she noted that "at least half of the race" was in need of social services; yet in nearly the same breath, Addams invoked specific notions of ethnicity and nationality when arguing that many disadvantaged Chicagoans were "held apart by differences of race and language" (Addams 98). As the novelist and historian Henry Adams dryly observed in 1918, despite the fact that "no one yet could tell [. . . him] what race was, or how it should be known," the concept itself was indispensable. Without race, Adams declared, "history was a nursery tale" (*Education* 411–12).

Despite its often ferociously reductive effects, race, as a causal agent in turn-of-the-century American social rhetoric, proved to have an expansive and curiously elastic range. This most disputed term could refer to anything from national origin, religious affiliation and aesthetic predilection, to geographic location, class membership and ancestral descent. In expressing her own concerns about America's future, Wharton drew freely on these protean possibilities. Although Wharton was not alone in making such claims (Henry Adams, Sarah Orne Jewett and Theodore Roosevelt expressed similar concerns), her unique position as a best-selling writer and a respected literary figure made her one of the most potent voices of her time. While Wharton could elicit passionate responses from everyday readers (as in the case of a woman who sent her a two-cent stamp and begged her to allow *The House of Mirth*'s Lily Bart to live happily ever after with Lawrence Selden), she could equally inspire the admiration of her highbrow literary peers (R. W. B. Lewis 152). T. S. Eliot, for one, declared Wharton "the satirist's satirist," while Pound solicited her to write for the *Little Review*.[2]

Wharton's readiness to engage in the heated cultural debates of her time may account for her diverse appeal. Her writings draw on a constellation of discourses, from the mundane to the sublime. She once remarked that "Every artist works, like the Gobelins weavers, on the wrong side of the tapestry" (*A Backward Glance* 197). In this sense, my methodology reveals my desire to take Wharton at her word – to follow her, that is, to the other side of the loom where the knotted and frayed cultural threads of her historical moment are interwoven. This study follows these discursive strands dialectically from their place within the text to their position outside of the work of fiction in order to formulate and explain their cumulative role within the novel itself. By taking Wharton's pre-war fiction as both my starting point and my destination, I examine not only the role of race and class in Wharton's fiction, but also the extent to which Wharton's writings registered and, in some instances, shaped the larger patterns of American cultural discourse in the early twentieth century.

In seeking to account for Wharton's conservative place within the framework of American politics and culture, I have been compelled to describe a political and historical position not my own. This necessity, however, has forced me to identify and defend certain core scholarly principles that my close engagement with Wharton's conservatism has brought to the fore. We need to evaluate Wharton's work on its own terms, unconstrained by either well-meaning protectionism or patronizing neglect. With this approach, we can better see how Wharton's resistance to popular culture and mass politics highlights not only the ongoing role of dissent in the United States, but also the unformulated and at times tenuous nature of America's multi-ethnic and multi-racial experiment. In seeking to critique and contain the *vox populi*, novels like *The House of Mirth* (1905) and *Summer* (1917) remind us afresh of the radical nature of the democratic project. Indeed, we ignore Wharton's conservative opinions at our own peril. By overlooking what we do not wish to see, we risk not only whitewashing the complexity of American cultural politics, but also underestimating the forceful arguments that drove writers like Edward Bellamy, Frances E. W. Harper, Upton Sinclair and Charlotte Perkins Gilman to respond.

I begin my exploration of this unfamiliar terrain by examining Wharton's role in the construction of certain basic American mythologies about race and national origin. "Invaders and Aborigines: playing Indian in the Land of Letters" examines Wharton's curious – and surprisingly various – comments on aboriginal identity. When *The Custom of the Country*'s Ralph Marvell identifies himself as an "aborigine" and his parvenu wife Undine as an "invader," he participates in a longstanding American practice of "playing Indian" that dates back to the Boston Tea Party. Although by the early twentieth century Native Americans had become synonymous with anti-modern simplicity and indigenous authenticity in the minds of many Americans of white European descent, the practice of masquerading as an Indian revealed the opposite possibility – that American identity was nothing more than a minstrel act. In a nation whose equivocal origins were mired in the indeterminacies of colonialism, slavery and western expansion, the danger of confusing an imitative identity with the real thing had a peculiarly visceral import. Wharton responded to the possibilities of racial and ethnic hybridity by forging a racial aesthetic – a theory of language and literature that encoded a deeply conservative, and indeed essentialist, model of American citizenship. If her native land generously welcomed the world's huddled masses, then the novel, under Wharton's neo-nativist laws of "pure English" and her colonial determination to suppress "pure anarchy in fiction," formed an architectural, aesthetic and political bulwark against the menacing possibilities of democratic pluralism (*The Writing of Fiction* 14).

Wharton puts this racial aesthetic into literary practice in *The House of Mirth*, her first best-selling novel. Faced with imminent Anglo-Saxon doom, Lily Bart sacrifices herself on the altar of racial purity and eugenic perfection. Chapter 2 examines how Lily's aestheticized decline functions as both a tragic extinguishment and a demographic climax: Lily's death, I suggest, simultaneously marks the annihilation of a rare, endangered species, and a stylized act of preservation. Wharton's heroine becomes a version of Carl Akeley's idealized taxidermic *tableaux* in the American Museum of Natural

History. Captured and immobilized at the peak of racial achievement, she embodies a stylized alternative to a slow decline in New York's competitive racial wilderness.

Like *The House of Mirth*, its successor, *The Fruit of the Tree* (1907), circulates around the prone, immobilized body of an elite American woman. After a paralyzing equestrian accident, Bessy Amherst, a wealthy mill heiress, falls prey to the impassive mechanisms of modern medicine. Her comatose body, plied with repeated rounds of stimulants and narcotics, incarnates what, for Wharton, was the nightmarish loss of upper-class agency. In this sense, *The Fruit of the Tree*, the subject of chapter 3, explores the threat posed by machine culture to the traditions of class entitlement. Only a merciful act of euthanasia at the hands of a well-meaning and well-born nurse can restore Bessy's imperiled agency. In marked contrast to Mattie Silver, the working-class victim of *Ethan Frome*'s climactic sledding accident, Bessy escapes the torture of a living death only through a singular act of elite compassion.

If technology represented one threat to elite hegemony, then changing sexual mores at the turn of the century posed another. In chapter 4, I suggest that sexuality effectively democratized the Victorian body by subordinating the mind's authority to the commonplace impulses of passion. Sex, according to Wharton, put all Americans on a common plane, blurring distinctions of race and class. In *The Reef* (1912), Wharton explores the relationship between the body human and the body politic, between the "regions perilous" of sexual desire and the "unmapped region outside the pale of the usual," where the country's other half dwelled (*A Backward Glance* 25). In likening her heroine's sexual awakening to a working-class rebellion, Wharton shows how sexuality can topple the sacred abstractions of the genteel tradition by unleashing the unwieldy chaos of direct experience. In this respect, *The Reef* marks Wharton's most immediate engagement with the pragmatism of William James. Sophy Viner, the novel's disruptive American governess, wreaks havoc on the codes of class and race by having an affair with her employer's fiancé. Like the *H.M.S. Titanic*, which sank into the North Atlantic several months before the novel was published, *The Reef* explores a comparable emotional shipwreck. Submerging class distinctions in the turbid waters of direct experience, sexuality threatens to sink everyone into a disastrously erotic democracy.

With the violent arrival of World War I, Wharton was forced to rethink her brief flirtation with democracy. If *The Reef* revealed the egalitarian temptations of pure sensation, then *Summer* marked the revival of Wharton's most austere brand of conservatism. As she toured the battle lines near Verdun, she saw countless French dwellings reduced to rubble, their private interiors brutally exposed to the pitiless sky. For Wharton, the shattered privacy of the roofless house came to epitomize the war's uncanny havoc. As I suggest in chapter 5, *Summer* represents Wharton's concerted effort to restore Europe's wartime refugees, and indeed America itself, to the conservative rites and rituals of the racially homogenous "old home." By engaging a number of contemporary discourses – from tourism and philanthropy to abortion and incest – *Summer* proposes a strategy of cultural containment and racial restoration that seeks to repair the fissures wrought by modern democracy.

In the years following the war, Wharton was forced to acknowledge the failure of the recuperative strategy she had explored in *Summer*. If *The House of Mirth* marked a monumental act of historic preservation, then *The Age of Innocence*, its Pulitzer Prize-winning successor, conceded the inevitability of elite defeat. As the novel's adulterous lovers gaze at Louis di Cesnola's Cypriot antiquities in the Metropolitan Museum of Art, they simultaneously recognize the hopelessness of their unconsummated passion and the transience of America's vanishing aristocracy. Someday, Ellen Olenska speculates, Old New York will similarly be the stuff of an antiquarian's collection, its obsolete artifacts labeled "Use unknown" (258). Despite its nostalgic poignancy, this moment, I argue in the coda, is a quintessentially American one. Despite the lovers' appeal to the museum's cultural authority, by the 1880s the Metropolitan had itself become a locus of controversy and debate. Rumor had it that Cesnola's artifacts were fakes. Their display in the gallery set off a public commotion that was followed, in turn, by a dramatic trial.

As her quiet allusions to the Cesnola controversy would seem to suggest, Wharton deplored the instability of American identity. Railing against the country's hybrid origins, she formulated a critique of American democracy that was as complicated as it was conservative. In exploring a number of strategies to contain what she saw as the pluralist excesses of American life, however, Wharton inadvertently profited from the cultural diversity she was determined to resist. In drawing on the considerable cultural resources of American popular discourse, Wharton gave her own fiction a hybrid force that could withstand and even countermand the limiting hauteur of her message. This pluralism, while a keen source of Whartonian anxiety, remains of palpable concern for scholars today. By limiting the range of critical inquiry, contemporary critics risk reifying a progressive genealogy that celebrates the pursuit of diversity, while – ironically – marginalizing its diverse opponents. To engage the complex conservatism of Edith Wharton is to take a step toward addressing this problem by confronting American pluralism in *all* of its manifestations.

CHAPTER I

Invaders and Aborigines: playing Indian in the Land of Letters

Edith Wharton's 1934 memoir, *A Backward Glance,* begins on a curious note of historical rupture. Recalling the New York birthplace of her father, George Frederic Jones, Wharton describes a "pretty country house with classic pilasters and balustraded roof" on land that eventually became East Eighty-first Street. Although the original dwelling has long since disappeared, an heirloom print shows a columned residence with "a low-studded log-cabin adjoining it under the elms" (17). According to family legend, the rustic cabin was actually the "aboriginal Jones habitation," and its colonnaded neighbor a later addition. Wharton, however, doubts the veracity of this account. The log cabin was not, in all likelihood, the family's ancestral seat, she remarks; it was "more probably the slaves' quarters" (18).

The rapidity with which this picture of Yankee self-reliance dissolves into its uncanny double – a repressed portrait of African enslavement – is as breathtaking as it is blunt. For all of its Lincolnian connotations, the Jones log cabin inexorably betrays the system of forced servitude that sustained the Jones family's economic, social and political ascent.[1] Indeed, Wharton's account betrays what Susan Scheckel calls "the fundamental ambivalences of American national identity . . . the deep ambivalence of a nation founded on the conceptual assertion of natural right and the actual denial of . . . natural rights" to Indians, African Americans and women (14). Despite the prescient observation of Mariana Griswold van Rensselaer, a nineteenth-century critic who remarked that "nothing . . . save the wigwam of the North and the pueblo of the South" could be a truly American home (19), Wharton craved a site of political, social and racial legitimacy that could offset the country's hybrid, disingenuous origins. Unlike France, the country of Wharton's "chosen peoplehood," America was Europe's derivative step-child, itself both a subject and an agent of domestic conquest (Sollors 128). This dichotomy was vividly encoded in the Jones home, whose classic pilasters testified to its share in "the great general inheritance of Western culture," and whose slave quarters bore witness to the moral ambiguity and racial pluralism of American origins (*French Ways* 96).[2]

Wharton's preoccupation with her country's beginnings were symptomatic of a wider set of anxieties at the turn of the twentieth century. At a time when even Warren G. Harding, then candidate for President, was rumored to have "black blood," America's fixation on the lurking possibility of "invisible blackness" made race a site of national hysteria (Williamson 106). As Eric Sundquist notes, by the mid-1890s America had begun its headlong "rush toward racial extremism in law, in science, and in literature." By abridging the equal protection guarantees afforded under the Constitution, state and federal courts sought to "render the African American population invisible or, what was more fantastic, to define color itself not by optical laws but by tendentious genetic theories that reached metaphysically into a lost ancestral world" (228). The "crisis in the loss of distinction" that ensued is evident in a letter from Wharton to her editor at Charles Scribner's Sons, William Crary Brownell, in 1902 (Sundquist 259). Admitting that she "hate[d] to be photographed because the results are so trying to my vanity," Wharton nonetheless agreed to have a new publicity photograph taken. "I would do anything to obliterate the Creole lady who has been masquerading in the papers under my name for the last year."[3] The comment is at once self-mocking and oddly self-defining. Wharton no doubt realized that the very methods of mass production that had made her first novel, *The Valley of Decision*, a popular success in 1902 were spawning a culture of imitation, replication and deception. Photography offered a particularly vivid locus for this concern. Summarizing nineteenth-century uncertainties about photography, Miles Orvell asks, could "the camera – a mechanical instrument – . . . deliver a picture of reality that was truthful," and if so, "what was a 'truthful' picture of reality?" (85). What truth did the Creole lady express? As a photograph put to the service of advertising and publicity, was it not doubly suspect, evoking the "carnivalesque tradition" that, T. J. Jackson Lears suggests, "subverted unified meaning and promoted the pursuit of success through persuasion, theatricality, and outright trickery"? (*Fables* 212). The Creole lady, however, embodies additional instability within the discourse of race. As P. Gabrielle Foreman has observed, while the camera was touted "as an antidote to illusion in an increasingly unstable and unreadable mid-century America," photography "also heightened 'the problem of racial discernment'" by challenging viewers' assumptions about the phenotypic status of light-skinned African Americans in photographs of the period (528). The Scribner's publicity shot had effectively transformed Wharton into an imitation white woman.

Undermining the guarantees of personal authenticity, mechanical reproduction transformed race into just another variable in the changeful algebra
of modernity.

Wharton found that American origins, like her own publicity photograph, were mired in a system of similarly fallible signs. Despite her longing for a more "subtle way of . . . indicating, allusively, [a nation's] racial
point of view" (*Uncollected Critical Writings* 92), these distinctions in the
United States were difficult, if not impossible, to make. After all, America
was a country in which a genteel family's "aboriginal habitation" could be
mistaken for the slave quarters. Under such circumstances, national origins
were uncertain at best.

Wharton saw her native land as "a world without traditions, without reverence, without stability," a "whirling background of experiment" incom-
patible with racial purity. Like the declining New England town at the
center of Wharton's 1908 short story "The Pretext," Yankee life was disappearing and taking its quaintly "inflexible aversions and condemnations"
with it. Villages like Wentworth, and other "little expiring centers of prej-
udice and precedent [made] an irresistible appeal to those instincts for
which a democracy has neglected to provide" (Wharton, *The Hermit and
the Wild Woman* 152). America's accommodating welcome to immigrants,
workers, feminists and newly minted millionaires had put an end to Yankee
rule. In the wake of the wildcat railroad strikes of 1877, the Haymarket
Square bombing in 1886, and the assassination of William McKinley by a
self-proclaimed anarchist in 1901, genteel Americans grew increasingly convinced that America was becoming "a society unhinged" (Wiebe 78). Josiah
Strong, a popular minister of the day, saw the "urban menace . . . multiplying
and focalizing the elements of anarchy and destruction" (qtd. in Boyer 131).
Looking down from his perch high above "the turmoil of Fifth Avenue,"
Henry Adams likewise compared New York to "Rome, under Diocletian."
One was aware of "the anarchy, conscious of the compulsion, eager for the
solution, but unable to conceive whence the next impulse was to come or
how it was to act" (*Education* 499–500). Rupture – not connection – was
to be the twentieth century's characteristic gesture. With the arrival of the
year 1900, "a new universe" had been born – one "which had no common
scale of measurement with the old." In this "supersensual world," Adams
could measure "nothing except by chance collisions of movements imperceptible to his senses, perhaps even imperceptible to his instruments, but
perceptible to each other" (*Education* 381–2). The scale, the pace and the
reach of modern America defied causal sequences; predictable trajectories
that had formerly connected origin to issue, and theory to practice, now

seemed irrevocably broken. As a result, formerly powerful elites, outspent and outvoted, cast about for a new source of self-justification. Gone was the "egalitarian vision of citizenship" that, according to Eric Foner, had been one of the legacies of the Civil War. In its place, Americans found themselves gravitating toward "definitions of American freedom based on race" (Foner, *Story* 131). Race became the essentialist axis orienting the patriciate's nostalgia for civic cohesion, social exclusivity and oligarchic permanence.

DEMOCRACY AND ITS DISCONTENTS: *THE VALLEY OF DECISION*

Like Josiah Strong and Henry Adams, Wharton saw early twentieth-century America as a "floundering monster" (*Backward Glance* 379). Her countrymen, she said, lacked the "blind sense in the blood of its old racial power" (*Motor-Flight* 178), for they had learned from their English forebears to "flout tradition and break away from their own great inheritance" (*French Ways* 97). *The Valley of Decision* captures this sense of loss and distress. Though ostensibly a historical romance set in eighteenth-century Italy, *The Valley* is in fact a sustained meditation on America itself. Despite Henry James's famous plea that Wharton turn her attention to "the *American subject*" – "DO NEW YORK!" – *The Valley* is a profoundly American book (Powers 34). The novel chronicles the rise and fall of Odo Valsecca, a reform-minded aristocrat whose reign over the northern duchy of Pianura collapses with the invasion of Napolean's troops and the unleashing of anarchy and class warfare. Suspended precariously between two historical epochs, Italy and the United States both face a comparable choice: should they align themselves with the decadent gentry, or embrace instead the forces of mass culture and revolutionary democracy?

It was a choice with which Wharton was all too familiar. Like Fulvia Vivaldi, *The Valley*'s intellectual heroine, Wharton saw herself the "child of a new era, of the universal reaction against the falseness and egotism of the old social code" (*Valley* 2: 217). On the one hand, she deplored the political apathy that had prevented her own immediate ancestors from playing a more significant role in affairs of state; on the other hand, however, she scrupled at embracing a future that seemed so unlike her own genteel past. *The Valley of Decision* explores this dilemma. Like the United States, Wharton's Italy is a "topsy-turvy land" whose aristocracy is soft and complacent, whose proletariat is explosive, and whose ascendant mercantile class is distinctly untrustworthy (1: 148). A "fat commercial dulness" pervades both countries, obstructing the development of "personal distinction which justifies magnificence" (2: 12). Mired in self-satisfaction, modern America wants "*a tragedy with a happy ending*," while eighteenth-century Italy "does not want tragedies – she wishes to be sung to, danced to, made eyes at, flattered and amused . . . anything that shall help her to forget her own abasement" (*French Ways* 65; *Valley* 1: 100).

An apathetic generation of leaders in both countries is responsible for the present predicament. Wharton frequently complained that her Knicker-bocker forebears were guilty of an "instinctive shrinking from responsi-bility" (*Backward Glance* 22). Despite their stately European origins, the "elders" of her New York youth had "[preached] down every sort of ini-tiative," a fact that Wharton found bewildering: "I have often wondered at such lassitude in the descendants of the men who first cleared a place for themselves in a new world, and then fought for the right to be masters there. What had become of the spirit of the pioneers and the revolution-aries?" Wharton could only speculate that "the very violence of their effort had caused it to exhaust itself in the next generation, or the too great pros-perity succeeding on almost unexampled hardships had produced, if not inertia, at least indifference in all matters except business or family affairs" (*Backward Glance* 55–6). Her own cohort of upper-class Americans had, unfortunately, inherited this apathy. In the words of Van Wyck Brooks, the elites of Wharton's generation were "the intellectual children of men who had ceased to believe in the country, who had no faith whatever in their place and their time" (450).

Wharton's grim appraisal of Old New York mirrors her gloomy depic-tion of Italy's "Old Order." Despite the "fighting blood" that Odo has supposedly inherited from his "rude Piedmontese stock" (*Valley* 1: 4), a "fatal lethargy . . . hung upon his race."[4] He depends almost entirely on the fortitude and conviction of his enlightened lover, Fulvia, for "[o]nly a woman's convictions, nourished on sentiment and self-sacrifice, could burn with that clear unwavering flame: his own beliefs were at the mercy of every wind of doubt or ingratitude that blew across his unsheltered sensibilities" (2: 182). Despite the fact that Fulvia exhorts him to "redeem the credit of his house," Odo vacillates (2: 139). When an angry throng later assassinates his high-minded lover, the feeble Duke loses what is left of his resolve. His enlightened theories cannot withstand the irrational impulses of the mob, and Odo himself cannot fight "the battle of ideas against passions, of reflection against instinct" (2: 262).

By dialectically equating political anarchy with unrestrained sexual desire, and the corrupt body politic with the sexualized body human, *The Valley of Decision* depicts the French Revolution as the barbarous result of the unfettered political id.[5] Unanimity, duty and social hierarchy give way to an unholy alliance of individualism, multiplicity and desire. Like Cantapresto, Odo's castrato manservant, whose sexual indeterminacy mirrors his political duplicity when spying on behalf of his master's enemies, Odo's predecessor to the throne creates civic instability by pursuing a homoerotic affair. Ignoring his Duchess, he turns his attentions instead to "the young Marquess of Cerveno, . . . a pale boy scented with musk and painted like a comedian, whom his Highness would never suffer away from him."[6] Not only does sexual license trigger revolution, however, but also democracy catalyzes sex. Thus, as the geographic epicenter of sexual activity in the novel, Venice is the city where "the mask [levels] all classes and [permits . . .] an equality of intercourse undreamed of in other cities" (2: 54). Odo and Fulvia discover that "every gondola [hides] an intrigue, the patrician's tabarro concealed a noble lady, the feminine hood and cloak a young spark bent on mystification, the friar's habit a man of pleasure and the nun's veil a lady of the town" (2: 60).

Because Wharton aligns unchecked sexuality with political anarchy, she finds it difficult to reconcile personal fulfillment with the public good. When Odo weds his predecessor's widow, thereby ensuring Pianura's political continuity, Fulvia must choose between "personal scruple" and the atomizing eroticism of an adulterous affair with her now married lover.[7] Despite her shaky conviction that, as Odo's mistress, she will have an "unlimited . . . power for good," Fulvia eventually falls victim to the public revolutionary forces that she has privately unleashed.[8]

In this respect, the French invasion plays out the novel's sexual fears on a geopolitical scale. After Napoleon's troops invade the Italian peninsula, "All the repressed passions which civilization had sought, however imperfectly, to curb, stalked abroad destructive as flood and fire. The great generation of the Encyclopædists had passed away, and the teachings of Rousseau had prevailed over those of Montesquieu and Voltaire" (2: 299). The Napoleonic invasion liberates the basest instincts of the "drunken mob" (2: 300), forcing Odo to admit that "all the old defences were falling": "Religion, monarchy, law, were sucked down into the whirlpool of liberated passions. Across the sanguinary scene passed, like a mocking ghost, the philosophers' vision of the perfectability of man. Man was free at last – freer than his would-be liberators had ever dreamed of making him – and he used his freedom like a beast" (2: 303). Political revolution becomes a force of sexual anarchy, while sexuality unleashes political revolution. Like the "fantastic procession of human races" that exceeds the borders of an ornate fresco in one of the novel's sumptuous Venetian ballrooms, a riot of sensual exoticism threatens to efface national and racial order. The fresco's "alien subjects of the sun" – "a fur-clad Laplander, a turbaned figure on a dromedary, a blackamoor and a plumed American Indian" – break out of the otherwise stylized parade (2: 48). Racial order can no more contain "the genius of Pleasure" than can the formal contours of the fresco's racial taxonomy compete with the bacchanalian possibilities of Wharton's orientalism. Pluralism vanquishes order, as "the sound and fury of the [revolutionary] demagogues" drown out the single voice. Under French occupation, Italy becomes "a very Babel of tongues" (2: 300).

Blinded by his own *volk*-ish aesthetic, Odo stands helplessly by as the French Revolution fragments Europe into a miscellany of "private ambitions and petty jealousies" (2: 305). He cannot understand the proletarian self-interest or the pluralist vitality that fuels the rebellion. To him, "the people" must be citizens of an idealized, pre-modern community, "tillers and weavers and vine-dressers, obscure servants of a wasteful greatness": "theirs had been the blood that renewed the exhausted veins of their rulers, through generation after generation of dumb labor and privation . . . Every flower in the ducal gardens, every picture on the palace walls, every honor in the ancient annals of the house, had been planted, paid for, fought for by the people" (2: 138). Because Odo believes that the burdens of the people are always transparent to their empathetic rulers, he thinks it "better to march in their ranks, endure with them, fight with them, fall with them, than to miss the great enveloping sense of brotherhood that turned defeat into victory."[9]

It is thus with some astonishment that Odo acknowledges the possibility that Pianura's workers have interests and desires other than his own. When a "brooding cloud of people" murders Fulvia as she is about to receive her doctoral degree, Odo's outlook undergoes a dramatic shift: no longer stylized peasants, the people become instead "his enemies [. . . and] he felt the warm hate in his veins" (2: 288). His subjects become a "terrible unknown people" who use their freedom like beasts. In this, Odo's disillusionment mirrors Wharton's own. If a progressive duke cannot prevent the "emissaries of the new France [. . . from] swarming across the Alps," Wharton seems to be suggesting, then surely her own tribe of listless New Yorkers cannot be expected to stanch the flood of immigrants or to slow the pace of social mobility in her native land (2: 304). As the Brahmin art historian Charles Eliot Norton pessimistically asked in 1888, could America impart "the highest results attained by the civilization of the past" to its common folk so that "all advantages shall be more equally shared"? Or would "the establishment of more democratic forms of society" inevitably "involve a loss"?

(Norton 313). These questions weighed heavily in the minds of northeastern elites who feared that the "Anglo-Saxon house of liberty" would topple under the weight of the country's sundry new inhabitants (Herman 180). Summing up these patrician anxieties, Arthur Herman asks, "what if the character of succeeding owners was drastically and catastrophically different from that of the original builders? What if the customs and habits needed to maintain as well as build that house of liberty depended on certain inborn instincts, which only those of Anglo-Saxon descent could bring to bear?"[10]

The Valley of Decision gives full voice to these anxieties. When Pianura collapses, judgment gives way to impulse, genteel restraint to unbridled passion and social hierarchy to mob rule. "[T]he multitude had risen – that multitude which no man could number, which even the demagogues who ranted in its name had never seriously reckoned with – that dim grovelling indistinguishable mass on which the whole social structure rested."[11] Like Napoleon's "eighteenth-century demogogues," America's striking workers and middle-class materialists were leveling a complex cultural edifice, and replacing "real men, unequal, unmanageable, and unlike each other" with a "hollow unreality" ingenuously labeled "Man" (*Uncollected* 155–6).

Despite its title, *The Valley of Decision* is a tale of vacillation and failure. Because they fail to implement their airy notions of the public good, the novel's elite activists are defeated by the popular insurgents from France. In the end, Odo's irritating impotence only invites anarchy and chaos. The Revolution's "new principles" are not "those for which he had striven. The goddess of the new worship was but a bloody Mænad who had borrowed the attributes of freedom. He could not bow the knee in such a charnel-house" (*Valley* 2: 305). In his quest to oversee "the formation of a new spirit," Odo foolishly armed "inexperienced hands with untried weapons" and thereby met a Mosaic fate, "destroy[ing] one world without surviving to create another" (1: 147, 91). In liberating "individual passions," his reforms blind the novel's restive democrats to the broader "needs of the race" (2: 217).

Odo inevitably succumbs to what Herman calls "racial pessimism" (180–1). Retrenching, he abandons his democratic theories and decides that the "real" state is the abstract fruit of hereditary precedent and not the result of direct social action. The nation, according to this revised vision, should be "the gradual and heterogeneous product of remote social conditions, wherein every seeming inconsistency had its roots in some bygone need, and the character of each class, its special passions, ignorances and prejudices, was the sum total of influences so ingrown and inveterate that they had become a law of thought" (2: 292). By aligning civic order with an ingrained "law of thought," Odo blurs the distinction between social custom and legislative decree, thereby distorting the difference between class and race. To borrow Sollors's pertinent formulation, Odo articulates "dissent" by "falling back on myths of descent" (6).

Near *The Valley of Decision*'s conclusion, Odo stages a final, futile feint of resistance. Acknowledging that "old associations" are "dragging [him] back to the beliefs and traditions of his caste," he vows that "If his people would not follow him against France he could still march against her alone" (*Valley* 2: 308, 307). Like the cowboy hero of Owen Wister's 1902 novel *The Virginian*, Odo stares the opposition down, rebuffing the rebel leader's final offer of "more power than you every dreamed of possessing." "Do not waste such poor bribes on me," the deposed Duke sneers. "I care for no power more but the power to wipe out the work of these last years. Failing that, I want nothing that you or any other man can give me" (2: 308–9). With these words, Odo rides off alone on horseback in true cowboy style, "away toward Piedmont" (2: 312).

"NATIVE" AMERICANS

Despite *The Valley*'s dime-western finale, Wharton condemned America's literary appetite for what she called "cowboys de chic" (*Letters* 91). In a 1904 letter to Scribner's Brownell, she confessed herself discouraged by recent reviews: "the continued cry that I am an echo of Mr. James (whose books of the last ten years I can't read, much as I delight in the man), & the assumption that the people I write about are not 'real' because they are not navvies & char-women, makes me feel rather hopeless. I write about what I see, what I happen to be nearest to" (*Letters* 91). Wharton's lament is twofold. Exasperated that she is not being taken seriously in her own right, she rails against those who would see her as a wan imitation of Henry James – a comparison as galling to her sense of creative independence as it was to her artistic authenticity. Her second objection is thus related to the first: the implication that only working-class people are real makes her bristle. "The idea that genuineness is to be found only in the rudimentary, and that whatever is complex is inauthentic, is a favorite axiom of the modern American critic," she later remarked (*Uncollected* 155). Nurtured in the "safe, shallow, and shadowless world" of the United States, modern critics were tasteless and indiscriminate, alienated as they were from "the deep roots of the past" (*Uncollected* 154).

Both grievances are central to Wharton's concerns about American identity. If Odo's reformist agenda had collapsed under the weight of democratic pluralism, then America was doomed to suffer a similar fate. As Raymond de Chelles, a French nobleman in *The Custom of the Country* (1913), caustically declares, Americans live in "towns as flimsy as paper, where the streets haven't had time to be named, and the buildings are demolished before they're dry, and the people are as proud of changing as we are of holding on to what we have" (*Custom* 307). Unlike the French, who were so habituated to their architecture that their own faces resembled the gargoyles adorning their country's ancient cathedrals, Americans were inexpressive, transient and ephemeral (see *Motor-Flight* 86). Only Ralph Marvell, *The Custom of the Country*'s ill-fated Knickerbocker hero,[12] takes a concerted stand against this transcendental homelessness, adopting what he sees as a more authentically American identity: he becomes one of the nation's "Aborigines . . . those vanishing denizens of the American continent doomed to rapid extinction with the advance of the invading race" (*Custom* 45).

This extraordinary act of impersonation vividly documents Wharton's struggle to resolve the indecision that she found in both the racially ambiguous Jones cabin and the dangerously democratic *Valley of Decision*. If divorce makes Undine Spragg, Ralph's parvenu wife, "internally alien, an identity-through-otherness," as Nancy Bentley has suggested (175), then *The Custom of the Country* would indeed seem to chart Ralph's decline from "ethnographic expert" to "grotesque museum artifact" (Bentley 171). To read Ralph's death as the condescending ethnographer's comeuppance, however, threatens to recapitulate the very self/other dichotomy that Bentley's reading of the novel so brilliantly contests. In identifying Undine's "cultural strangeness and menace" (Bentley 209), might we not bring a similar level of mistrust to our reading of Ralph? As I hope to show, Ralph shares his wife's protean quality. Oscillating between invader and aborigine, self and other, Ralph discloses his own complex investment in the racial masquerade of imitation and identification. Under such circumstances, suicide seems at best a Janus-faced gesture, one that threatens to collapse into its own mimetic performance. As the vanishing aborigine, Ralph risks becoming the figure he scorns – the invader who, appropriating an alien identity, seeks to fill the void he perceives in himself.

Like the turn-of-the-century ethnologists whose rhetoric he uses, Ralph recognizes cultural study as a potentially threatening act of Conradian identification. His heavily foreshadowed demise, with its self-conscious reference to what Lora Romero called the "cult of the Vanishing American"

(35), betrays his central role in the novel's racial crisis. Ralph's ironic but elegiac characterization of "Washington Square as the 'Reservation,'" whose inhabitants will "before long . . . be exhibited at ethnological shows, pathetically engaged in the exercise of their primitive industries," locates his own narrative not outside of, but within, the vexed context of racialized decline (*Custom* 45). Indeed, Ralph's wistful vision echoes many popular requiems for the vanishing Indian (45). When the Nez Percé chief Joseph died in April 1897, for example, *The New York Times* claimed that "The American bison is scarcely more completely extinct than the savage, unspoiled by civilization, of which the chief of the Nez Percés was a very typical specimen" (*A Race at Bay* 126).

At once elegiac and smug, the discourse of native decline climaxed in 1911 when a starving, ill-clad Yahi Indian was discovered outside of an Oroville, California slaughterhouse late that summer. Quickly touted as "the most uncontaminated aborigine in the known world," the man subsequently knows as Ishi was thought to be the last survivor of California's decimated Yana tribe ("Find a Rare Aborigine"). Under the supervision of Arthur Kroeber, the lead anthropologist on the case, Ishi was taken to the University of California's Museum of Anthropology, where ethnologists, reporters and curiosity seekers alike came to see this genuine "survivor from the past" (Kroeber 308). For the next five years – until his death from tuberculosis in 1916 – Ishi lived in the university museum, working as an ethnographic informant, an anthropological exhibit and a part-time janitor.

Curiously, neither Kroeber nor his colleagues ever learned Ishi's real name. "[T]he strongest Indian etiquette in Ishi's part of the world demands that a person shall never tell his own name, at least not in reply to a direct request," Kroeber explained (305). The name "Ishi," the Yana language word for "man," only underscored the tribesman's endangered and racially representative status. A quintessentially generic subject, Ishi was the last of his kind, an assumption only accentuated by his refusal to utter his real name. Without another Yahi Indian to confirm his identity, Ishi remained nameless and unassimilated. As Kroeber remarked in 1912, "He feels himself so distinct from his new world, that such a thing as deliberately imitating civilized people and making himself one of them has apparently never dawned upon him. He is one and they are others; that is in the inevitable nature of things, he thinks" (307). Ishi was synonymous with the real: he embodied a kind of non-imitative authenticity that transcended linguistic representation altogether.

While it is not clear whether Wharton ever heard of Ishi, her familiarity with the rhetoric surrounding him is plain. When Ralph Marvell appropriates the identity of an imperiled aborigine, he gains access to the "singularly coherent and respectable [ideals]" that Americans had come to associate with the Indian (*Custom* 45). To be like Ishi, a museum piece "exhibited at ethnological shows, pathetically engaged in the exercise of their primitive industries," is, for Ralph, to win the guarantee of non-imitative authenticity.[13] Ralph's appropriative act thus places him within the long European-American tradition of "playing Indian." From the Boston Tea Party in the late eighteenth century, to such wildly popular scouting groups as Ernest Thompson Seton's Woodcraft Indians in the early twentieth, Americans have repeatedly turned to Indian play as a way of claiming a fixed, non-European, and thus geographically specific national identity.[14] As Dana D. Nelson has remarked, "imagined projections into, onto, against Indian territories, Indian bodies, Indian identities" served as one means by which the "abstracting identity of white/national manhood" could stabilize "internal divisions and individual anxieties."[15]

If dressing up in war-paint and feathers gave eighteenth- and nineteenth-century Americans of European descent the opportunity both to assert the young nation's cultural independence and to register their own ambivalence with the violent means used to achieve those ends, the twentieth century witnessed the transformation of Indian play into an anti-modern antidote to what Philip J. Deloria terms the "empty sense of self generated by the historical chasm that served as a signpost of the modern."[16] As the concrete rigors of the Revolutionary and Civil Wars faded from memory, only to be replaced by the "hazy moral distinctions and vague spiritual commitments" that Jackson Lears associates with turn-of-the-century "weightlessness," Indians represented authenticity, reality and truth (Lears, *No Place of Grace* 32). As Sura P. Rath notes, "a civilized culture without its indigenous tribal past risks the authenticity of its process of change to challenge and doubt" (61). Early twentieth-century Americans felt precisely this danger. Indian play gave them a compensatory assurance of their authority and authenticity. Indeed, by 1900, Native Americans had been so seamlessly woven into the nation's mythical past that, according to Leah Dilworth, they had come to embody an "idealized [version] of history, spirituality, and unalienated labor" (3). Deprived of their recent, often violently confrontational history, these newly rehabilitated Indians became ironic icons for what Alex Nemerov has called the "mythic American values – pride, defiance, freedom – in whose name actual Indian cultures had been decimated" (311). Although they were often themselves the direct descendants of the very pioneers who had destroyed Native American culture in the first place, early twentieth-century Indian impersonators did not hesitate to participate in a sort of historical revisionism. By transforming the Indian into a "living relic" (Dilworth 3), European Americans successfully recast their former adversary as a vibrant, if painfully artificial, metaphor for the nation's, and therefore their own, elusive past.

Ralph's identification with the doomed aborigine draws both its wry force and its curious ambivalence from the contradictions inherent in Indian play. If aboriginal American identity stood in self-conscious opposition to the derivative legacy of European colonialism, playing Indian itself enacted a form of racial cross-dressing that dramatized America's anxious relationship to its own internal others. As Eric Lott has argued in his important analysis of nineteenth-century minstrelsy, racial impersonation evinces both fear and fascination: "American fears of succumbing to a racialized image of Otherness" are intensified by the audience's own act of racist voyeurism (Lott 40). The mimetic claims to authenticity that fueled Indian play in the early twentieth century laid bare not only America's precarious jurisdiction over its newly subjugated peoples and territories, but also the hybridizing consequences of those imperial impulses in the first place. Dilworth distills this paradox: "The Indian, supposedly a model for authenticity, was conceived of as an oppositional other to the self, and so, paradoxically, authentic states of being were apparently only accessible through acting, impersonation, and/or acquisition" (209). This contradiction, predicated on the assumption that the real thing was always just beyond the self's reach, made authenticity inaccessible. Playing Indian only exacerbated this problem, producing what Deloria finds to be "powerful doubled identities that granted one access to an authenticity that became legitimate only when one could not gain access" (200).

This contradiction is at the center of *The Custom of the Country*. If playing Indian therapeutically eased America's transition into modernity by staging what Deloria sees as "a heuristic encounter with the primitive" (105), then it did so only by making a travesty of American origins. To be an old-stock American, Ralph's metaphor implies, is to play the "aborigine" to the arriviste's "invader" – to align oneself with the besieged Indian who must, in turn, defend himself against the crude incursions of the mimetic intruder. It is, in effect, to perform a charade of authenticity in order to fend off the invader's spectacular hybridity. In this respect, Ralph's ethnographic paradigm seems to be that of Frank Hamilton Cushing, an amateur ethnologist who became widely known as the "White Indian" in the late nineteenth century. Between 1879 and 1884, Cushing introduced a new approach to anthropological fieldwork by taking up residence with his subjects, New Mexico's Zuñi tribe. Rejecting the conventional pose of scholarly

objectivity, Cushing effectively "went Native": he wore Zuñi garb, participated in Zuñi rituals, lived in a Zuñi home, and ultimately adhered to Zuñi
practices (including piercing his ears) (L. C. Mitchell 236–41). Despite the
resemblance between Marvell's rhetorical disguise and Cushing's adaptive
posture, Ralph aligns himself not so much with the mimetic White Indian,
as with the hapless Zuñi tribesmen who endured Cushing's mimetic incursion. It is Undine, not Ralph, who resembles Cushing. Like the audacious
anthropologist who boasted that he could "live entirely on Zuñi food, dress
as a Zuñi, sleep on a bed of skins and blankets, and in fact, in all outward
things, to conform my life exactly to those of the natives" (J. Green 105),
Undine is "modified by contact with the indigenous" (*Custom* 47). When
Ralph's sister, Laura Fairford, mentions a new art exhibit, Undine immediately sets off for the gallery, where she flings "herself in rapt attitudes
before the canvases, scribbling notes in the catalogue in imitation of a tall
girl in sables, while ripples of self-consciousness played up and down her
watchful back" (30). As Ralph belatedly recognizes, his wife is hollow on the
inside, and wholly mimetic on the outside. She adopts "the speech of the
conquered race . . . though on [her] lips it had often so different a meaning"
(47). Like Cushing who, after eight months among the Zuñi, reported that
he could speak "a strangely complicated tongue not perfectly but fluently
and easily; a tongue . . . difficult to the Anglo-Saxon" (J. Green 105),
Undine can ape the gestures and locutions of the New York and European
elite.

In casting America's arrivistes as imitative invaders, Ralph is clearly open-
ing himself up to similar accusations. If Undine seems to be a latter-day
Cushing, then Ralph resembles the rogue anthropologist's tolerant host, a
Zuñi tribal governor who permitted the disruptive white man to live in his
home. Ralph fully captures the palimpsest of Indian play: he is a European
American, pretending to be an Indian, who discovers that white people
(Undine, the invaders, Cushing) like to imitate aboriginal people. The
complexity of these layered acts of mimicry informs and betrays Wharton's
anxiety: is authenticity, she asks, even possible in the United States, or is
American identity invariably an act of minstrelsy?

These issues circulate with startling persistence around the body human
and the body politic in *The Custom of the Country*. Ralph's anxiously aboriginal performance mirrors his own restless quest for a virgin wilderness
unsullied by racial alterity or cultural fakery. Blinded by his romantic search,
Ralph tragically misreads his deceptive bride, whom he considers "still at the
age when the flexible soul offers itself to the first grasp" (*Custom* 49). Theirs
will be the pristine adventure of "a primeval couple setting forth across a

virgin continent" (85). As their disastrous honeymoon ensues, however, Ralph's "remote and Ariel-like" wife turns out to be little more than "a stranger . . . insensible to the touch of the heart" (88, 129). Despite their unhappy marriage, scandalous divorce and bitter child-custody dispute, however, Ralph doggedly refuses to abandon his core belief in Undine's "virgin innocence" (49). It is not until he discovers Undine's early marriage to the ruthless tycoon, Elmer Moffatt, that Ralph's illusions are finally shattered. As Moffatt brutally recalls the night that he and his prairie bride were "made one at Opake, Nebraska," Ralph begins to feel a "mounting pang of physical nausea." "[T]hey caught us too soon," Moffatt pruriently adds; "we only had a fortnight" (264). As he grows increasingly aware of Moffatt's "bodily presence," Ralph is forced to acknowledge his predecessor's phallic advantage. Moffatt begins "to loom, huge and portentous as some monster released from a magician's bottle. His redness, his glossiness, his baldness, and the carefully brushed ring of hair encircling it . . . all these solid witnesses to his reality and his proximity pressed on Ralph" (264). A serpent in Ralph's frontier garden, Moffatt has a previous claim on Ralph's virgin terrain. Undine is sexually tainted: she embodies neither Ralph's fantasy of pure genealogical origin nor his continental dream of an unadulterated American past. Despite the watery "coolness of the element from which she took her name," Undine is, in fact, the human equivalent of the tainted well water that served as the source of her father's corrupt wealth in the "Pure Water Move."[17]

The Custom of the Country dramatizes America's racial dilemma. Like the country whose initials she bears, Undine Spragg is not a virgin wilderness at all: instead, she is an example of what Lauren Berlant calls the "postvirginal bride." She is "simultaneously the source of our historical consciousness, our historical amnesia, and our personal nostalgia for those moments before her 'knowledge' atomized our whole bodies and destroyed our utopian . . . dreams" (32). Undine's tainted origins are mired in the contaminated costs of conquest and hybridity.

For Wharton, this was a source of crisis. In *French Ways and Their Meaning* (1919), her most sustained treatment of race and nation, Wharton stakes the country's future on its possession and knowledge of an unobstructed racial past. As a series of articles written to justify and encourage America's involvement in World War I, *French Ways* is an unabashed paean to Wharton's adopted home. The French enjoy an unprecedented level of artistic and racial continuity, she declares; indeed, they can trace their culture back to the cave painters of prehistoric Europe. This "old, almost vanished culture doubtless lingered in the caves and river-beds," Wharton speculates, and therefore "handed on something of its great tradition, kept alive, in the hidden nooks which cold and savages spared, little hearths of artistic vitality" (*French Ways* 81). By resisting the repeated "invasions of savage hordes," the French were able to protect their ethnic purity and to foster "the most homogenous and uninterrupted culture the world has known."[18]

By contrast, America could claim neither ethnic uniformity nor aesthetic continuity. Without a convincing link to the aboriginal past, national authenticity remained an elusive vision. Even if "The traces of a very ancient culture discovered in the United States and in Central America [were to] prove the far-off existence of an artistic and civic development unknown to the races found by the first European explorers," Wharton argued, "they would not count in our artistic and social inheritance, since the English and Dutch colonists found only a wilderness peopled by savages, who had kept no link of memory with those vanished societies. There had been a complete break of continuity" (*French Ways* 79). By summarily rejecting a genealogical link between North America's aboriginal inhabitants and the Native Americans who were living in the United States in the early twentieth century, Wharton presents a vision of America as an orphaned nation isolated from the past and unprepared for the future.

Wharton grounded this verdict in contemporary archeological debates that were circulating around the question of American origins. Her comments reveal her especial familiarity with the Mound Builder controversy. Since 1781, when Thomas Jefferson reported a "spheroidical [land] form" in Virginia, the geometric mounds scattered over the lands west of the Appalachians had puzzled American observers (Jefferson 223). Who had built these arithmetically precise circles, squares and octagons? Were they the ancestors of the present-day Indians, or were they a lost European or Greco-Roman tribe? Speculation was divided into two major schools of thought. On one side were those who believed in the existence of an American Paleolithic period whose structures and artifacts indicated the existence of a separate, prehistoric race – possibly related to European Paleolithic peoples or even the Eskimo – but clearly distinct from later, "historically encountered" Native Americans (Meltzer 18). J. W. Foster, the President of the Chicago Academy of Sciences, and subscriber to this theory, insisted in 1873 that the American Indian "has been signalized by treachery and cruelty. He repels all efforts to raise him from his degraded position . . . He has never been known voluntarily to engage in an enterprize requiring methodical labor . . . To suppose that such a race threw up . . . symmetrical mounds . . . is . . . preposterous" (qtd. in Kennedy, *Hidden Cities* 238).

Sympathizers with Foster argued that the mounds drew a direct line from North America to "Herodotus and Homer, to Rome and the Vikings, to England's barrows, to all the mounds of Europe and Asia that had been known so long" (Silverberg 6). "In a stroke," Robert Silverberg notes, North America was "joined to the world's past, and no longer floated traditionfree [*sic*] and timeless" (6). Late nineteenth-century Indians were not descended from the Mound Builders at all; instead, insisted supporters of the American Paleolithic, modern-day Indians were heirs to the savage tribes who had destroyed their more advanced mound-building peers (Trigger 105).

At the Smithsonian's Bureau of American Ethnology (BAE), a competing school disputed this view. In 1893, Cyrus Thomas, the Bureau's archeology director, led a coordinated investigation of the mounds of the Mississippi and Ohio valleys. Declaring himself "a pronounced believer in . . . a race of Mound Builders distinct from American Indians," Thomas was surprised to find that his research had turned up countervailing evidence (qtd. in Kennedy, *Hidden Cities* 238). When he published his *Twelfth Annual Report of the Bureau of Ethnology* in 1894, he debunked the theory of the "lost tribes," presenting evidence instead that linked the Mound Builders to contemporary indigenous tribal practices (J. A. Brown 399). As the report's co-author John Wesley Powell declared, the "alluring conjecture that a powerful people, superior to the Indians, once occupied the valley of the Ohio and the Appalachian ranges," only to be swept away by "the invasion of copperhued Huns from some unknown region of the earth," had now been exposed for the "romantic fallacy" that it was (qtd. in S. Williams 61–2).

Wharton evidently remained unconvinced. Modern-day Indians, she insisted, were not conduits but, rather, obstacles to American identity. Violent encounters with such fierce tribal opponents had indeed contaminated the European pioneers. Although the "English and Dutch settlers no doubt carried many things with them, such vital but imponderable things as prejudices, principles, laws and beliefs, even these were strangely transformed when at length the colonists emerged again from the backwoods and the bloody Indian warfare" (*French Ways* 83–4). Europe's confrontation with the Native American tribes had been a fatally hybridizing experience. In the heat of national expansion, European Americans had forfeited their salutary racial intolerance in order to meet the slipperier demands of racial assimilation and cultural accommodation. Herein lay the fundamental difference between America and France: "The stern experience of the pioneer, the necessity of rapid adaptation and of constantly improvised expedients formed a far different preparation from that dogged resistance to invasion, that clinging to the same valley and the same river-cliff, that have made the French, literally as well as figuratively, the most conservative of western races" (84).

While Wharton shared Frederick Jackson Turner's belief that the frontier had encouraged assimilation, she rejected his sanguine interpretation of this phenomenon. Far from being a source of civic pride, the pioneer experience for Wharton was a site of regrettable racial corruption. Frontiersmen had survived their bloody encounters in the wilderness only by assuming a posture of regrettable racial pliancy.[19] Forced to mingle indiscriminately with their enemies, the European pioneers had won the national battle, but lost the racial war. As Wharton shows in *The Valley of Decision*, the victory was pyrrhic at best. Like the "new man" of the eighteenth century, who "prided himself on being a citizen of the world, on sympathizing as warmly with the poetic savage of Peru as with his own prosaic and narrow-minded neighbors," the offspring of the Enlightenment had accommodated "the savage's mode in life," and thus transformed "civilized Europeans" into nothing more than "a passing phase of human development." (*Valley* 2: 186). "To cast off clothes and codes, and live in peaceful socialism 'under the amiable reign of Truth and Nature,'" *The Valley*'s narrator sardonically remarks, "seemed on the whole much easier than to undertake the systematic reform of existing abuses" (2: 186). Like the "uprooted colonists" in America, who had "change[d] so abruptly all their agricultural and domestic habits" after coming to the new world (*French Ways* 82–3), the denizens of *The Valley of Decision* underestimate the value of stoic intransigence and chary parochialism. Instead, they fall victim to the haphazard complacency of "peaceful socialism," adapting where they should have resisted.

Wharton's belief that "the sudden uprooting of our American ancestors and their violent cutting off from all their past" had tainted the continent's racial character forms the backbone of her conservative critique in *The Custom of the Country* (*French Ways* 82). If Undine's "pliancy and variety" are evidence of the imitative aesthetic of mass production (Bentley 196), then they are also symptomatic of a more pervasive racial decline (*Custom* 86). The "pioneer blood" that fuels Undine's restless quest for "ampler vistas" is precisely the compound that makes her vulnerable to the amalgamating chemistry of the frontier (35). Her indiscriminate mind, "as destitute of beauty and mystery as the prairie school-house in which she had been educated," embraces novelty and change at the expense of bias and tradition. The resulting pliancy informs her frequent declarations of independence.

"I don't believe an American woman needs to know such a lot about . . . old rules," she flippantly remarks, tossing her head in a "movement she had learned in 'speaking' school-pieces about freedom and the British tyrant" (86, 94). Derivative and capricious, Undine embodies the racial taint that Wharton associated with "pioneer blood."

If the frontier threatens its European explorers with racial hybridization, then playing Indian demanded something equally dislocating: a mimetic acknowledgement of ancestral absence. The same historical rupture that Wharton associated with America's aborigines makes Ralph Marvell's appropriative act particularly puzzling in so far as he takes his impersonating cue from the very plasticity that Wharton had condemned in the pioneers. The paradox is striking. While Wharton enviously observed in 1908 that everything "In France . . . speaks of long familiar intercourse between the earth and its inhabitants . . . every blade of grass is there by an old feudal right which has long since dispossessed the worthless aboriginal weed" (*Motor-Flight* 5), she claimed in 1919 that the Dordogne's prehistoric cave-painters *were* the aborigines, and therefore the prehistoric forebears of subsequent French artists. "Even if it seems fanciful to believe that the actual descendants of the cave-painters survived there can be little doubt that their art, or its memory, was transmitted."[20] Wharton's is a peculiarly American uncertainty: who are the invaders and who are the aborigines? Did American culture flower because of the conquest of the "aboriginal weed," or did it spring instead from its roots in the aboriginal? Are a nation's citizens authentic because they displace the aborigine, or because they *are* the aborigines?

THE RACIAL AESTHETIC

These issues were both personal and political for Edith Wharton. Having spent much of her early childhood in Rome, London, Paris and Seville, Wharton returned to New York in 1872 only to face "the mean monotonous streets" of Manhattan (*Backward Glance* 54). From a young age, Wharton's relationship with the United States was vexed. What "could New York offer to a child whose eyes had been filled with shapes of immortal beauty and immemorial significance?" (54). As she matured into a brainy socialite, Wharton felt herself an outsider at every turn: "I was a failure in Boston . . . because they thought I was too fashionable to be intelligent, and a failure in New York because they were afraid I was too intelligent to be fashionable" (119). Her frequent journeys back to Europe only exacerbated her sense of displacement: a "traveller from a land which has undertaken to get on without the past," she was suddenly a tourist where she longed to dwell (*Motor-Flight* 11).

It was only with the publication of her first collection of short stories, *The Greater Inclination* (1899), that Wharton experienced a genuine sense of place. "I felt like some homeless waif who, after trying for years to take out naturalization papers, and being rejected in every country, has finally acquired a nationality. The Land of Letters was henceforth to be my country, and I gloried in my new citizenship" (*Backward Glance* 119). Compensating Wharton for the gross inadequacies of her own native land, the Land of Letters took the United States as its point of resistance. If America played indiscriminate host to the world's huddled masses, then the Land of Letters, by contrast, enforced more stringent immigration policies. Like Lawrence Selden's "republic of the spirit" in *The House of Mirth*, the Land of Letters was less a Platonic republic than a "close corporation" where "arbitrary objections . . . keep people out."[21] Citizenship in Wharton's literary nation required one to pledge allegiance to "routine, precedent, tradition, [and] the beaten path" (*French Ways* 32). In the Land of Letters, English was the official language, but only English "as spoken according to the best usage" (*Backward Glance* 48).

On this latter point, Wharton was adamant. Writing in the midst of the post-war "language panic" of 1918 to 1928 (Daniels 53), Wharton insisted that the national idiom was a barometer for political stability, racial cohesion and cultural civility. Without "accepted standards and restrictions," she warned, English would deteriorate into "a muddle of unstable dialects," a language no better than the hybrid tongues "found among any savage tribe" (*French Ways* 49–50). Energized by her frustration with America's racial and ethnic diversity, Wharton's critique offered a conservative alternative to Whitman's sanguine view that "The English Language is grandly lawless like the race who uses it" (qtd. in Baron 51). For Wharton, by contrast, linguistic instability was a symptom of political volatility. The "heterogeneous hundred millions" of immigrants coming into the United States were indifferent to the "recognised guidance" of the country's hereditary elite and therefore agents of chaos and decline (*French Ways* 50). As H. L. Mencken acknowledged in his encyclopedic 1919 study, *The American Language*, the United States was the hub of impulse and gullibility. In rejecting Great Britain's "relatively stable social order," America had launched itself into a cultural free-for-all. A "new fallacy in politics spreads faster in the United States than anywhere else on earth," Mencken remarked, "and so does a new fashion in hats, or a new revelation of God . . . or a new shibboleth, or metaphor, or piece of slang" (32–3).

Wharton deplored this fickle adaptability. "[T]he lover of English need only note what that rich language has shrunk to on the lips" of the sundry public in modern America, who were "being suffered to work their many wills upon it" (*French Ways* 50). These speakers were eliminating "hundreds of useful [social and linguistic] distinctions" by contaminating "Pure English" (*Uncollected* 62). Many of America's newest citizens "[shuffled] along, trailing [the English language] after [them] like a rag in the dust, tramping over it, as Henry James said, like the emigrant tramping over his kitchen oil-cloth" (*Backward Glance* 51). Citizenship in the United States had become a dingy amalgam of household and highway, clean and dirty, private and public. Wharton's bitter complaint that "the interchangable use of 'shall' and 'will' has passed from Irish-English speech to our own . . . and past participles manufactured out of nouns are weakening the few inflected verbs we have left" speaks to her larger anxiety about the collapse of social barriers (*Uncollected* 61). The grammar of America's class and race relations was undergoing a similarly dramatic shift. Interchangeability, in its broadest sense, had altered the syntax of social relations, replacing authentic signs with manufactured idioms, and diminishing the impact of elite actions by undermining "the few inflected verbs we have left." As Theodore Roosevelt insisted in 1919, "We have room for but one language here and that is the English language, for we intend to see that the crucible turns our people out as Americans and not as dwellers in a polyglot boarding house" (qtd. in Farb 163). As Lily Bart's death in one such polyglot boarding house suggests, Wharton found such possibilities "unpardonable": "there deterioration and corruption lurked" (*Backward Glance* 51).

In an undated manuscript entitled "The Bitter End," Wharton adds a cantankerous twist to this socio-semantic critique. Vowing to fight the good fight in the "great campaign for Pure English" (2), Sheraton, an American magazine editor, vows to uphold linguistic standards in "our poor polyglot country" (8). He begins by "impos[ing] on all who were connected with the New Magazine the moral obligation to speak & pronounce the English language as if it were English & not Choctaw" (1–2):

People talk about the conservatives turning English into a "dead language," because they respect usage & are aware of etymology. But if fluidity is what you want, say savage dialect is fluid, & stability is the essence of any speech that has a great historie [*sic*] and intellectual past. A language made over every six months by emigrants & drummers can never provide the material for great literature – or even for civilized human intercourse. (5)

Pure English maintains political-linguistic order by insisting that ethnically fluid Americans conduct themselves according to the best usage. It is a linguistic sanctuary for the educated few, a refuge for those who share Wharton's distaste for the culture of Indians, immigrants and peddlers that has overtaken modern America.

Such itinerant Americans "trample on & destroy [our language] every hour of the day," whereas citizens of the Land of Letters dwell in "that magnificent house not built with hands, that temple of our race, the English tongue" (Wharton, "Subjects and Notes 1918–1923"). By turning English into "a mere instrument of utility," modern pluralists degraded "relations between human beings to a dead level of vapid benevolence, and the whole of life to a small house with modern plumbing and heating, a garage, a motor, a telephone, and a lawn undivided from one's neighbors" (*Uncollected* 154). American English was the linguistic equivalent of the dull uniformity of suburbia. Choicer real estate was to be found in the Land of Letters, where elite grandees lived on magnificent hereditary estates.

Pure English, however, not only policed difference within the Land of Letters; it also ensured the country's imperial jurisdiction over competing ontological domains. In this sense, the novel was the Land of Letters' politically dominant form. While the short story could offer the "temporary shelter of a flitting fancy," the novel was something mightier and more substantial: a "four-square and deeply-founded monument" erected in commemoration of the author's mastery over the heterogeneous "welter of existence" (*Writing of Fiction* 75, 14). Unlike the "pompous" Statue of Liberty in New York Harbor (*Fighting France* 177), who wantonly welcomed the indiscriminate hoards to her accommodating shores, the novel granted citizenship only to those "born of the creator's brain."[22] When "real people" were haphazardly "transported" into a novel, undetached from the welter of existence – as in the *roman à clef* – they "instantly cease[d] to be real; only those born of the creator's brain can give the least illusion of reality" (*Backward Glance* 210). In the Land of Letters, there was no Ellis Island that assimilated "navvies & char-women"; immigrants were not even real. At best, they could only drift around in "a resuscitated *real world* (a sort of Tussaud Museum of wax figures with actual clothes on)" (*Writing of Fiction* 59). Theirs was an imitative limbo that bore no resemblance to "that other world which is the image of life transposed in the brain of the artist, a world wherein the creative breath has made all things new" (*Writing of Fiction* 59). The novel represented its own cognitive empire, a dominant and incomparable force among the otherwise sham colonies of the real.

In formulating a theory of language and literature, Wharton fashioned a deeply conservative model of citizenship and writing. If the United States opened its arms to the world's tired, poor and huddled masses, the novel, under the neo-nativist laws of Pure English and Wharton's colonial determination to suppress "pure anarchy in fiction," imposed sharp restrictions on foreign immigration (*Writing of Fiction* 14). By repeatedly emphasizing that works of art were first and foremost the "products of conscious ordering and selecting," Wharton theorized an artistic form that could withstand the menacing indeterminacies of democratic pluralism (*Writing of Fiction* 16). While she shared what one critic calls the "Victorian rage for order," she also added something specific to the mix – a determination to write simultaneously *about* and *through* her conservative principles.[23] As Frederick Wegener rightly notes, "Wharton's regressive social and political views . . . are closely intertwined with her convictions about the writing of fiction and the making of art" ("Form" 134).

When Wharton wrote that the "universal French sense of form" had "led the race to the happy, momentous discovery that good manners are a short cut to one's goal, that they lubricate the wheels of life instead of obstructing them," she implicitly reminded her readers that formal principles not only governed fiction, but equally organized the world's assorted inhabitants into a disciplined rubric of race (*Motor-Flight* 28–9). Fixed within a stable aesthetic, race guarded against the potential slippages of class. The French collectively realized this: class mobility was pointless because race was at the core of national identity. The French worker's "admirable *fitting into the pattern*" thus bore quiet testimony to the Gauls' shared commitment to a civic racial aesthetic (*Motor-Flight* 29, Wharton's italics). Each artisan contributed to the overall effect: "Every one . . . from the canal-boatman to the white-capped baker's lad . . . had their established niche in life, the frankly avowed interests and preoccupations of their order, their pride in the smartness of the canal-boat, the seductions of the show-window, the glaze of the *brioches*, the crispness of the lettuce." Because daily life both conditioned and reproduced French art, the "requirements of the average Frenchman in any class are surprisingly few, and the ambition to 'better' himself socially plays a very small part in his plans" (*French Ways* 94). From the glazed brioche to the stylish shop window, French culture revealed the pleasing consequences of class hierarchy subordinated to the ordered fixity of race.

If Wharton's formalism was grounded in a "wider antiliberal, indeed antidemocratic, critique," as Wegener suggests ("Form" 133), then her conception of the Land of Letters assumed a racialized conception of national identity, one that was authorized to withstand the ambiguity of class.[24] Everyone in France "was more or less 'marked'" by the "sharp accents" of a common national identity, she said ("The Intruders" 3). In an unfinished short story entitled "The Intruders," Gertrude Arch, an American expatriate, wistfully admires the French people's "expressive abridgement" and their "vivid and pictorial side," for she herself is the "child of a blurred race" ("The Intruders" 3). The difference "between a race that has had a long continuance and a race that has had a recent beginning" is clear (*French Ways* 83). By foolishly exchanging their great biosocial inheritance for "everything which does not rise above the very low average in culture, situation, or intrinsic human interest," America had perverted Europe's cultural algebra that held geography constant and varied for time – time that perpetually drifted into the past (*Uncollected* 153). The upstart citizens of the United States, by contrast, held time constant and varied for place. Immature nomads, they were neither indigenous to the soil, nor deferential to historical precedent. America, in short, remained "intellectually and artistically . . . in search of itself" (*French Ways* xxiii).

Wharton's often self-contradictory argument with modernism stemmed from this socio-political critique. In accusing writers like Joyce, Woolf and Eliot of ascribing "exaggerated importance to . . . trivial incidents," and thereby wasting their talents on "trivial lives," Wharton, of course, was selectively overlooking her own representations of common folk – from the Bunner Sisters to Ethan Frome (*Writing of Fiction* 102). Her Tory sympathies, however, are clear: "If the novelist wants to hang his drama on a button, let it at least be one of Lear's," she insisted (*Writing of Fiction* 103). "Better a bad King than the Populace, any day" (letter to Elisina Tyler, July 29, 1936). Wharton's central complaint against modernism, however, had less to do with content than with form. Again and again, she criticizes the modernists' innovations in language and narrative, their replacement of the structured grammar of the nineteenth century with the shapeless logorrhea of the twentieth. By promoting the babbling commoner over the syntactical elite, the modernists had unleashed a revolution in language and politics. In so far as stream-of-consciousness privileged "amorphous and agglutinative" impulses over carefully selected incidents (*Uncollected* 172), modernism represented a threat to the most basic statutes of social and formal order. In her adamant insistence that any "incident, insignificant in itself, must illustrate some general law," Wharton sought a method that would enable her to regulate both narrative and nation (*Writing of Fiction* 103).

Modernism turned the racial aesthetic on its head by substituting the pseudo-originality of modish experiment for the authenticity of established literary origins. "True originality consists not in a new manner but in a new vision," Wharton insisted – a new vision that could come only from an "accumulated wealth of knowledge and experience" (*Writing of Fiction* 17–18). Wharton's pecuniary metaphor is telling: because intergenerational stability was a function of accumulated wealth, cheap originality was for those who put things "to uses for which they were not intended" (*Decoration of Houses* 19). Consumed with a "fear of being unoriginal," the modernists wasted their energies on verbal high jinks that were stylistically surprising but aesthetically unremarkable (*Writing of Fiction* 15). "[T]he book closed," Wharton remarked, the reader of the modernist novel "seems to stand on the scene of a drunken revel 'whence all but he have fled' – so rapidly have the wraiths he has been reading about vanished from his memory" (*Uncollected* 172). When discount feats of syntactical acrobatics replaced the rich traditions of meaningful content, social collapse was imminent. In such situations, cowardice took the place of courage, and puerility crowded out sophistication. "Original vision is never much afraid of using accepted forms," Wharton observed, "and only the cultivated intelligence escapes the danger of regarding as intrinsically new . . . a mere superficial change, or the reversion to a discarded trick or technique" (*Writing of Fiction* 109).

Ultimately, Wharton worried that modernism would open the way for "pure anarchy in fiction" (*Writing of Fiction* 15). Faux originality would undermine the social architecture. "To be original at any cost is apparently the first quality demanded of the modern architect, and the popular interpretation of originality in architecture is the application of structural forms or ornamental detail to uses for which it was not intended," she told Rhode Islanders in an 1896 letter to the *Newport Daily News* (*Uncollected* 55). Newport's citizens must protect their historic homes, and thereby resist the siren call of modern design. True originality combined form and function into an organic, indivisible whole, while sham innovation divorced the decorative from the structural, substituting pretense for substance.[25] In this respect, formlessness was the aesthetic equivalent of lawlessness. Only strict compliance with "the necessary laws of thought" could adequately protect a civilization from the damage of creative excess. To realign innovation with inheritance was thus to render "the supposed conflict between originality and tradition . . . no conflict at all," for originality resumed its respectful place as a law-abiding citizen in the Land of Letters (*Decoration of Houses* 11).

What made modernist originality particularly pernicious was its threat to racial continuity. The modernist's capricious approach to language, Wharton insisted, only accelerated the "deplorable loss of shades of difference in our blunted speech" (*French Ways* 83). To render shades of difference imperceptible was to intensify linguistic and ethnic confusion. America's blurry racial and class boundaries thus found an uneasy equivalence in the formal relativism of stream-of-consciousness. Wharton's criticism of *Mrs. Dalloway* as a "formless rush of sensation," an indiscriminate "flow of gelatinous mass" ("Documentation in Fiction" 10), and *Ulysses* as "a turgid welter of pornography (the rudest schoolboy kind) & unformed & unimportant drivel" (*Letters* 461) reveals this correlation between social and aesthetic formlessness. Until "the raw ingredients of a pudding *make* a pudding," Wharton told Bernard Berenson, "I shall never believe that the raw material of sensation & thought can make a work of art without the cook's intervening" (*Letters* 461). Only the "creative intelligence [. . . who is] irresistibly sorting and rejecting" could make the necessary judgments and decisions (*Uncollected* 172). While modern democracy and modern literature subordinated the singular password to the repetitious byword, traditional society had "its old-established distinctions of class, its passwords, exclusions, delicate shades of language and behavior" (*Uncollected* 155). The homogenous demographics of Main Street – that "common mean of American life" – threatened to crowd out the richly idiosyncratic values of "old-time Americans" (*Uncollected* 156).

Repetition endangered originality. According to Edward Said, "Repetition shows nature being brought down from the level of natural fact to the level of counterfeit imitation. Stature, authority, and force in the original sink through each repetition into material for the historian's scorn" (124). Wharton worried that repetition would deprive origin of its singular basis in the real. Each iteration would compromise the original statement, transforming origin into little more than a matter of historical contingency, "at a remove from any timeless or fixed standard of truth" (Quint 7). In such situations, originality became just another facet of the written record, the "large pattern [which] domesticates the single act, the order [. . . which] overtakes the idiosyncrasies even of script" (Said 134). The unique utterance became a relative linguistic event, indelibly enmeshed in the man-made weave of history. Origin was no longer the beginning of history; it was the *subject* of history.

For Wharton, the prospect of origin's being rendered a historically relative event raised a number of political and aesthetic questions. If "repetition is useful as a way of showing that history and actuality are all about human

persistence, and not about divine originality," as Said suggests, then intergenerational repetition undercuts not only the transcendent status of
divine genealogical origin, but also the reliability of origin altogether.
Wharton alludes to precisely this possibility in her travel narrative, *Italian
Backgrounds* (1905). In the "intermediate world" of Italy's medieval
hermits – a "twilight world of the conquered, Christianized, yet still lingering gods" – pagan spirits still remained a vital part of hermetic cosmology
(81). "Shapes which have once inhabited the imagination of man" only
reluctantly pass "out of existence" (78). Because early Christians were loath
to banish the "half-human, half-sylvan creatures" that they had worshipped
for centuries, they continued to pay tribute to "the gods their own forbears
had known" (80, 81). Many additional centuries would have to pass before
these former pagans were willing "to lay their ghosts" aside (78–9). In the
meantime, though, idolatrous rituals would supplement Christian sacra-
ments, and God's Incarnate Word would remain on a historical continuum
with pagan practice.

This indeterminate state was for Wharton a familiar one. Like the inhabitants of Plato's cave, Americans in the early twentieth century "attribute[d]
timelessness and truth to the only meaning they know, the meaning they
have created for themselves" (Quint 11). As Wharton remarks in *The Age of
Innocence*, the citizens of Old New York "all lived in a kind of hieroglyphic
world where the real thing was never said or done or even thought, but
only represented by a set of arbitrary signs" (41). A locus of unwieldy signi-
fication, America posed a threat to the real. "Every sham and substitute for
education and literature and art has steadily crowded out the real thing,"
Wharton complained (*French Ways* 72). When Newland Archer, in *The Age
of Innocence*, impetuously implores his fiancée to elope with him ("Can't
you and I strike out for ourselves . . . ?"), May Welland's placating response
registers Wharton's alarm:

> "You *do* love me, Newland! I'm so happy!"
> "But then – why not be happier?"
> "We can't behave like people in novels, though, can we?"
> "Why not – why not – why not?"   (*Age of Innocence* 72)

Archer's pleading rejoinder betrays the obvious: Newland and May *are*
people in novels. Despite the book's evocative simulation of the real thing,
its characters are, in fact, "sham[s] and substitute[s]" – creations constituted
through a system of arbitrary signs. Without what David Quint calls "an
original meaning, a meaning which exists temporally prior to the sign itself,"

the United States and narrative itself would remain tangled in a network of displacement and play (Quint 18).

Archer's reaction to May's wondrous exclamation – "'Newland! You're so original!'" – underscores Wharton's central dilemma. "'Original!'" the genteel New Yorker replies. "'We're all as like each other as those dolls cut out of the same folded paper. We're like patterns stenciled on a wall'" (*Age of Innocence* 72). Because Archer and May are fictive characters, and therefore truly paper dolls, their seeming reality depends on a series of pre-existing syntactical patterns that make them seem lifelike. Like the shadows in Plato's cave, they are stencils of the real thing. Their originality is as elusive as their origin in the real; their authenticity is as unreliable as fiction itself. Americans, however, could not see past the shadows flitting across the walls of their national cave'. As Charles Bowen tells Laura Fairford in *The Custom of the Country*, Americans are epitomized by their women. "All my sympathy's with them, poor deluded dears, when I see their fallacious little attempts to trick out the leavings tossed them by the preoccupied male – the money and the motors and the clothes – and pretend to themselves and each other that *that's* what really constitutes life!" Only the odd exception could see "through the humbug" and recognize "the big bribe she's paid for keeping out of some man's way" (*Custom* 120). In practicing what Quint calls a "narcissistic oblivion to history" (11), American women must content themselves with the "semblance of freedom, activity and authority," and must ignore the fact that this facsimile bears no more "likeness to real living than the exercises of the Montessori infant" (*French Ways* 102).

The prospect of the counterfeit's passing for the real was an ever-present danger in the early twentieth century, especially in a country whose national roots were mired in slavery, colonialism and frontier violence. As Myra Jehlen observes, "To be born an American is simultaneously to be born again" – outside of the temporal relativism of old-world historicity, and into the "absolute, timeless natural laws in the new" (9). For Wharton, this was an uncertain prospect at best. Brought up in a country where chance collisions replaced the orderly teleology of time and space, Wharton might have agreed with Werner Sollors, who identifies "the central drama in American culture" as "the conflict between contractual and hereditary, self-made and ancestral, definitions of American identity – between *consent* and *descent*" (5–6).

A Francophilic exile who took unpopular positions on women's higher education (she was against it), foreign policy (she declared herself a "rabid Imperialist"), and post-industrial democracy (she deplored the "man with the dinner-pail"), Wharton articulated a wide-ranging and intellectually voracious brand of American conservatism.[26] To understand Wharton's conservative positions on racial pluralism, unfettered immigration, industrial reform and even gendered equality is not to diminish her central place in American letters; rather, it is to enrich and complicate our understanding of this intense woman and the political divides that informed her work. To study Wharton's politics is to understand at once the inventiveness of her fiction and the complex ways that she interacted with the issues of her day. Doubtful of her nation's beginnings, Wharton nonetheless mined America's ambiguity for all of its protean promise.

CHAPTER 2

"The real Lily Bart": staging race in The House of Mirth

"But what *is* your story, Lily? I don't believe any one knows it yet." Gerty Farish's question, coming as it does near the end of Edith Wharton's 1905 best-seller *The House of Mirth*, is certainly ironic. Within the context of a novel that labors precisely to tell the whole "story" of Lily Bart, Gerty's question suggests the absence or concealment of the text's central narrative. Lily's response, moreover, is disconcertingly opaque:

"From the beginning?" Miss Bart gently mimicked her. "Dear Gerty, how little imagination you good people have! Why, the beginning was in my cradle, I suppose – in the way I was brought up, and the things I was taught to care for. Or no – I won't blame anybody for my faults: I'll say it was in my blood, that I got it from some wicked pleasure-loving ancestress, who reacted against the homely virtues of New Amsterdam, and wanted to be back at the court of the Charleses!" (*House* 226)

Lily decides that her flaws are not the work of environment alone; they are also the result of hereditary traits "in [the] blood," passed down from a sybaritic ancestress. Such logic represents a prime example of what Laura Otis calls "organic memory" – the belief that "repeated patterns of sensations, whether of the recent or distant past, had left traces in the body, making the individual an epitome of his or her racial history" (3). Indeed, Lily's intimation that she embodies a racial past responsible for "all of her instinctive resistances, of taste, of training, of blind inherited scruples" was a popular Spencerian notion of the day (104). As Forbes Phillips queried in 1906, "Is it not possible that the child may inherit some of his ancestor's memory? That . . . flashes of reminiscence are the sudden awakening . . . of something we have in our blood . . . the records of an ancestor's past life?" (980). For Wharton, the answer was self-evident: Lily's "ancestral memory" reveals not only her deep racial consciousness but also, more importantly, her embodiment of race itself.

Wharton's early fiction was profoundly invested in the imbricated logic of race, class and national identity. If, on one level, *The House of Mirth* famously documents a woman's disinheritance – from familial money, from maternal support, from timely true love, from political power and from the material comforts of social position – I will suggest that the novel in fact pursues precisely the opposite end. Although Wharton indicates that Lily's status as a 29-year-old unmarried socialite renders her vulnerable to the whims of what Charlotte Perkins Gilman called "the sexuo-economic relation" (*Women and Economics* 121), she equally insists that her heroine's racial status is reassuringly immutable. Race becomes an essentialist – if deeply problematic – answer to the cultural vulnerabilities of class and gender. Wharton uses Lily's disinheritance, in other words, to underscore and consolidate the permanence of her racial inheritance, effectively reworking the amorphous possibilities of class and gender into a seemingly inviolate teleology of blood. In this sense, *The House of Mirth* highlights the tensions inherent in the now familiar trinity of race, class and gender: while class and gender have conventionally structured Wharton criticism, race is the missing but historically crucial component complicating progressive interpretations of Wharton's project.

Lily's body becomes a supreme emblem of her race in all of the turn-of-the-century senses of the term.[1] As a figure for whiteness, class pedigree, western European origin and incipient nativism, Lily articulates a central set of early twentieth-century patrician anxieties: that the ill-bred, the foreign and the poor would overwhelm the native elite; that American culture would fall victim to the "vulgar" tastes of the masses; and that the country's oligarchy would fail to reproduce itself and commit "race suicide."[2] What links these concerns is an implicit belief – held by Wharton and a number of her elite compatriots – in a genealogical conception of American citizenship, one that transformed the contingencies of gendered disadvantage and class decline into an anthropology of racial extinction. Here, one hears the echoes of Hippolyte Taine, the French historian whom Wharton hailed as "one of the formative influences of my youth – the greatest after Darwin, Spencer & Lecky" (*Letters* 136). By bringing Lamarckian theories of evolution to bear on pre-Mendelian notions of blood, Taine, in Thomas Gossett's estimation, "did the most to translate race theory into an explicit force in [nineteenth-century] literature" (199). Not only were "the French and the Italians . . . 'races,'" according to Taine, but their defining traits were also discernable in their national literatures (Gossett 200). While some of Wharton's vocabulary of race might sound familiar to those versed in the late twentieth century's semantics of skin, other components of Wharton's racialized idiom demand a more historically nuanced interpretation. It was with Taine-inspired insouciance, for example, that Wharton could confidently declare in 1905 that "far-sighted altruism savours of the romantic northern races; beneath a hot sun there is less weighing of remote contingencies" (*Uncollected* 112).[3]

To examine the pervasive and instrumental role of Wharton's racial strategy, this chapter will locate *The House of Mirth* within a diverse range of cultural phenomena that together condition the novel's complex treatment of race. In this respect, I hope to add a cultural dimension to the growing debate over Wharton's racial politics. This debate, by turns reproving, apologetic, defensive and ambivalent, originated in large part with the work of Dale Bauer, Hildegard Hoeller and Elizabeth Ammons, who, in the mid-1990s, began to look into Wharton's treatment of race. In *Edith Wharton's Brave New Politics* (1994), Bauer described Wharton as "unable or unwilling" to see race for the "restrictive [category]" it was and thus a constraining element on a par with sex and class in Wharton's work (54, 55). "[S]he never recognizes the reprehensible oversimplification of her own racial politics," Bauer remonstrated, "– the hatred of 'nigger society' and 'dirty Jews'" (111). Hoeller saw Wharton's reductive attitude toward race somewhat differently. Borrowing a formulation from Henry Louis Gates Jr., she argued that, as "Wharton's only 'trope of ultimate, irreducible difference,'" race was central to her thinking and her writing ("Impossible Rosedale" 14). Ammons even tempered her own early insistence that gender was at the root of Edith Wharton's "argument with America." "[W]hen pushed to choose," she admitted, "Wharton's racial and class allegiances overpowered her gender ones" ("Race" 81).

These arguments proved to be a watershed in Wharton scholarship. Since the mid-1990s, new critical work has emerged that actively interrogates what Stuart Hutchinson mordantly terms Wharton's "recurrent and creatively unexplored prejudices about sex, race, and class" (431). This overdue interest, while welcome, at times suffers from some definitional constraints that were inadvertently put in place by Ammons, Hoeller and Bauer. In particular, these critics tended to define race in narrowly phenotypic terms. Bauer, for example, privileges Wharton's post-war material in large part because, after 1920, Wharton began "to see race as a biologically specific category and not, as [she] had more loosely used the term, as a line of descent" (15). Wharton's turn toward a more essentialist "conscious[ness] of race," Bauer implies, makes her late novels more racially legible. Thus, in *The Children* (1928) and *The Buccaneers* (1938), Bauer finds race embodied in "the American racial other, the Negro" (183). Ammons likewise confines race to the limited constraints of phenotype. Lily's "dazzling, overdetermined whiteness" in *The House of Mirth* thus emphasizes the "shiny, Semitic" alterity of Simon Rosedale (79). Subsequent critics, among them Anne MacMaster and Augusta Rohrbach, have retained this phenotypic logic to substantiate more sympathetic portraits of what they see as Wharton's shrewd, ironic and ultimately self-knowing deployment of race. MacMaster regards Ellen Olenska as the "dark heroine" of *The Age of Innocence*, an embodiment of the novel's "Africanist presence" (191, 188), while Rohrbach reads *The House of Mirth* as a latter-day incarnation of the tragic mulatta narrative, with Lily as the doomed slave awaiting her fate at the auction block.[4]

While color has clearly played a central and insidious role in America's ongoing obsession with race (we need only look at the passing narratives of Charles Chestnutt, James Weldon Johnson and Pauline E. Hopkins for confirmation), phenotype alone does not account for the multi-faceted hermeneutics of race that animated early twentieth-century American culture. In this respect, Victoria C. Hattam's observation that "we frequently invoke rather timeless notions of race as if we can move from 1860 through 1960 . . . without attending to the very dramatic shifts in languages of race over this period" is a keen one (63). While my own views have been challenged and enriched by current Wharton scholarship, I share the concerns of historians like Barbara J. Fields, Eric Foner and Eric Arnesen who worry that, in Arnesen's words, those who focus on phenotype generally, and whiteness more particularly, "often conflate the ubiquity of racial thought – scientific and popular racisms which hierarchically ranked a variety of European 'races' – and whiteness" (17). Eugenicists and immigration restrictionists at the outset of the twentieth century were not in the habit of invoking whiteness as a category of racial differentiation. Rather, according to Arnesen, "they talked of multiple races, which, depending on the particular classification, could number in the dozens for Europeans alone" (14). As Ruth Frankenberg acknowledges in her work on twentieth-century conceptions of whiteness, "Were one to undertake a history of . . . 'generic' white culture, it would fragment into a thousand tributary elements, culturally specific religious observances, and class survival mechanisms as well as mass-produced commodities and mass media" (204).

Barbara Fields has underscored and elaborated on these problems. Despite the fact that it is "all the rage" to figure out how the European immigrant became white, "no one deems it pertinent to such exploration to ask how African and Afro-Caribbean immigrants became black. Whiteness, according to its bards, may be identity; but blackness, their silence confirms, is identification, authoritative and external" (51). The assumption that race boils down to a question of blackness or whiteness is itself a bitter legacy of the one-drop rule, Fields maintains. "Whether as a rough-and-ready ideology or as a legal definition, racism in America has served, not to classify or categorize people, but to specify who is black and who is not" (51). Despite efforts by black Americans to wrest self-definition away from the semantic stranglehold of race, "the equation of self-definition and race for Afro-Americans – and for them alone – is an axiom, no more in need of proof than susceptible of it" (50). If we reduce race to a Manichean question of color (however problematically determined or construed), we risk forgetting, in Lucius Outlaw's words, that while "'race' is continually with us as an organizing, explanatory concept, what the term refers to – that is, the origin and basis of 'racial' differences – has not remained constant" (61–2).

I take my cue from this appeal to historical specificity. Eric Foner's observation that we must "examine the specific historical circumstances under which one or another element of identity comes to the fore as a motivation for political and social action" thus informs my own approach (Foner, "Response" 58). Like Judith Sensibar and Frederick Wegener, who have responded to the "challenge of Wharton's imperialist aesthetics" by launching a discerning and closely analyzed investigation of the archival, documentary and literary materials that informed Wharton's work (Wegener, "Rabid" 805), I see my project as further testimony to the "mutual embeddedness of art and history" (Gallagher and Greenblatt 7). Wharton's representation and deployment of race is best understood within the context of early twentieth-century American culture. As Peggy Pascoe reminds us, "the important point was not that biology determined culture" in post-Civil War America, "(indeed, the split between the two was only dimly perceived), but that race, understood as an indivisible essence that included not only biology but also culture, and intelligence, was a compellingly significant factor in history and society" (48). The logic of race in *The House of Mirth* similarly transcends issues of skin, encoding instead a complex semiotics of class, genealogy, ethnicity and nation.

Wharton's own multiform dialogue with the racial questions of her day demonstrates at once her profound investment in the hybridity of American culture and her simultaneous rejection of the country's elastic accommodations. On one level, the very multi-vocality of race within turn-of-the-century American rhetoric made it quintessentially useful to Wharton's purposes. If race could expansively embrace the changing dimensions of class, family, ethnicity and nation, it often did so precisely to transform these fluctuating categories into an "indivisible essence" – a static vision of the organic, the permanent and the real. Expediency was central to this strategy. As cultural democratization, class mobility and ethnic pluralism eroded the elite's belief in the social exclusivity of Darwinian fitness, hereditary distinction increasingly seemed neither permanent nor unique. The patrician rationale behind race thus underwent a perceptible shift, becoming less a function of nature – with its manifest susceptibility to change, excess and ruin – and more a function of culture, the rarefied domain of beauty, order and permanence. Caught on shifting ideological ground, Wharton strategically exploited the meaning that best suited the situation at hand. Thus, she variously insisted that race was natural and hence inimitable, that it was cultural and thus durable and, ultimately, that it was spiritual and therefore intangible. Because this pliant notion of race could encompass everything from class affiliation and genealogical origin, to physical appearance and aesthetic preference, it served as an all-purpose ideological epoxy, fixing disparate and often unpredictable orders of meaning within a seemingly structured, essentialist taxonomy.

This protean approach is evident in *The House of Mirth*, a text that, along with Thomas Dixon's *The Clansman*, captured the popular imagination of 1905. Wharton famously observed that her first New York novel had explored how "a frivolous society can acquire dramatic significance only through what its frivolity destroys" (*Backward Glance* 207). Critics have long assumed that Wharton was criticizing her own affluent Knickerbocker set, an interpretation bolstered by her scathing indictment of the elite self-interest and moral cowardice that catalyze Lily's demise. But Wharton's remark equally condemns American culture more generally – a culture in which entrenched class distinctions had given way to what her friend Barrett Wendell called "the dangers of democratic tyranny" ("Democracy" 188). In a 1905 letter to Morgan Dix, rector of Trinity Church in New York, Wharton noted that "Social conditions as they are just now in our new world, where the sudden possession of money has come without inherited obligations, or any traditional sense of solidarity between the classes, is a vast & absorbing field for the novelist" (*Letters* 99). Who are these rich new Americans? Surely they are not Lily's wealthy friends who, despite their instrumental role in her demise, hardly qualify as the disruptive *arrivistes* of Wharton's complaint. Rather, the author seems to fault other, less genealogically privileged citizens, whose ascendancy has fostered the culture of materialism and mobility that spells Lily's doom. Because their advantages are bought goods rather than birthright, these Americans have challenged the very foundations on which the social hierarchy is based. A potent combination of urbanized labor and robber-baron industry had dealt "a double blow" to the complacent American patriciate (Herman 166). As Arthur Herman points out, elite intellectuals felt themselves doubly besieged: "anarchy and despotism" threatened from below, and "incorporated power and greed" menaced from above (168). Even more perilously, the old stock found itself strangely attracted to the invader's clamorous ways (Kaplan 92–3). Wharton's response to these conditions was adamant: an upstart culture that could not value Lily Bart, she insisted, could itself have no value.

This seems to be what Wharton had in mind when she remarked in 1905 that a "handful of vulgar people, bent on spending and enjoying, may seem a negligible factor in the social development of the race, but they become an engine of destruction through the illusions they kill and the generous ardors they turn to despair" (*Uncollected* 110). If vulgarity, like frivolousness, was a symptom of egalitarian leveling, then Wharton crucially reinscribed this phenomenon within the context of racial decline. Inherited distinctions, she contended, were disappearing in a democratic quagmire of spending and enjoying. As her admired mentor, the Harvard art historian Charles Eliot Norton, observed, "Quantity tells against quality": "Vulgar people" were cultural vandals, eradicating "the common inheritance . . . of thought and experience of the race" and accelerating national disintegration (321, 322). The "shallow and the idle . . . always rest on an underpinning of wasted human possibilities," Wharton agreed in *The House of Mirth*'s 1936 preface (*Uncollected* 266). Lily personifies this squandered Anglo-Saxon promise. She is caught in a complex web of racial discourses that require at once her apotheosis and her extinction.

THE VICE OF BREEDING

From its opening moments when Lawrence Selden encounters Lily in Grand Central Station, *The House of Mirth* meticulously describes its heroine's eugenic superiority: "He led her through the throng of return-ing holiday-makers, past sallow-faced girls in preposterous hats, and flat-chested women struggling with paper bundles . . . Was it possible that she belonged to the same race? The dinginess, the crudity of this average section of womanhood made him feel how specialized she was" (5). The female throng highlights Lily's evolutionary specialization. Echoing the work of the American neurologist George M. Beard, who had declared in 1881 that "the lower must minister to the higher . . . millions perish that hundreds may survive" (302), Selden theorizes that "a great many dull and ugly people

must . . . have been sacrificed to produce her" (*House* 5). Lily's evolutionary advantages are evident. Her vulnerabilities, however, are equally so.
Despite the appearance that Lily belongs to the "same race" – the human
race – Wharton will gradually insist that Lily represents an exclusive, albeit
imperiled race – at once superior and fatally overspecialized.

Lily is, in a sense, *over*bred: "She could not figure herself as anywhere but
in a drawing-room, diffusing elegance as a flower sheds perfume" (100).
Beard had warned that "development . . . along any one line of . . . race,
family, or tribe, in time reaches its limit, beyond which it cannot pass" (300),
and this vulnerable perfection is crucial to Wharton's logic. Too refined for
her own good, Lily is racially doomed. As Henry Adams would grimly
predict in 1919, when "man [is] specialized beyond the hope of further
variation . . . he must be treated as . . . a degraded potential" (*Degradation*
195).

Lily's very survival requires certain choice conditions:

The dreary limbo of dinginess lay all around and beneath that little illuminated
circle in which life reached its finest efflorescence, as the mud and sleet of a winter
night enclose a hot-house filled with tropical flowers. All this was in the natural
order of things, and the orchid basking in its artificially created atmosphere could
round the delicate curves of its petals undisturbed by the ice on the panes. (*House*
150)

Lily is a hyperevolved specimen whose purity demands a life sheltered
from the encroaching dinginess of American democracy. The hothouse
with frosted windows thus perfectly captures her evolutionary dilemma:
once breeding has become a rarefied art, akin to the skilled horticulture of
lilies and orchids, the well-bred can no longer survive in the chill air of a
potentially heterogeneous world.[5]

The hothouse, we know from John Auchard, is also the quintessential site of aesthetic decadence – a place "rich in discriminated delicacy,
but . . . foster[ing] little or no hardy growth" (1–2). Lily's effete hyper-
aestheticism in fact reveals Wharton's unexpected place in the discourse most often associated with the flamboyant Oscar Wilde.[6] Indeed,
despite her prim persona, Wharton professed the "keenest admiration" for her friend Paul Bourget's *Essais de psychologie contemporaine*
(1883), a collection that contained his landmark analysis of decadence
(*Uncollected* 213). Bourget described decadence as the inevitable consequence of a stratified culture's capitulation to the forces of anarchy and
barbarism. Under such circumstances, he said, the elite inevitably relin-
quished its commitment to social unity and embraced instead an "aesthetic

individualism" (Calinescu 171). The results, for Bourget, were appealing: "Let us indulge in the unusualness of our ideal and form, even though we imprison ourselves in an unvisited solitude. Those who come to us will be truly our brothers, and why sacrifice what is most intimate, special and personal?" (qtd. in Calinescu 171).

Lily dramatically personifies this lonely prisoner. Unwilling to tolerate America's crass compromises, she is prepared to sacrifice herself to the "intimate, special and personal" – a sincere gesture that requires the height of artifice. As the French poet and critic Théophile Gautier had asserted in 1868, decadence was the "inevitable idiom of . . . civilizations in which factitious life has replaced natural life," in which art exists for itself alone.[7] Lily is Wharton's answer to these contradictory imperatives: at once personal and artful, intimate and factitious, she is a portrait of American decadence.

Is Lily's hair "ever so slightly brightened by art" (5)? Was it her "streak of sylvan freedom . . . that lent such savour to her artificiality" (13)? Selden's speculations arguably beg the question. The issue for Wharton is not whether Lily is natural or artificial but how nature can be transformed into an acculturated art. Lily's mysterious blend of the sylvan and the synthetic captures natural perfection in the realm of aesthetic permanence. She projects what Alan Trachtenberg calls "an official American version of reality" – the natural reconceived by the upper classes and recast as an emphatic rejection of ethnic and racial pluralism (143). In a world transformed by urbanization, immigration and social mobility, Wharton insists that Lily's racial perfection is not simply natural (and thus presumably vulnerable to loss); rather, she is the product of Gilded Age culture – the "privileged domain of refinement, aesthetic sensibility" and continuity (Trachtenberg 143). In this sense, Lily's "art of blushing at the right time" fuses nature and culture in a deeply class-specific way (*House* 6): Lily effectively transforms the biological into a culturally engineered aesthetic. Surpassing unaffected beauty, she controls the natural, projecting a decadent vision of racial permanence.[8]

The novel's opening "sight of Miss Lily Bart," motionless in Grand Central Station, dramatically stages this strategy. Standing "apart from the crowd, letting it drift by her to the platform or the street" (3), Lily's pose stresses her stylized distinction. While sallow women hurry through the terminal, itself the very symbol of industrial movement and commerce, Miss Bart's unmoving presence not only forces Selden to "pause," but also stops anonymous passers-by, "for Lily Bart was a figure to arrest even the suburban traveler rushing to his last train" (4). Wharton's choreography suspends Lily in a moment of arrested dynamism: fixed in one of her many ensuing *tableaux* of racialized stasis, Lily distinguishes herself from the mobile American crowd by performing a fantasy of equilibrium, wholeness and aesthetic singularity. Having "learned the value of contrast," she is "lifted to a height apart" (47, 116).

Wharton, of course, was not alone in attempting to stage racial perfection by capturing an ideal image of the endangered Anglo-American. As Nancy Bentley has shown, Carl Akeley's 1908 taxidermical displays of African mammals in New York's American Museum of Natural History (AMNH) are also relevant to Wharton's project. Building on Donna Haraway's assertion that the Akeley specimens resist the vulgarity of industrial modernism by representing nature as a permanent totality, Bentley argues that *The House of Mirth* deploys a similar aesthetic, transforming the modern woman's "chaotic subjectivity" into "a social or medical artifact" (192). Despite her innovative approach, however, Bentley's argument ironically serves a somewhat conventional purpose, emphasizing Wharton's preoccupations with gender, class and authorial agency.[9] Taxidermy's central role in the novel's racial critique remains unexplained.

The art of endowing the natural with "factitious immortality," and the unnatural with the "illusion of . . . life itself," taxidermy engendered a fantasy of plenitude in which eugenic specimens were held in poses of ideal strength, transcending the potential concessions of time (Walton 555, 556). By 1900 a growing number of urban elites shared Theodore Roosevelt's alarm at the "extensive and wasteful slaughter of strange and beautiful forms of wild life" by the "forces of greed, carelessness, and sheer brutality" (Roosevelt, "Conservation" 424, 426; see also Judd 209–22). Fearing the annihilation of the country's "leading species," the director of the New York Zoological Park, William T. Hornaday, urged American hunters to collect "examples of . . . beautiful and interesting animal[s]." "[I]f you must go and kill things," he declared in 1900, at least "save their heads and mount them as atonement for your deeds of blood" (ix, 158). This logic, at once sporting and strangely spiritualized, informs Lily's racial fate. Like the nation's imperiled wildlife, she is a Miranda among Calibans, an innocent creature who requires the staged naturalism of a protective Prospero (*House* 135). Indeed, *The House of Mirth* reveals a moment of self-recognition, however subliminal: America's elite had glimpsed the future and realized that they, like Akeley's gorillas, were an endangered species.

Mark Seltzer's observation that "the naturalist art of taxidermy" seems "to hover midway between the *tableau vivant* and the *nature morte*" offers a provocative correlation in this regard (170). Like the AMNA dioramas, the art of *tableaux vivants* immobilizes the mobile, rendering life still. The real is represented in a stylized simulacrum that fixes nature in an attitude utterly controlled by human technology. Consider, then, the continuity between Akeley's spectacles and Lily's motionless poses which culminate in a ballroom tableau of Joshua Reynolds's "Mrs. Lloyd." The logic informing both styles of exhibition reveals a stunning instance of nature's unnaturalness, the decadent preservation of the organic in the service of a perfect but failing racial myth.[10]

If the patrician impulse to glorify racial culture and the taxidermic quest to capture eugenic nature shared a common desire – to secure an American identity impervious to hybridization and change – then, as Stuart Culver notes, such "arresting" displays also ran a significant risk, for "The image of a complete body is also the picture of death or dehumanization" (100). Wharton acknowledged this hazard in the final pages of her 1905 travel narrative, *Italian Backgrounds*. Recalling a Venetian museum where "life-sized mannikins" stiffly displayed costly eighteenth-century apparel, Wharton regards "the very rigidity of their once supple joints" as a poignant "allegory of their latter state" – a sumptuous nobility laid waste by Napoleonic republicanism (213). "[D]iscarded playthings of the gods," these lifeless aristocrats now embody an inanimate fate that threatens Lily's own stylized stasis. Like them, she risks becoming a "poor [doll] of destiny," a wooden aristocrat collapsing the distinction between person and thing (213).

The novel's very title encodes this anxiety. Taken from Ecclesiastes 7.4 – "The heart of the wise is in the house of mourning; but the heart of fools is in the house of mirth" (*New Oxford Annotated Bible*) – the novel poses a crucial choice: is the American "house" to be the artificial construction of fools or the racially authentic home of oligarchic mourning? In the final pages of *The Decoration of Houses* (1897), the interior design treatise she wrote with architect Ogden Codman Jr., Wharton begins to tackle this question:

Modern civilization has been called a varnished barbarism: a definition that might well be applied to . . . modern decoration. Only a return to architectural principles can raise the decoration of houses to the level of the past. Vasari said of the Farnesina palace that it was not built, but really born – *non murato ma veramente nato*; and this phrase is but the expression of an ever-present sense – the sense of interrelation of parts, or unity of the whole. (192)

Scornful of modern American barbarism, Wharton appeals to the principles of the past – a European past in which dwellings were not built, but born.[11] Every house, she maintains, is an "organism" whose essential integrity is compromised by the "superficial application of ornament totally independent of structure" (1). This organism, as her biological language suggests, is more than just a house: it is a metaphor for the country's elite, and a metonym for the United States at large. "It is a fact recognized by political economists that changes in manners and customs, no matter under what form of government, usually originate with the wealthy or aristocratic minority, and are thence transmitted to other classes," Wharton remarks. "This rule naturally holds good of house-planning" (7). Throughout *Decoration* and later in *The House of Mirth*, Wharton attempts to restore America's "aristocratic minority" to a sense of "interrelation of parts," a sense, that is, of eugenic plenitude, strength and continuity.

Wharton's repeated analogy between people and their houses is by now familiar: "The Fullness of Life," an 1893 short story, provides perhaps the best-known example of a woman whose "nature is like a great house full of rooms" (22). In *Decoration*, however, the home operates as the central metaphor in a cautionary tale of democracy. The entrance to America's house, Wharton notes, "should clearly proclaim itself an effectual barrier," preventing the "hordes of the uninvited" from trespassing on hallowed ground (*Decoration of Houses* 107; *House* 87). These "other classes" – immigrants, workers and middle-class capitalists – are the human equivalents of Wharton's much-deplored decorative "cheap knick-knacks": they are mass-produced human beings, built – not born – to menace the American patriciate by democratically cluttering the national home.[12] Wharton remarks that "Vulgarity is always noisier than good breeding, and it is instructive to note how a modern bronze will 'talk down' a delicate Renaissance statuette or bust."[13] Unable to make herself heard amid the many-voiced din of modern America, Wharton uses *Decoration* to talk down the abundant agents of varnished barbarism.[14]

The problem in both *Decoration* and *The House of Mirth* is that of staging racial perfection without sacrificing the privileges of personal specificity. If America's elite was threatened by what Edwin Lawrence Godkin caustically called "chromo-civilization" – a mass-produced "pseudo-culture" that "diffused through the community a kind of smattering of all sorts of knowledge"– then blue-blooded Americans were urged to vigilance ("Chromo-civilization" 202). The ubiquitous chromolithograph – a cheap printed copy of an original work of art – had come to represent a dangerous accessibility that would undermine the exclusivity of upper-class privilege. Wharton thus insists in *Decoration*'s nursery section that teaching a child to distinguish between "a good and a bad painting" is a "civic virtue" – one easily destroyed by popular chromos that confused the hierarchical sensibility by imitating authenticity (*Decoration of Houses* 175).

For Wharton, such perils were the inevitable consequence of mass production. In an important 1903 essay, she mockingly connected "the vice of reading" to "[t]hat 'diffusion of knowledge' commonly classed with steam-heat and universal suffrage" (*Uncollected* 99). This "diffusion," like other dubious emblems of modern progress, had produced the dangerously undiscerning "mechanical reader."[15] "To read is not a virtue; but to read well is an art, an art that only the born reader can acquire" (100). By contrasting born readers with their mechanical counterparts, Wharton draws a distinction between Americans who inherit culture and those who acquire it artificially. Here as elsewhere, moreover, she translates modern industrial changes into an ontological opposition between the animate and the inanimate, between the traditional race and those who would erase tradition. Mechanical readers, she laments, "seem to regard literature as a cable-car that can be 'boarded' only by running; while many a born reader may be found unblushingly loitering in the tea-cup times of stage-coach and posting-chaise" (100). The contrast between an older, more exclusive form of "locomotion" and modern mass-transit is telling: mechanical readers represent the newly mobile citizenry rushing through Grand Central Station in *The House of Mirth*; guided by the capricious "*vox populi*" and given to the "socialistic use of certain formulas," they threaten to propel themselves over and beyond the horse-drawn American patriciate (102, 103). Wharton's political and economic critique is clear: democracy threatens the nation with civic unrest, cultural decline and even the wholesale redistribution of wealth.

LIVING PICTURES AND THE CRISIS OF THE REAL

Like *The Decoration of Houses*, *The House of Mirth* offers a blueprint to separate the born from the built. Indeed, *tableaux vivants* perfectly capture the politics of replication and reproduction so fundamental to the novel's racial concerns. New York's "living picture" controversy, fueled by the titillating possibilities of scantily clad performers representing classic works of art, had become a staple of vice debates by the 1890s. In 1894, Susie Kirwin, poseur and design artist, wrote a spirited defense of the entertainment which, she insisted, offered "rational, wholesome enjoyment" for the whole family. Audiences were amazed, not aroused, by the "wonderfully counterfeited" spectacles. The "human model" became "an inanimate thing, no more than so much paint or canvas or marble" (7).

Kirwin's insistence on the lifelessness of *tableaux vivants* indicates at once the fears and fantasies that underwrote the form. If complete mimesis was the longing of realism more generally, then an additional anxiety is equally palpable. *Tableaux vivants* involved a representational shell game in which the person (Lily, in this case) represented a thing (a painting by Reynolds), which in turn represented a person (the original "Mrs. Lloyd"), who then represented a thing (a classical archetype). As we have seen, however, the risk of such sleight of hand is that the person will be confused with the reproducible thing. The very fact that Reynolds's portrait is the subject of parlor theatrics at all proves the case in point: *tableau vivant*, as Henry James made comically clear in his 1899 short story "Paste," was the democratic illusionist's genre of choice. When James's heroine Charlotte Prime questions the appropriateness of using her dead aunt's seemingly faux jewels for a tableau of *Ivanhoe*, her friend Mrs. Guy retorts, "*Our* jewels, for historic scenes, don't tell – the real thing falls short. Rowena must have rubies as big as eggs" (459). The real thing always "falls short" precisely because *tableaux* deliberately conflate the genuine and the counterfeit. The distinction between paste (sham markers of class status) and pearls (authentic essence) is intentionally reversed: the fake suddenly appears real while the real seems fake. "Living pictures" played on this possibility: the authentic was displaced, the original was duplicated, and high art was democratized into yet another American commodity.

Lily's famous appearance midway through the text in an elaborately costumed *tableau* arguably climaxes both the Wellington Bry ball and the novel as a whole. The setting is itself significant. Like Simon Rosedale, the Jewish financier with whom they are repeatedly linked, the "Welly" Brys have made their fortune at the expense of the Knickerbocker elite (121). They are invaders "advancing into a strange country with an insufficient number of scouts" (130). It is no surprise, then, that the Bry gala functions as a journey into the *terra incognita* of a new, democratic America. The ballroom itself is immediately marked as a space of illusion – a *trompe-l'œil* in reverse: "so recent, so rapidly-evoked was the whole *mise-en-scène* that one had to touch the marble columns to learn they were not of cardboard, to set one's self in one of the damask-and-gold arm-chairs to be sure it was not painted against the wall." This is not the real America, linked in the novel to the rituals of an elusive European past; instead, this is a strangely improvised country associated with fairy tale and fantasy, a "boundary world between fact and imagination" (132, 133).

The Bry entertainment opens with a series of *tableaux* "in which the fugitive curves of living flesh . . . have been subdued to plastic harmony without losing the charm of life" (133). Wharton's socialite performers, accommodating themselves to the limitations of theatrical form, effectively become "types." Carry Fisher's "short dark-skinned face," for instance, makes a "typical Goya," while a "young Mrs. Van Alstyne, who showed the frailer Dutch type . . . made a characteristic Vandyck" (133–4). Such classifications participate in the novel's pervasive discourse of racial typology. Rosedale, for example, is earlier described as "a plump rosy man of the blond Jewish type" (14), while Selden has "keenly-modelled dark features which, in a land of amorphous types, gave him the air of belonging to a more specialized race" (65). A staple of Victorian vocabulary, *type* indicated a distinct racial ontology of permanent (if often peculiar) genetic characteristics – a way of determining the general by extrapolating from the specific (Cowling 184).

Typology met its logical extreme in the strange composite photography of the eugenicist Francis Galton, whose work is curiously relevant to Wharton's *tableaux*. By superimposing fractional exposures of individual faces on top of one another, Galton created "portraits" in which distinguishing features faded into a hazy common face. His best work, he claimed, was a composite of the definitive "Jewish type," a synthesis of boys from the London Jews' Free School that captured the Jew's "essence" – his "cold scanning gaze . . . coolly appraising [one] at market value" (243). Galton's work reveals, if nothing else, typology's propensity to erase human specificity in order to mass-produce images of the generic subject. Indeed, if the camera had democratized the formerly elite aesthetic of portraiture, then composite photography introduced a new possibility – what Allan Sekula has called an "essentialist physical anthropology of race" (370).

Wharton's familiarity with Galton's enterprise is evident from a 1905 review of Maurice Hewlett's novel *The Fool Errant*. After criticizing Hewlett's previous heroines, who blur "into a kind of composite portrait, while their moral idiosyncrasies fail to leave any impression at all," Wharton praises the present protagonist whose "certain definiteness of outline [is] marred only by an occasional reversion to type" (*Uncollected* 111). The edges of this critique are sharp, for such typological lapses could hardly be more anathema to Wharton's singular representation of Lily Bart:

[S]o skillfully had the personality of the actors been subdued to the scenes they figured in that even the least imaginative of the audience must have felt a thrill of contrast when the curtain suddenly parted on a picture which was simply and undisguisedly the portrait of Miss Bart.

Here there could be no mistaking the predominance of personality – the unanimous "Oh!" of the spectators was a tribute, not to the brush-work of Reynolds's "Mrs. Lloyd" but to the flesh and blood loveliness of Lily Bart . . . It was as though she had stepped, not out of, but into, Reynolds's canvas, banishing the phantom of his dead beauty by the beams of her living grace. (134)

As an astonishingly vibrant portrait of herself, Lily cannot be reduced to "type." Indeed, by choosing "a type so like her own that she could embody the person represented without ceasing to be herself," Lily transcends typology altogether: she effectively performs the impossible, subordinating the Galtonian composite to her own personal specificity (*House* 134). Unlike her assimilating peers, Lily resists the generic abstraction of "plastic harmony," preserving instead her own "flesh and blood loveliness." Were she to become the portrait she represents, she would risk losing the eugenic quality that makes her previous *tableaux* so arresting and racially loaded. She would risk, in short, becoming a mere type – either the equivalent of the racially typologized Jew or what Seltzer describes as "the American *as* typical, standard, and reproducible" (5).

Wharton rescues Lily from these possibilities by stressing the "predominance of personality" – the "serious purity of the central conception" which can "break through the strongest armour of stock formulas."[16] "Undisguisedly" herself, Lily stands in stylized opposition to the generic and the mechanized – a strategy not without risk. Indeed throughout the novel, Wharton implies that Lily is imperiled by the very racial economy she represents – an economy consumed with purity and terrified of sham. Lily's embodiment of the William Jamesian double self – "there were two selves in her, the one she had always known, and a new abhorrent being to which it found itself chained" – crystallizes this vulnerability (148; see W. James, *Varieties* 142 and Lears, *No Place of Grace* 38). Struggling to define her real self in a world where distinctions between the genuine and the imitative, the natural and the cultural, have all but collapsed, Lily's crisis reveals the instability of race as an ontological category. Indeed, Wharton can only tenuously resolve this problem by shifting the grounds of the debate. To be a "real" self, she increasingly suggests, is to be realigned with a racial "soul" – the "slowly-accumulated past [that] lives in the blood" (319). Walter Benn Michaels's contention that race in this period becomes essentially invisible – something spiritually inherited rather than physically acquired ("Souls") – is thus central to Wharton's logic. Hovering over Lily's deathbed, Selden fantasizes that he can distinguish the "sleeping face" from "the real Lily" who was "close to him, yet invisible and inaccessible" (326). Only in her final tableau of death is Lily truly transmogrified into her authentic racial personality – a disembodied soul, at once real and invisible.[17]

RACIAL ELEGY IN THE HOUSE OF MOURNING

The overreaching effort to consolidate Lily into an authoritative real self reveals at once the imperiled condition of the oligarchic body and Wharton's insistence on its transcendent possibilities. Part of an endangered species, Lily is not so much a circulating commodity as she is a rare museum piece, desirable precisely because she is out of circulation. Stephen Greenblatt's notion that the museum retains its "mystery" by displaying the masterpiece "in such a way as to imply that no one, not even the nominal owner or donor, can penetrate the zone of light and actually possess the wonderful object" is thus pivotal to Wharton's vision. As Rosedale eventually realizes, "It was [Lily's] very manner of holding herself aloof that appealed to his collector's passion for the rare and unattainable" (113). Miss Bart is fundamentally – indeed, ontologically – inviolate.

Rosedale's very presence in the novel underscores this perfect inaccessibility. If the appearance of the Jewish businessman in a "paternal rôle," "kneeling domestically" before Carry Fisher's daughter, seems to reveal the sympathetic "fireside man" (249), then Lily's eventual rejection of Rosedale's proposals indicates the alarming nature of the Jew's familial persona. Although later scenes appear calculated to make Rosedale less sexual and thus more socially admissible, *The House of Mirth* remains what Ammons calls the story of "the flower of Anglo-Saxon womanhood . . . not ending up married to the invading Jew" ("Race" 80). Rosedale as father raises the horrifying specter of reproducing with a Jew – indeed reproducing Jews. The novel's working title, "The Year of the Rose," thus inadvertently reveals one of its central anxieties: were Lily to marry the Jewish millionaire, the country's future might only bring racially degenerating years of the Rosedale.[18]

To prevent this outcome, Wharton commits herself to the iconic preservation of a perfect American museum piece. The Whartonian hothouse thus functions as a gallery – a decadent house of mourning designed to preserve and exhibit a vanishing species.[19] Like the rare "Americana" so lovingly collected by Jefferson Gryce in the opening sequences of the novel, Lily is of interest to the curator, the historian and the "real collector [who] values a thing for its rarity" (11). The acquisition of antiquarian books, by definition "an unmarketable commodity" (20), is in fact crucial to Lily's status. Susan Stewart's point that the "antiquarian sensibility" presumes "a rupture in historical consciousness" which makes "one's own culture *other* – distant and discontinuous," suggests that Lily is simultaneously the object and source of antiquarian desire (142). She is not only a rare, talismanic beauty, but she is also a disenfranchised patrician orphan nostalgically determined to retrieve "an imagined past" (Stewart 142). In this sense, the failure of the Hudson Barts to provide their daughter with "the house not built with the hands but made up of inherited passions and loyalties" marks Lily as the quintessential site of antiquarian loss and nostalgic recuperation

(*House* 319). In her reawakened desire for aristocratic rootedness, Lily embodies the patrician quest for a "homogenous and uninterrupted culture" (*French Ways* 80).

Such impulses reveal Wharton's sympathy with a group of like-minded northeastern intellectuals who, fearing for the country's future, increasingly forged a rhetoric of "racial nativism" (Higham, *Strangers in the Land* 137). Norton, writing in 1888, had descried "a predominance of . . . the uneducated and unrefined masses, over . . . the more enlightened and better-instructed few" (321). Under such circumstances, he worried, the republic surely could not survive the melting pot. As the *New York Tribune* editor Whitelaw Reid told a posh gathering of the New England Society in 1903, "We have emphatically and even vociferously made everybody else, from all over the world, at home in our Fathers' house. But as we look around at the variegated throng, do we always feel just as much at home ourselves?" (46)

Voicing a growing sense of racial siege, the Williams College minister John H. Denison declared in 1893, "We have tried to share our freedom with foreigners, only to discover that freedom is not transferable . . . The higher force cannot be dominated by the lower. Nature will not tolerate it; she prefers disintegration and reorganization" (18). The imagined world of the racially uniform New England village was crumbling into what Henry James in 1904 called "a prodigious amalgam . . . a hotch-potch of racial ingredients" (*Writings* 456). Social Darwinism armed patrician intellectuals with a fitting vocabulary to predict imminent Anglo-Saxon extinction. Denison's warning that old-stock Americans had "entered upon a struggle for survival" and would soon share the fate of "the American Indian and the bison" (17) found its most famous spokesman in Theodore Roosevelt, who urged well-born Americans to resist "race suicide" ("Letter"). Cheap immigrant labor, the president of the Massachusetts Institute of Technology, Francis A. Walker, agreed, had forced America's "native" stock to reduce family size in order to preserve a higher standard of living – a socio-economic strategy that spelled biological ruin (Higham, *Strangers in the Land* 143–4). As Henry Adams observed, Kelvin's second law of thermodynamics – the "Law of Entropy" – made the dissipation of America's "vital energies" inevitable (*Degradation* 184–5, 155). Henry's brother Brooks, an occasional guest at Wharton's Berkshire estate, spoke for a generation of Brahmins when he gloomily predicted that "when the waste of energetic material is so great that the martial and imaginative stocks fail to reproduce themselves, disintegration may set in, the civilized population may perish, and a reversion may take place to a primitive form" (x–xi). Fearful for their cultural survival, upper-class nativists could only look forward to eventual reorganization in the wake of imminent racial disintegration.

In 1902, Wharton began writing the novel she would abandon after some seventy pages to begin work on *The House of Mirth*. It was entitled "Disintegration." The story of an ambitious woman who deserts her shabbily genteel husband and daughter only to win social redemption after marrying an upstart millionaire, "Disintegration" was clearly a dress rehearsal for *The Mother's Recompense* (1925; see Joslin, *Edith Wharton* 114–16). More fundamentally, however, Wharton's unfinished project outlines the racial concerns that were to dominate *The House of Mirth*.

The narrative charts the spiraling decline of the cuckolded Henry Clephane, whose loyalty to the "family pieties" and the "honourable past," "six or seven generations of upright and gentle living," magnifies the gravity of his wife's betrayal. "To continue the family tradition . . . had been part of his conception of life . . . to have failed in this continuance meant the rending of innumerable fibres with which his own were inwoven" (48–9). Alice Clephane's infidelity strikes a number of chords simultaneously: not only does she sever Henry's affiliation to an unblemished genealogy, but she also does so as a direct result of democratic license. Henry cynically proposes to write a book on the subject:

"It's to be a study of the new privileged class – a study of the effects of wealth without responsibility. Talk of the socialist peril! That's not where the danger lies. The inherent vice of democracy is the creation of a powerful class of which it can make no use – a kind of Frankenstein monster, an engine of social disintegration . . . The place to study [the results] is here and now – here in this huge breeding-place of inequalities that we call a republic, where class-distinctions, instead of growing out of the inherent needs of the social organism, are arbitrarily established by a force that works against it!" (64)

Railing against counterfeit class distinctions and pining for what Denison called "the Anglo-Saxon organic nation" (26), Clephane becomes Wharton's case-study in "the disease" of racial decline ("Disintegration" 64). He is the end of the line, the victim of a culture untethered from its legitimate fixtures of racial demarcation. As his friend George Severance predicts, when South Dakota divorcees outnumber Old New Yorkers, society "will have ceased to exist": "There will be nothing to hold it together. You can't found a state on a penal settlement. But before that happens, the social instinct of self-preservation will assert itself: society will not let itself be destroyed by a band of robbers and murderers" (61). "Disintegration" reveals the more extreme edges of Wharton's conservative critique. The invaders of American life are robbers and murderers, threatening to transform a consecrated nation into a penal settlement. The socialist peril cannot rival the menace of these democratic impostors – artificial Frankenstein monsters, built, not born, to threaten oligarchic dominion and social cohesion.

If "Disintegration" demonstrates Wharton's share in the abundant gloom of her intellectual milieu, her failure to finish the manuscript indicates an important shift in her thinking. Like a number of contributors to the discourses of racial nativism and aesthetic decadence, Wharton eventually came to believe that Anglo-Saxon extinction, however inevitable, would take place not in the depths of Henry Clephane's demise, but at the peak of Lily Bart's brilliant racial achievement. Barrett Wendell's exhilarated 1893 pronouncement that "[t]he songs that live are the swan-songs" speaks to this realignment (*Stelligeri* 113). A great culture would only vanish at its aesthetic summit, Wendell insisted, for "Artistic expression is apt to be the final fruit of a society about to wither" (*Literary History* 462). This singular combination of elation and elegy found its most ardent spokesman in George Edward Woodberry, a professor of comparative literature at Columbia University. "Race-history," Woodberry declared in 1903, had always documented the process of Christian sacrifice whereby eugenic peoples, "at the acme of achievement," bequeathed their civilized legacy to their inferiors – what he called the "absorption of aristocracies in democracies" (29, 5). If "a vanquished nation [alone] can civilize its victors," as Wharton's friend Vernon Lee had maintained (45), then Woodberry's conclusions were compelling. "[F]or a race, as for an individual," he rapturously declared, "there is a time to die, and that time, as history discloses it, is the moment of perfection" (4).

Lily Bart fully embodies this paradigm of apotheosis, sacrifice and extinction. Wharton captures and immobilizes her heroine at the moment of racial perfection, a fate clearly preferable, she implies, to monitoring Lily's slow demise in New York's competitive wilderness. Lily's final tableau of death thus transforms her into the period's quintessential museum piece – the perfectly preserved taxidermic specimen. As Selden enters Lily's boardinghouse room, he discovers "a delicate impalpable mask over the living lineaments he had known" (325–6). Lily becomes the site of racial elegy: she incarnates the house of mourning. Despite her social decline, she embodies a decadent fantasy of oligarchical wholeness that, like Akeley's dioramas and the Gryce Americana, preserves an iconic instance of completion and permanence.[20] Wharton's description is thus rich in the language of eugenic preservationism:

But at least he *had* loved her . . . and if the moment had been fated to pass from them before they could seize it, he saw now that, for both, it had been saved whole out of the ruin of their lives.

It was this moment of love, this fleeting victory over themselves, which had kept them from atrophy and extinction . . .

He knelt by her bed and bent over her . . . and in the silence there passed between them the word which made all clear. (329)

It is precisely this battle against "the influence of her surroundings," now suddenly democratic and accessible, that Wharton wages throughout *The House of Mirth*. Like Roosevelt and Hornaday, she is committed not only to protecting Lily from "atrophy and extinction," but also to the larger project of preserving her "whole out of the ruin of their lives."

This commitment supersedes all others in *The House of Mirth* as it does in the logic of taxidermy. The emphasis on Lily's completeness in fact outweighs the possibility that she might eventually produce future generations of eugenic offspring. She is more useful dead and stuffed, as it were, than alive. The messy contingencies of motherhood, Wharton seems to suggest, would compromise – indeed diminish – Lily's status as a racial icon. The longing for an ancestral past with the "power of broadening and deepening the individual existence, of attaching it by mysterious links of kinship to all the mighty sum of human striving," is realized not in the quest for an individual family (Lily, after all, rejects her own stifling kin) but in the desire, in Wharton's vocabulary, for "Family" – for the sense of genealogical continuity that can only originate in those elusive centers "of early pieties" that are born of aristocratic blood (319). Wharton sacrifices Lily to these values: she is to stand for a kinship that must of necessity supersede individual, mortal families, and instead represent a timeless tableau of racial stasis.

Lily's final hallucination of cradling the infant daughter of working-class Nettie Struther thus enacts the novel's most fundamental fantasy: Lily appropriates the child of the reformed laboring class as her own, a switch that marks at once working-class acculturation and the "mysterious," immaculate reproduction of the elite – what Candace Waid calls Lily's "virgin sacrifice" (47). Indeed, if the novel's conclusion seems to envision class convergence, it does so on fundamentally oligarchic terms. The striking absence of any proletarian consciousness in Nettie's fawning idolatry of Lily ("Sometimes, when I . . . got to wondering why things were so queerly fixed in the world, I used to remember that *you* were having a lovely time . . . and that seemed to show there was a kind of justice somewhere" [312–13]) implies that a "just" world is one governed by a "traditional sense of solidarity between the classes." In such a world, one knows one's place.

Nettie's decision, then, to name her infant daughter "Marry Anto'nette . . . after the French queen in the play at the Garden – I told George the actress reminded me of you," satirically captures at once the dynamics of class emulation and, for Wharton, their racial impossibility (314). The baby's silly name only has meaning in a democratic society that transforms doomed aristocrats into the stuff of cheap melodrama, and real nobility into the site of mimetic, mass-produced distortion. *The House of Mirth* will ultimately insist that Lily's racial markers are inimitable. Despite Nettie's maternal ambitions, Wharton reassures us that, in the end, "Marry Anto'nette" will only be a doubly displaced theatrical imitation of the disappearing real thing.

Indeed, if Wharton acknowledges the inevitable Darwinian doom of America's insular elite, she equally envisions a form of cultural production that transcends the mutating mechanics of mere survival. Lily embodies a sacrificial transmission of culture only possible within the walls of the most hallowed of museums – the ancient cathedral, the site where preservation becomes veneration and the specimen becomes the relic. Without the untidiness of mating, Lily enacts a purified form of cultural reproduction, mystically incorporating Nettie's baby: "[it was] as though the child entered into her and became part of herself" (319, 316). Like the sacred mother in Henry Adams's famous anti-modern critique, Lily embodies "the force that created it all – the Virgin, the Woman – by whose genius 'the stately monuments of superstition' were built."[21] She offers an elegiac answer to the mechanized culture of the dynamo – what Wharton saw as society's "atoms whirling away from each other in some wild centrifugal dance" (*House* 319). In "sacrificing her pleasures to the claims of immemorial tradition," Lily incarnates J.-K. Huysmans's "Christian Venus," the *mater dolorosa* of the "word which made all clear."[22] A plaintive paragon of "spiritual motherhood," she bears the pathos and promise of Anglo-Saxon deliverance. Her "passion of charity for [the] race" in the end engenders the word (Wharton, *Sanctuary* 112) – a word "not . . . for twilight, but for the mo[u]rning" (*House* 324).

CHAPTER 3

"A close corporation": the body and the machine in The Fruit of the Tree

Between 1905 and 1911, Edith Wharton published three novels, each of which circulated with fascinated horror around the prone body of an immobilized woman. At the conclusion of *The House of Mirth* (1905), Lawrence Selden discovers "on a bed, with motionless hands and calm, unrecognizing face, the semblance of Lily Bart" (325). Six years later, in the culminating moments of her bleak New England tale, *Ethan Frome* (1911), Wharton's narrator discovers the dreadful source of Ethan's grief: the incapacitated body of a "much smaller and slighter" Mattie Silver:

She sat huddled in an arm-chair near the stove, and when I came in she turned her head quickly toward me, without the least corresponding movement of her body. Her hair was as grey as her companion's, her face as bloodless and shrivelled, but amber-tinted, with swarthy shadows sharpening her nose and hollowing the temples. Under her shapeless dress her body kept its limp immobility, and her dark eyes had the bright witch-like stare that disease of the spine sometimes gives. (125)

While Wharton would return to this image six years later in *Summer's* harrowing description of Mary Hyatt, whose body lies atop the Mountain "like a dead dog in a ditch" (*Summer* 163), *The House of Mirth* and *Ethan Frome* form an oddly compact trilogy with the less well-known novel that links them, *The Fruit of the Tree* (1907), Wharton's peculiar foray into the worlds of industrial reform, bodily paralysis and euthanasia.

Wharton began work on the manuscript within months of publishing *The House of Mirth*. Unlike its terse literary successor, *Ethan Frome*, which was "only an anecdote in 45,000 words," *The Fruit of the Tree* turned into a sprawling saga of social change, paresis and death (letter to Bernard Berenson, May 19, 1911). As the narrative opens, John Amherst, an idealistic, reform-minded mill manager, has come to plead the case of a maimed factory worker before the company's widowed owner, Bessy Westmore. Captivated by the beautiful proprietor and the institutional power she represents, Amherst marries Bessy, only to discover later that she is more concerned with her social life than with the welfare of her workers. The couple grow increasingly estranged until, midway through the novel, Bessy suffers an excruciating spinal injury after being thrown from a horse. Despite the professional ministrations of her childhood friend Justine Brent, a former Westmore factory nurse, Bessy's condition grows steadily worse. Unwilling to see her friend endure such agony any longer, Justine disobeys a narcissistic doctor's orders and secretly administers a fatal dose of morphine. Amherst, having received word of his wife's accident, returns from South America to find himself a widower. He falls in love with Justine, and the two marry, sharing custody of Bessy's young daughter, Cicely, and their common dream of industrial reform. Predictably, however, their passion permanently sours when Amherst discovers his wife's role in Bessy's death.

Shortly after its publication, Henry James dismissed *The Fruit of the Tree* as a disappointing and deeply flawed novel. With trademark ambiguity, he remarked that though the book contained "a great deal of (though not perhaps of a completely) superior art," he continued to have reservations as to "the composition & conduct of the thing."[1] Subsequent critics have generally followed James's lead. Faulting the novel's construction, R. W. B. Lewis complains that "There are too many 'subjects' in the book" (181). Euthanasia, industrial reform, the war between the sexes, the limits imposed on American women, "the list could go on and on," Cynthia Griffin Wolff remarks. Indeed, "what is the 'problem' in the novel?" (Wolff 139). A book that ought to focus on Justine Brent's inability to separate her own needs from those of her active imagination or, more generally, life from art, instead lapses into "a series of evasions: [Wharton] introduces other 'subjects' – many, many other subjects" (Wolff 142). Dale Bauer concurs: Wharton's third novel "fails to weave together the complicated issues of reform, scientific engineering, and medicine and the effects of these on the inner lives of the main characters" (xiii). According to Robert M. Crunden, Wharton lacked "the middle class, evangelical psychology necessary for commitment to social reform" (94). As a result, she delivers what Elizabeth Ammons deems "a comparatively sloppy, vague picture of factory life" (*Edith Wharton's* 44–5). What begins as a fictional treatise on industrial reform devolves, midway through the text, into a weird euthanasia plot.

Yet it was precisely the novel's ambitious agenda that Wharton most enthusiastically embraced. She told Charles Scribner in 1905 that her new book would explore "life in New York & in a manufacturing town, with the House of Mirth in the middle of the block, but a good many other houses adjoining" (letter to Charles Scribner, Nov. 22 [1905]). When *The Fruit of the Tree* appeared in 1907, she sent a similarly sanguine note to Edward

Burlingame: "I do hope this book will be liked, for it seems to me so much better built up than the H. of Mirth" (letter to Edward Burlingame, March 30 [1907]). These hopes went largely unrealized, of course, making Wharton's aesthetic choices all the more puzzling: why detour into all of these "other houses" – houses of technology, dismemberment, reform and euthanasia?

One clue may be Wharton's 1906 decision to call the book "The Fruit of the Tree." After toying with titles like "The Cup of Mercy," "The Shadow of a Doubt," "The Chariot of the Gods" and "Justine Brent," she settled on a title that cast a backward glance at the opening moments of *Paradise Lost*. Here, Milton describes "man's first disobedience, and the fruit / Of that forbidden tree, whose mortal taste / Brought death into the world" (Milton 36). According to Deborah Carlin, the Miltonic paradigm of "female sin" structures Wharton's narrative of female-initiated euthanasia (Carlin 63). The title, however, equally invites more literal readings. Writing from aboard a trans-Atlantic ocean liner in 1907, Wharton thanked Eunice Maynard for sending a gift basket of "delicatessen." The delectable treats, she noted, were far superior to the usual ship-fare of "grapefruit & mandarins" which she self-mockingly designated "'The Fruit of the Sea'" (Wharton, *Letters*, Jan. 7, 1907). The pun indicates that, from at least one perspective, the "fruit of the tree" could quite literally refer to edible produce. Indeed, given Wharton's depiction of the writing process as "the growth and unfolding of plants in my secret garden," her use of floral imagery to encode images of eroticism, and her ongoing interest in landscape design, this interpretation may not be entirely far-fetched.[2] A palimpsest of fertility, reproduction and artistic creativity, the eventual title had the added advantage of being "easy to say & effective, & leaving the problem unsolved, as I wish to leave it" (letter to Edward Burlingame, July 30 [1906]).

This unresolved "problem," while formally troublesome, circulates around the central issue of agency. Who controls the yield of industrial production and the issue of genealogical reproduction? Who, in effect, manages "the fruit of the tree"? On this count, the title is elusive: agency and intent are conspicuously absent. While the act of production linking the fruit to the tree is assumed, it is never explicitly shown. By masking this relationship, moreover, Wharton betrays her own uncertainty about the novel's status as a product itself. Coming on the heels of *The House of Mirth*'s extraordinary success, *The Fruit of the Tree* could only be regarded as a commercial disappointment. Wharton's literary earnings in 1907 dropped to half of what they had been in 1906. Charles Scribner attributed the book's limited success to the "great and sudden change in business conditions" caused by the financial panic of 1907 (Scribner, letter to Edith Wharton, undated). Though the novel had been "well received everywhere," he said, the country's larger economic machinery had impaired its commercial potential (Scribner, letter to Edith Wharton, Nov. 22, 1907). Caught in the economic machinery of her time, Wharton was forced to agree: "It is too bad that I coincided with the Knickerbocker Trust!" (letter to Charles Scribner, Dec. 18, 1907).

Lead by plummeting copper shares and the sudden failure of the venerable Knickerbocker Trust Company, the stock market collapsed in early October 1907.[3] By the mid-1900s, industrial production had begun to outpace gold. The resulting capital shortages sent waves of fear throughout world markets, moving financial observers to warn that a drop in demand or a wave of bank withdrawals could create a panic that, in the words of railroad financier Jacob Schiff, would "make all previous panics look like child's play" (qtd. in Sobel 303). Schiff's 1906 prediction came vividly true the following year. Jumpy brokers, hoping to escape possible losses, dumped stocks on to the Exchange, and alarmed depositors rushed the banks. Wall Street spiraled into full-blown crisis.[4]

The panic of 1907 sent shock waves from New York to Washington. Fearful of a national débâcle like the market upheaval that had rocked the 1890s, Theodore Roosevelt dispatched Treasury Secretary George B. Cortelyou to Wall Street. Cortelyou offered J. P. Morgan and his team of financiers $25 million dollars of federal money to pacify and stabilize the markets. Roosevelt's long-standing anger at corporate unaccountability boiled over with renewed frustration: "I am doing everything I have power to do," he complained, "but the fundamental fact is that the public is suffering from a spasm of lack of confidence." Corporate "trickery and dishonesty in high places" were the causes (letter to Douglas Robinson). Roosevelt's anger typified many Americans' response to the collapse. Although Morgan and his associates restored order to the markets, the incident remained a glaring reminder of the economic havoc possible in a country plagued by "chronic overproduction" (Trachtenberg 39). As Isidor Straus, a senior partner at R. H. Macy's, warned:

When times are prosperous and the demand for all sorts of commodities appears to be insatiable, the manufacturer enlarges his plant, the merchant extends his undertakings and the railroads try to build apace[,] all of them unmindful of the fact that sooner or later there must come a halt to continuous, progressive growth and power of consumption, which will necessarily compel reduced production. (Straus 52)

As early as 1891, Josiah Strong, author of the enormously popular polemic *Our Country*, had sounded the alarm: "Increasing wealth will only prove the means of destruction, unless it is accompanied by an increasing power of control, a stronger sense of justice, and a more intelligent comprehension of obligations" (164).

The panic of 1907 alarmed many Americans: was the country's developing system of industrial production under proper management? Some argued that Americans would be wise to put their financial future in the hands of private industrialists like J. P. Morgan, who were "vastly better qualified for their work than were the thousands of small men who were in control, and were working at cross purposes with one another, in the same fields twenty years ago" (J. F. Johnson 462). Others maintained that these magnates and trusts were themselves the enemies – greenback conspirators consolidating America's wealth in their own greedy hands. Alfred O. Crozier spoke for many progressives when he warned in 1908 that an "elastic currency," unfettered by the gold standard, could move economic power away from the government, "where the Constitution put it," and into "private hands in a way to makes it possible to contract the currency when the demand and volume of business is the greatest. This," he concluded, "would create fearful panic" (274).

The Fruit of the Tree, itself a casualty of the panic, anticipates this national discussion. Before contemporary commentators debated the lessons to be learned from the collapse, Wharton had already mapped out a strategy of elite control. Marshaling a complex set of images, *The Fruit of the Tree* articulates Wharton's deep-seated fears of political and cultural democratization. A country adrift in the twentieth century, America would only experience further economic and social instability were it further alienated from its genealogical and class-based traditions. *The Fruit of the Tree* is consumed not only with the problem of regulating and controlling industrial production, but also with the related demographic challenges of managing working-class ascendance while staving off further elite dislocation. Within this context, Lily Bart, Bessy Amherst and Mattie Silver come to embody the abject loss of agency. Incarnating a complex web of class, gender and authorial anxieties, the prostrate woman incarnates Wharton's fear of oligarchic collapse.

THE VISIBLE HAND

We can begin see this fear in Wharton's equivocal attitude toward modern machinery. Though she was enamored of technology, *The Fruit of the Tree* allegorizes the underside of modern invention.[5] Like Henry Adams, she was wary of mechanisms that could generate forces that utterly defied human measurement and regulation.[6] An industrial economy powered by such forces seemed altogether unmanageable. The mighty dynamo, with its "aura of supreme power," mocked human agency (Trachtenberg 41). As Alan Trachtenberg has remarked, the machine represented "an autonomous force that held human society in its grip" (41). Like an unpredictable Frankenstein monster, machinery appeared dangerously capable of displacing and superseding human control.

This ontological crisis haunts *The Fruit of the Tree*. As the body and the machine intertwine in complex, overlapping ways, Wharton corporealizes the machine, and mechanizes the body. As in Upton Sinclair's 1907 exposé of Chicago's meat-packing industry, *The Jungle*, technology is dangerously carnivorous in this novel, indiscriminately annexing and absorbing human bodies. Westmore is a monstrously vampiric body, sucking the life-blood from its human workers. The factory incarnates "the dark side of monotonous human toil, of the banquet of flesh and blood and brain perpetually served up to the monster whose insatiable jaws the looms so grimly typified" (57). The town, as a result, is "'dead – stone dead: there isn't a drop of wholesome blood left in it'" (23). If the closing whistle can transform the subjects "of the giant machine [. . . into] men and women again," the effect is only temporary (126). As Bessy Westmore reflects, the factory's looms are mechanical minotaurs – "meaningless machines, to which the human workers seemed mere automatic appendages" (59).

If the machine is a huge, outrageous body – one in which "the throb of the great engines . . . fed the giant's arteries" (56) – the body, in turn, is a soul-less "human machine" (48). From the wealthy "weekend automata" who visit Lynbrook, Bessy's posh Long Island estate, to the mill operatives who are treated as "half machine, half man, and neglecting the man for the machine," Wharton's characters behave automatically (216, 458). "[T]he mechanical performance of [Amherst's] duties" thus finds its mirror image in "the hum of a controlled activity" with which Justine grinds out her own routine (98, 386). Wharton's deliberate confusion of the body and the machine is crucial to the novel's anxiety of agency. As human will threatens to disappear into a cyborg-like jumble of mortal and mechanism, neither the mechanized body nor the corporealized machine definitively regulates the other. Agency is in fact located nowhere.[7] The body and the machine are so thoroughly intertwined that the very status of conventional ontology hangs precariously in the balance. The novel explicitly allegorizes this imbrication in its startling opening scene.

Wharton's first chapter focuses with stark immediacy on the prone, partially dismembered male body of Dillon, a hospitalized worker recovering from a mutilating mill accident. As Justine, the Westmore nurse, hovers over his bedside, Dillon's "bandaged right hand and arm lay stretched along the bed" (3). In what will emerge as a significant detail, the wounded member in question is the worker's hand: "As she leaned over, he lifted his anxious bewildered eyes, deep-sunk under ridges of suffering. 'I don't s'pose there's any kind of a show for me, is there?' he asked pointing with his free hand – the stained seamed hand of the mechanic – to the inert bundle on the quilt" (3). Although the young nurse urges her patient to rest, Dillon continues to writhe painfully: "His free left hand continued to travel the sheet, clasping and unclasping itself in contortions of feverish unrest, left without work in the world now that its mate was useless" (4). "[L]eft without work" Dillon's hand has been rendered useless by an accident that itself underscores the intimacy of man and machine. While operating his "carding machine," Dillon had mistakenly placed his hand in the mechanism: "on the day of the accident his 'card' stopped suddenly, and he put his hand behind him to get a tool he needed out of his trouser pocket. He reached back a little too far, and the card behind him caught his hand in its million of diamond-pointed wires" (10). The text suddenly literalizes what the narrative repeatedly analogizes: the body and the machine have become so dangerously and unmanageably intertwined that agency is located in neither. The unregulated carding machine devours Dillon's hand, forcing him later to have his entire arm amputated. The body – as it is constructed by industrial capitalism – in turn fetishistically imitates the machine: the company eventually offers Dillon "an artificial finger or two."[8]

Wharton's powerful opening scene begins to gain importance as one unpacks the multiple meanings embedded in the term "hand." The factory workers in the novel are metonymically referred to as the "mill hands" (8) or simply "the hands" (1). Dillon's machine, a dislocating emblem of mechanization and the corresponding threat of overproduction, not only displaces but in fact destroys "the hand" – or the worker – altogether. Because the carding machine works too efficiently in an overcrowded room, its rapid movements menace the unfortunate worker. As it turns out, either man or machine must go. To Bessy's innocent question, "'But why do they crowd the rooms that way?'" Amherst can only reply, "'To get the maximum of profit out of the minimum of floor space. It costs more to increase the floor-space than to maim an operative now and then'" (11). It is cheaper, in other words, to lose a "hand," thereby forcing down production and raising prices, than it is to keep the "hand" employed. To borrow Mark Seltzer's formulation, the appendage becomes "at once radically embodied" (hand as body), "and strangely generic" (hand as alienated, replaceable worker) (106).

The possibility that workers would soon be displaced by a newly mechanized industrial order controlled by newly rich capitalists was, of course, the source of widespread concern in Wharton's lifetime. As Alfred D. Chandler Jr. acknowledges, by the mid-nineteenth century, the "visible hand of management" had replaced what Adam Smith famously termed the "invisible hand" of the market. In the place of small entrepreneurs whose cumulative gains determined economic health came a new, multi-leveled system of industrial supervision (Chandler 1). Josiah Strong, for one, deplored the change. Speaking on behalf of American workers, he deplored industrial planners, stratified bureaucracy and Taylorized conglomerates:

Many industries are combining to force down production – that means that working men are thrown out of employment; and to force up prices that means increased cost of living. There are great numbers of "syndicates" or "trusts," all formed in the interest of capitalists. Small dealers must enter the combination or be crushed. Once in, they must submit to the dictation of the "large" men. Thus power is being gathered more and more into the hands of conscienceless monopolies. (149)

Industrial control was literally changing "hands." Wrested from the worker's grasp, power was being reconsolidated in "the hands of conscienceless monopolies," Chandler's "visible hand" of management. Dillon thus vividly embodies the transaction Strong describes: he is one more "hand" (in both senses) eliminated by the sheer momentum of a mechanized market.

Strong's views on the intersections of agency and class could hardly have differed more radically from Wharton's own. This becomes abundantly clear in *The Fruit of the Tree*'s complicated treatment of hands. However sympathetically it is presented, Dillon's accident vividly suggests that the concentration of power in the hands of the working man was for Wharton an intolerable prospect. Discovering that his carding machine has suddenly stopped, the Westmore worker "put[s] his hand behind him to get a tool he needed out of his trouser pocket." In gesturing toward his pocket to get his tool, however, Dillon's hand accidentally slips into the dismembering machine. The text enacts a form of castration. Instead of applying the pocketed tool to the machine, Dillon employs his hand. The slippage is apparent: hand and phallic tool become interchangeably vulnerable.[9]

The metaphoric association between hand and phallus is a familiar trope in Wharton's *œuvre*. In the famously pornographic "Beatrice Palmato" fragment, Mr. Palmato refers to his penis as his "third hand."[10] The analogy, however, appears even earlier in Wharton's 1904 tale "The House of the Dead Hand." In this veiled story of incest, an eccentric Dr. Lombard confines his daughter Sybilla to their Gothic mansion, where he compels her to guard his cherished Leonardo da Vinci painting of a "dead hand." The hand, though that of a woman, is described in explicitly phallic terms, "thrust forth in the denunciation of evil mystery within the house" (146). If the painting gestures at the incestuous connection between Lombard and his daughter, it equally reveals Wharton's more parodic critique of phallocentric hyperbole.[11] Lombard's excessive interest in the hand ("'Beautiful – *beautiful!*' the doctor burst out. '. . . There are no adjectives in the language fresh enough to describe such pristine brilliancy . . . Think of the things that have been called beautiful, and then look at *that!*'") is matched only by his hysterical injunction to the narrator – "'Don't ask what [the hand] means, young man, but bow your head in thankfulness for having seen it!'" (150).

Wharton would return to the image of the phallic hand again and again. In one of *The House of Mirth*'s climactic scenes, for instance, Gus Trenor (described at one point as "a fat stupid man almost old enough to be [Lily's] father") threatens to rape the novel's heroine (124). Wharton articulates the scene's menace by focusing on Trenor's ominous hand. Blocking Lily's exit, Gus "[squares] himself on the threshold, his hands thrust deep in his pockets" (143). As he grows increasingly reckless, Trenor lurches toward Lily, "closer still, with a hand that grew formidable" (146). As the more sexually equivocal Selden later observes, "the way [Trenor's] jewelled rings were wedged in the creases of his fat red fingers" is repulsive. "[A]ll the way back to his rooms [Selden] was haunted by the sight of Trenor's fat creased hands" (154). The menacing financier's corpulent fists fully embody his phallic threat.

Given the phallic content of Dillon's accident, his wound is significant not only to his status as an industrial producer but equally to his role as a working-class reproducer. Violently emasculated, the machinist can no longer father additional members of the working class.[12] Wharton develops this implication in answer to the novel's central but deeply encoded question: who will secure and control the machinery of twentieth-century economic production?

Wharton shared Theodore Roosevelt's belief that a strong hand was needed to direct the nation's economy. In late 1911, Roosevelt proclaimed that the general public was best served when American business gave "adequate power of control to the one sovereignty capable of exercising such power – the National Government" (qtd. in Blum 117). Disturbed by the growing influence of large corporations commandeered by powerful new industrialists like J. P. Morgan, James J. Hill, John D. Rockefeller and James B. Duke, Roosevelt sought to exercise the power of the federal government to reign in corporate power. In 1902 the Justice Department brought a suit against Morgan's and Hill's Northern Securities Company under the Sherman Anti-Trust Act, and in 1903 Roosevelt established the Bureau of Corporations, an agency mandated to monitor and investigate the activities of inter-state corporations. As his famous 1899 paean to the "strenuous life" suggests, Roosevelt envisioned a dynamic coalition of patrician and working-class Americans who could together unite against their common enemy: the middle-class industrialist. Although he insisted that "All honor must be paid to the architects of our material prosperity, to the great captains of industry who have built our factories and our railroads, to the strong men who toil for wealth with brain or hand," he nevertheless criticized the "base spirit of gain and greed which recognizes in commercialism the be-all and end-all of national life" (*Strenuous* 323). The country's true debt, he concluded, was "yet greater to the men whose highest type is to be found in a statesman like Lincoln, a soldier like Grant . . . who recognized that there were yet other and even loftier duties – duties to the nation and duties to the race" (*Strenuous* 323). In privileging the statesman over the businessman, Roosevelt made his case for a vibrant and powerful executive branch. In explaining his decision to run again for President in 1908, he remarked, "I don't think that any harm comes from the concentration of power *in one man's hands*, provided the holder does not keep it for more than a certain, definite time" (qtd. in Blum 122, *emphasis added*).

In Roosevelt, Wharton saw a strong leader with a fine pedigree and a regal air (she privately called him "Theodore the First") (*Letters* 210). Although she may not have shared all of his enthusiasms (she protested to Sally Norton that the President was "not all – or nearly all – bronco-buster"), she did identify with his distaste for the corporate *nouveaux riches* and their increasing economic clout (*Letters* 68, n.2). When Roosevelt stopped in Lenox to give a brief speech on the Anti-Trust Act in 1902, Wharton found "the few very quiet and fitting words he said to the crowd gathered to receive him" affecting and appropriate (*Letters* 68, n.2). Like the President, she believed that a well-chosen (and therefore well-born) executive could rein in the greedy machinations of a middlebrow corporate elite. Only a powerful patriciate could control the excesses of America's unregulated marketplace.[13]

Within this scheme of social engineering, well-born women were to play the lead role. According to the precepts of "educated motherhood," middle- and upper-class American mothers were inimitably qualified to supervise social improvement. "In a woman's hands is placed the destiny of the race," Harriet Anderson argued in 1912. "*She* controls the quality of posterity. *She* has her hand on evolution's course" (180). Indeed, as the educator Mary Stanley Boone observed in 1904, "Everyone will concede . . . that it is the mother's hand that moulds, but she greatly needs preparation for the process" (qtd. in Rothman 97). To be a good mother, one needed skill and training. In the words of Elizabeth Harrison, a kindergarten advocate, "the destiny of nations lies far more in the hands of women – the mothers – than in the hands of those who possess power."[14]

Indeed, the hands most frequently commended in *The Fruit of the Tree* are precisely those of upper-class women. The hands of Amherst's well-born mother are admiringly depicted "shaping garments, darning rents, repairing furniture, exploring the inner economy of clocks" (25). It is no surprise, then, that the dutiful son looks for similar qualities in his bride. He contemplates Bessy's reformist potential with glowing optimism:

"Think of what it means . . . for a young woman like Mrs. Westmore, without any experience or any habit of authority, to come here, and at the first glimpse of injustice, to be so revolted that she finds the courage and cleverness to put her little hand to the machine and reverse the engines – for it's nothing less than she's done!" (117–18)

Bessy's ambitious physician, Dr. Wyant, admires Justine's nursing skills in similarly tactile terms: "'How you do back a man up! You think with your hands – with every individual finger!'"[15] Simultaneously producers and potential reproducers, Wharton's patrician women are "manual laborers" in the best sense.[16] Their demonstrated skill as dexterous workers and enlightened mothers forms the double hinge on which the novel's larger strategy turns – a class-based strategy of social control.

CORPORATE THINKING

Despite her self-conscious effort to portray working-class concerns in *The Fruit of the Tree* (she would have better success in *Ethan Frome*, "Bunner Sisters" (1916) and *Summer*), Wharton was bound by her own elitism. Her third novel is singularly concerned with the reproduction of a natural elite capable of dominating America's rising proletariat and newly ascendant middle class. Throughout *The Fruit of the Tree*, familial narratives and narratives of industrial reform repeatedly overlap, fusing the novel's concerns with economic production and social reproduction. The Westmore factory is first and foremost a family business. As the sole heir to the Westmore fortune, Bessy's daughter Cicely *is* the "fruit of the tree." She represents familial and industrial continuity in a narrative mandated to safeguard patrician entitlement. Indeed, this implicit directive helps explain why, despite a sequence of marriages, the novel contains no births.[17] Even after Amherst's wedding to Justine, step-father and new step-mother are inexplicably committed to ensuring Cicely's sole inheritance of Westmore. The couple celebrates Cicely's birthday each year by planning an elaborate party at the factories to ensure their step-daughter's emotional attachment to her inheritance. Indeed, the novel's final scene takes place on one such occasion: Cicely knows "that this shining tenth birthday of hers was to throw its light as far as the clouds of factory-smoke extended" (622). By linking Cicely's birth with the prosperity of her factories, the novel invokes a compelling analogy between the reproduction of the moneyed classes and their capital-producing commodities – in short, "the continuance of a beautiful, a sacred tradition" (630).

The narrative is complicit with ensuring such dynastic succession. Wharton is careful to certify that all of the characters who are in the position to control industrial production are in fact sufficiently "aristocratic." Despite his bona fides as the son of a "mechanical genius," John Amherst is in reality the descendant of a long line of genteel Americans. He recalls "with a touch of bitterness how he had once regretted having separated himself from his mother's class, and how seductive for a moment, to both mind and senses, that other life had appeared" (184). Although he masquerades as a working man, Amherst is in fact a blood-member of the upper class. In fact, "it was only by living among the workers that he had learned to care for their fate" (97).

The novel correspondingly reveals that Justine, despite her nursing job, is in fact the descendant of an old-stock family that has fallen on hard times. Bessy thus expresses appropriate shock when she recognizes her childhood friend: "'Then it *is* Justine Brent! I heard they had lost their money – I haven't seen her for years. But how strange that she should be a hospital nurse!'" (107). Like Amherst, Justine is a class tourist, observing the plight of the working poor without permanently participating in their lives. After making a medical visit to the Dillon family, she makes an outrageous confession: "'It's the same kind of interest I used to feel in my dolls and guinea pigs – a managing, interfering old maid's interest. I don't believe I should care a straw for them if I couldn't dose them and order them about'" (458). For Justine, "Philanthropy is one of the subtlest forms of self-indulgence" (156).

By insuring not only Cicely's succession, but also the pedigrees of her two step-parents, Wharton explores the possibility of continued upper-class dominion through controlled reproduction. In this connection, the novel's love plots, each engineered within the context of industrial reform, play a crucial role. If novelistic marriage traditionally sanctions the existing social order, as Joseph A. Boone has shown, then both of the novel's courtship narratives are designed to preserve a mode of production dominated by America's elite (Boone 80). This strategy emerges most clearly in two particular episodes. After an erotic sleigh ride that prefigures its more famous counterpart in *Ethan Frome*, Amherst informs Bessy that he has been dismissed from the factory. The wealthy widow anxiously responds,

> "Then what will happen to the mills?"
> "Oh, some one else will be found – the new ideas are stirring everywhere. And if you'll only come back here, and help my successor –"
> "Do you think they are likely to choose any one else with your ideas?" she interposed with unexpected acuteness; and after a short silence he answered: "Not immediately, perhaps; but in time – in time there will be improvements."
> "As if the poor people could wait! Oh, it's cruel, cruel of you to go!"
> Her voice broke into a throb of entreaty that went to his inmost fibres. (138)

The language of love and the rhetoric of industrial reform here become indistinguishable. If Amherst leaves, he abandons not only the "poor people" but the rich widow as well. The courtship methods of the wealthy metonymically reinforce their resolve to run American industry, a pattern that is then repeated when Amherst proposes to Justine in chapter XXXI:

> He began abruptly. "Wouldn't you marry, if it gave you the chance to do what you say – if it offered you hard work, and the opportunity to make things better . . . for a great many people . . . as no one but yourself could do?"
> It was a strange way of putting his case: he was aware of it before he ended. But it had not occurred to him to tell her that she was lovely and desirable – in his humility he thought that what he had to give would plead for him better than what he was. (465)

If courtship seems to be a form of social philanthropy, it is only because marriage consolidates elite corporate control. By accepting Amherst's offer, Justine is capable of producing and reproducing the country's economic future. Thus Bessy's father, Mr. Langhope, has every right to worry about Cicely's inheritance in light of his former son-in-law's remarriage: "'with

Amherst unmarried, the whole of the Westmore fortune would have gone back to Cicely – where it belongs'" (469). The widower's marital status directly affects the dispensation of the Westmore family's lucrative industrial holdings.

The procreative status of Amherst's body is therefore crucial to the economic logic of the novel. His capacity to reproduce future heirs to the family fortune directly corresponds to his ability to command industrial production. If, as we have seen, Wharton's text dismembers the working-class body, it equally and implicitly foregrounds Amherst's corporeal unity. "His life was in truth one indivisible organism, not two halves artificially united. Self and other-self were ingrown from the roots – whichever portion fate restricted him to would be but a mutilated half-live fragment of the whole" (588). Amherst embodies what Bill Brown has called the "perfected, eugenic American body": he is "the converse, diegetic symptom of technology's disintegration of the body" (140). Wharton draws a marked contrast between this living "organism" and its antithesis, the "artificially united" self we have come to associate with the body of Dillon. The mechanized, prosthetic worker's body threatens corporeal – and indeed "corporate" – unity.[18] The word "corporate" itself – "united or combined into one body" – functions in its dual capacities. Amherst literally embodies the oligarchical corporation: he is, in Brown's words, "a transcendent, metasocial guarantee of wholeness, of totality" (140). Without this unity, the corporate body is "no more than a machine": it is uncontrollable, dangerously democratic and unmanageable (407). To exist as a "mutilated half-live fragment" – to live, that is, as Dillon does – is not to live at all.[19] Despite this kind of corporate thinking, however, the novel's central paradox remains unresolved. Indeed, within this context of bodily integrity and class-based eugenic fitness, it is all the more perplexing that Wharton populates her pages with so many prone, incapacitated women.

THE CUP OF MERCY

If, as Michael Fried has observed, the work of Stephen Crane is populated by disfigured upturned faces, then it is equally true that the early fiction of Edith Wharton is replete with immobilized female bodies. From Lily Bart's "motionless hands and calm unrecognizing face," to Mattie Silver's "limp immobility, and . . . bright witch-like stare," Wharton represents the female body as a mere husk, a "semblance" at once "bloodless and shrivelled," demanding an outside observer's puzzled interpretation. Indeed, these famously immobilized women are linked to the "poor, powerless body" of Bessy Amherst by a logic of agency that informs and explains the discourse of euthanasia in *The Fruit of the Tree* (432).

The confusion surrounding the term "euthanasia" at the turn of the century is indicative of the cultural debate generated by assisted death itself. Alternately "a gentle and easy death" or the "means" of bringing about such a death, euthanasia could equally describe the "action of inducing" a peaceful passing ("Euthanasia," *OED*). Depending on its meaning, euthanasia was either a mild, passive form of "sleeping," or an artificial and belligerent act of "murder." In either case, human volition was determinative. As the *Journal of the American Medical Association* pointed out in 1899, "Euthanasia is at best an ambiguous word; while it may mean only rendering certain death painless, it is liable to another construction" ("Euphoria vs. Euthanasia"). The debate oscillated between these two viewpoints. While supporters argued that the procedure was the only humane and merciful response to incurable suffering, euthanasia's foes – many of them physicians – charged that the practice amounted to nothing less than homicide, the violent removal of personal agency. As New York doctor S. E. Gibbs asked in 1906, "Who is to decide that the patient cannot live? Certainly a surgeon who has seen many extraordinary cases of recovery would hesitate" (10). Both positions straddled an essentially hermeneutic dilemma: who was authorized to interpret the desires of the prone body?

In 1902, Herbert Spencer proposed a strangely elaborate experiment in which the human body would be placed on a rapidly spinning table, thereby registering the effect of motion on the circulation of blood to the brain. While acknowledging the "extremely dangerous" nature of the test, Spencer nonetheless proposed the bizarre procedure as an effective method of capital punishment: "Supposing the sentiment of revenge to be excluded, and supposing it decided that criminals of an extremely degraded type may best be put out of existence, there would thus be provided for them a simple means of euthanasia" (231–2). Eliding euthanasia and execution, Spencer's modest proposal crucially hinges on intent. In his view, the impartial doctor or legal official can assume responsibility for the active infliction of "euthanasia" on the patient/criminal. Mechanized and deprived of self-determination, the convict's whirling body would then become the site of state and medical jurisdiction.

While Spencer's essay may be an extreme contribution to the euthanasia debate, his central question goes to the heart of the matter: who is authorized to control the immobilized body, the individual himself or some other entity like the state? Writing for the *Law Quarterly Review*, Herbert Stephen insisted in 1889 that medically assisted death "would undoubtedly be murder by our law."[20] Euthanasia, others warned, would unravel the whole social fabric, concentrating the body's "unalienable rights" [*sic*] in undetermined hands ("Shall We Legalize Homicide?" 252). "To give all a legal right to administer poison on demand without responsibility," one commentator objected, "would be to arm every profligate heir with a most dangerous weapon. Who is to tell after death whether the patient has consented to his own departure, or whether the last ray of hope had really disappeared or not?" ("Euthanasia," *Littell's* 636). To be "poisoned" by medical technology raised the intolerable specter of self-determination run amuck. "When shall it be said that the patient has already suffered enough, when that he has not," a Dutch physician, H. Pinkhof, asked in 1906. "As soon as it can be reasonably concluded that the disease is incurable, or as soon as the patient no longer desires to live? To whom shall be adjudged the right of passing the sentence of death?" (*Euthanasia from the Physician's View-Point* 628).

Euthanasia proponents responded by insisting that the procedure only reified the body's "natural" relinquishment of agency. By easing the patient's organic descent into a peaceful death, drugs and doctors merely added a humane period to the mortal sentence. As one 1906 commentator rapturously concludes, "Take me, Death that art a birth, Grave that art a womb! I am on the brink; my heart is light; to thy arms I commit myself. Light, Beauty, Benediction, Love, take me! Behold, I come" (Dickinson 447).

By early 1906, a sequence of widely publicized events had brought the euthanasia debate to a crescendo. In October 1905, Anne E. Hall, daughter of an Arctic explorer and herself a wealthy Cincinnati widow, put a resolution before the American Humane Association in Philadelphia requesting AHA approval of "the practice of physicians who in cases of hopeless suffering make painless the last hours of life by an anaesthetic," and protection against "the practice of prolonging by artificial means the agonies of incurable diseases" ("Kill to End Suffering"). Though the resolution went down in defeat, Hall continued her campaign, enlisting the support of Charles Eliot Norton, distinguished Harvard art professor and Wharton's "beloved friend."[21] Norton had long supported euthanasia: when his mother died after a protracted illness in 1879, Norton wrote that "Euthanasy [*sic*] would have been a blessing at any time for a year and more past; and, of late, to abridge her life would have been a duty in any society more civilized than ours" (Norton and Howe 92). At Hall's request, Norton wrote an open letter to the *Washington Post* in January 1906, in which he condemned the prolongation of suffering as "criminal cruelty":

There is no ground to hold every human life as inviolably sacred and to be preserved, no matter with what results to the individual or to others. On the contrary, there are cases to which every reasonable consideration urges that the end should be put. Setting aside all doubtful cases, no right thinking man would hesitate to give a dose of laudanum, sufficient to end suffering and life together, to the victim of an accident from the torturing effects of which recovery was impossible, however many hours of misery might be added to conscious life by stimulants or surgical operations. ("Kill to End Suffering")

Norton's letter, which not only anticipated the "torturing effects" of Bessy Amherst's paralysis, but which also rationalized Justine's merciful response, received a swift and derisive reaction. Norton was not only suffering from a "curious delusion," but he was in fact "scientifically wrong," the *New York Times* insisted the next day ("Dr. Norton on Euthanasia"). Only an "amazing representative of feminine gentleness and wisdom" like Hall would want "to legalize the murder of the aged, the sick, and the injured," and only those "with unregulated enthusiasms" like Norton would fail to recognize that they had "shocked and angered the entire medical profession . . . and . . . been judged as utterly abominable by all who have studied them under some other light than that of sentimentality gone quite mad" ("'Euthanasia' Bobs Up Again"). "The Halls and the Nortons," the *Times* concluded, ". . . apparently do not remember that the doctrine they preach is the common practice of savages" ("Euthanasia and Civilization").

Nonetheless, fortified by Norton's support, Hall sponsored a bill on January 23, 1906 in the Ohio state legislature that would have legalized euthanasia for patients suffering intolerable and incurable pain. The widely publicized bill stipulated that if the patient wished to die, he or she could inform a physician in the presence of three witnesses. Once the doctor concurred that the case was indeed terminal, he could then administer a fatal dose of anesthetic. Unlike those it proposed to assist, the Hall bill suffered a long and protracted death: languishing in committee, it was subsequently rejected and vanished into legal obscurity (Kuepper 37–8).

The day after the Hall bill was introduced in the Ohio statehouse, Walter Kempster, a Milwaukee doctor, made front-page news in New York by admitting that he had given a fatal dose of morphine to a burn victim. Kempster's disclosure, coming right on the heels of the Hall bill, fueled months of heated debate in New York, where Wharton was preparing to leave for Europe on March 10. While opponents condemned and lampooned the bill, comparing it to a fantastic "Statute of Murders" in "savage" Tierra del Fuego, supporters, who were in the minority, denounced protracted and senseless suffering (Tomlinson). Writing in support of "the advocates of the cup-of-merciful oblivion" in March 1906, Army Captain W. E. P. French told the *New York Times*, "I hope that if I ever become . . . an inert mass of hopeless agony, or if some incurable malady should make me a horror to the tender hearts that would minister unto me – I hope some merciful, compassionate, gently brave hand will 'medicine me to that sweet sleep'" (8).

Though Wharton insisted to Scribner's that "my story is not a thesis for or against 'euthanasia,'" her private letters underscore the novel's sympathies (letter to Edward Burlingame, March 12, 1906). In early June 1901, Wharton wrote to tell Sara Norton that her mother had died in Paris. "She had been hopelessly ill for fourteen months, paralyzed & unconscious for nearly a year – but it was one of the cases in which it seemed that life – that kind of life – might go on for years; & there is no room for anything but thankfulness at this sudden conclusion of it all." Death had come "suddenly & unexpectedly," relieving Lucretia Rhinelander Jones (and her daughter) of additional suffering (letter to Sara Norton, June 3, 1901). Four years later, in July 1905, Ethel Cram, the former owner of the Jones summer home in Newport, was thrown from a pony-cart, her skull fractured by the horse's kick. Doctors initially predicted a full recovery, though Wharton was skeptical. "She is still quite unconscious, but that is perhaps as well," she told Norton three weeks after the accident. "If she recovers it will be one of the most remarkable cases in modern surgery, I believe" (letter to Sara Norton, July 25, 1905). Despite early optimism, Cram died after "two months' agony" in mid-September. "One can only give thanks," Wharton remarked in a letter to Norton, "for the bitterness of death is long past . . . I am sure I should have the 'triste courage,' in such a case, to let life ebb out quietly – should not you?" (letter to Sara Norton, Sept. 15, 1905). Wharton had the opportunity to develop this conviction when Mrs. Hartmann Kuhn, a Lenox neighbor, died in October 1908, after a prolonged and painful illness. Wharton had seen Kuhn throughout the summer, "& her vitality grows more amazing as she becomes more death-like to look at. She even laughed at a joke the other day!" Nevertheless, the woman's lingering demise only confirmed Wharton's opinion: "oh, if I had morphia in reach, as she has, how quickly I'd cut the knot!" (*Letters* 159). By early October, Kuhn had arrived at a mercifully peaceful end: "Mrs. Kuhn does not suffer, & is barely conscious – in a kind of dream . . . Ah, well, the best thing of all is to know that once we're asleep they can't wake us!" (letter to Sara Norton, Oct. 5, 1908).

Such thoughts were undoubtedly soothing to Sara Norton, whose father was dying at their summer home in Shady Hill, Massachusetts. On

October 19, 1908, the day Charles Eliot Norton died, Wharton wrote Sally from the Mount to say that she had just received her friend's missive of the day before. Wharton's supportive response make the content of Sally's letter unmistakable:

Oh, how *glad* I am you wrote me! And how *right* & admirable you were in your choice – both you & he, worthy of the ideas you hold by, of the new light & of the old loyalties, which are so inextricably & tragically blent. It has helped me to know of such a fine thing being done so near me. You could *not* have done otherwise. (letter to Sara Norton, Oct. 19, 1908)

The Nortons had made good on their belief in euthanasia. As Wharton consolingly wrote to her grieving friend: "you will at least know, all through, that it is better so than the alternative of prolonged life could have been" (letter to Sara Norton, Oct. 21, 1908).

Wharton's fiction registers this belief that a peaceful death "is infinitely better than a gradual failure of body & mind" (letter to John Hugh Smith, March 9, 1910). In this respect, Lily Bart and Mattie Silver embody the two extremes of the euthanasia debate. While one woman drifts peacefully into a deathly sleep, the other suffers the prolonged agony of a failed suicide. Dr. E. P. Buffet, as if anticipating *The House of Mirth*'s penultimate scene, described a euthanasic death in 1891 as "a slumberous condition, not unlike that at the end of a toilsome day" (233). "Should this person to whom chloroform is administered be of a certain temperament, resigned, ready to assist, eager to inhale the vapor which is to cause forgetfulness, he may, without the least indication of discomfort, pass into a state of oblivion. This process may be compared to the easy, painless death" (236). Lily's final sensations after swallowing a lethal dose of chloral correspond almost directly to Buffet's description: "the recovered warmth flowed through her once more, she yielded to it, sank into it, and slept" (*The House of Mirth* 323). By contrast, Mattie Silver's distorting agony is *Ethan Frome*'s central horror. Paralysis transforms the once lively young woman who danced with a "cherry-coloured 'fascinator'" into the human equivalent of the smashed pickle dish of "gay red glass" that Wharton later describes as "a dead body" (21, 59, 92).

Between these two examples lies the disabled figure of Bessy Amherst. As her handsome suitor realizes early on, control over Bessy's body and control over her factories are one and the same thing. Without self-determination, however, Bessy's prostration risks effacing human agency altogether. As the subject of Dr. Wyant's "implacable scientific passion," Bessy degenerates into a "mere nameless unit," a mechanized experiment in Taylorism and scientific management (421, 587). Justine considers Wyant a torturer. "Just so a skilled agent of the Inquisition might have spoken, calculating how much longer the power of suffering might be artificially preserved in a body broken on the wheel" (401). While she deplores the synthetic appropriation and protraction of the body in pain, the nurse nonetheless obeys the doctor's orders, dosing Bessy with a succession of stimulants and narcotics.

[Bessy] was wrapped in a thickening cloud of opiates – morphia by day, bromides, sulphonal, chloral hydrate, at night. When the cloud broke and consciousness emerged, it was centred in the one acute point of bodily anguish. Darting throes of neuralgia, agonized oppression of the breath, the diffused misery of the helpless body – these were reducing their victim to a mere instrument on which pain played its incessant deadly variations. (423)

Throughout the novel, Wharton equates drug use with the dangers of scientific artifice and the wholesale loss of bodily control. Wyant's addiction to morphine and his attempt to blackmail Justine to support his habit reflect his own bitter loss of self-direction after Bessy's death. Similarly, Justine's obsessive love for Amherst works like "a narcotic in her veins," preserving the "almost artificial quality of her happiness" and depriving her of the will to confess her role in Bessy's death (489, 490). Such synthetic love stands in marked opposition to the couple's former passion. Indeed, Justine can only wistfully recall "when their love was not a deadening drug but a vivifying element that cleared thought instead of stifling it" (534).

A persistent fear runs through *The Fruit of the Tree* that medical technology will ultimately transform the specificity of "natural" agency into a replaceable cog within an anonymous human machine. Euthanasia articulates this fear. In Wyant's feverishly ambitious hands, Bessy is "a case – a beautiful case."[22] Transformed into what Seltzer calls a "statistical person," the prostrate upper-class woman becomes the locus for the novel's pervasive anxiety of agency. As the source of productive and reproductive agency, Bessy's transformation into a scientific "case" threatens not only her power to govern her own body, but also her corporeal/corporate specificity as well. The heiress's diseased body threatens what Walter Benjamin defines as "aura" – a unique human agency, embedded in tradition, that resists mechanical reproduction. "To pry an object from its shell, to destroy its aura, is the mark of a perception whose 'sense of the universal equality of things' has increased to such a degree that it extracts it even from a unique object by means of reproduction," Benjamin asserts (223). This is precisely the outcome that both Wharton and Justine dread. The potential democratization of Bessy Amherst's body signifies the wresting of mechanical reproduction from oligarchic control. Justine's act of euthanasia is thus deeply embedded in the novel's logic of class, for by administering the fatal dose, the nurse effectively restores a measure of her friend's integrity, specificity and bodily control – the very qualities denied to Dillon, the automatized, prostheticized worker.

This class logic helps explain why Lily Bart's suicide is a success, while Mattie Silver's is a dismal failure. Like Bessy's euthanized death, Lily's suicide restores both personal sovereignty and genealogical succession. Her final vision of herself as a mother, gently cradling Nettie Struther's baby, enacts at once a restoration of genealogical continuity and the appropriation of working-class progeny. Nettie's child becomes Lily's own imagined infant, and the heroine's death successfully – albeit fantastically – re-engineers the class dynamics of social reproduction. As she dreamily drifts off, Lily achieves in death what she could not accomplish in life: hugging a baby in her arms, she is no longer "rootless" and ephemeral, but instead connected "by mysterious links of kinship to all the mighty sum of human striving."[23]

If drugs successfully ease Lily into an anesthetized death, they do precisely the opposite in *Ethan Frome*. Mattie Silver arrives in Starkfield a destitute orphan because of her father's failure to make good on the "thriving 'drug' business" he inherited from his father-in-law (*Ethan Frome* 43). Orin Silver and his wife die in poverty, leaving their daughter to fend for herself.[24] While drugs are symptomatic of class dislocation and personal isolation in *The House of Mirth* and *The Fruit of the Tree*, in *Ethan Frome* they fail to consume the very social evils they represent. In marked contrast to Lily and Bessy, who are humanized by narcotics, Mattie suffers like a "little animal twittering somewhere near under the snow" (123). While death transforms Lily into her "real" self, Mattie's accident is radically alienating: Ethan's lover no longer appears the way she "*was*, before the accident" – vivacious and alive (130). In her place, a new inauthentic Mattie survives, indistinguishable from "the Fromes down in the graveyard" (130). Whereas Selden gets a romantic – even erotic – charge from Lily's death, bending over her bed and "draining their last moment to its lees," paralysis destroys Mattie's sexual vibrancy (*The House of Mirth* 329). When Ethan introduces his wife and her disabled cousin to the narrator, his use of full courtesy titles – "This is my wife, Mis' Frome . . . And this is Miss Mattie Silver" – underscores Mattie's status as a terminally single woman, barred from a future of marriage and motherhood (126). Threadbare and sterile, Mattie is doomed to live in perpetuity under the care of her querulous cousin Zeena. In marked opposition to Justine's compassionate care for Bessy and eventual adoption of Cicely, Zeena is a resentful nurse who thinks her cousin "'a pauper that's hung onto us'" (83). By appealing to this Dickensian discourse of institutional obligation, Zeena emphasizes Mattie's conclusive alienation from "her people" – from a familial source of identity, continuity and agency. The novel's conclusion thus finds its working-class heroine trapped, incapacitated and alone. Wharton paralyzes the poor in a torpor of hopelessness. Mattie offers a bleak counterpart to the personal specificity and reproductive agency of Lily and Bessy.

DEATH AND THE AUTHOR

Both *The House of Mirth* and *Ethan Frome* pose the question that lies at the heart of the euthanasia debate: what is (or was) the intention of the prone body? *The House of Mirth* leaves Selden, the reader and generations of future critics to wonder whether Lily's overdose was an accident or a suicide. Faced with his lover's enigmatic form, Selden must "[construct] an explanation of the mystery" (329). Because Lily's "mute lips on the pillow refused him more," he can "read into that farewell all that his heart craved to find there" (329). Lily's prone body becomes a text in which her hesitant lover can "read" his own reconstruction of her story. Her own intent, however, remains a mystery.

The narrator of *Ethan Frome* feels similarly compelled to rationalize Mattie's crippled frame: "It was that night that I found the clue to Ethan Frome, and began to put together this vision of his story" (17). As was the case in *The House of Mirth*, the text provides no authoritative account of the prone body's choices. Mrs. Hale admits as much: "'the folks here could never rightly tell what she and Ethan were doing that night coasting'" (129). Mattie's recollection of the fatal sleigh-ride, in fact, becomes something of a teasing enigma. Even Mrs. Hale abruptly interrupts her retelling of the event:

"When she came to I went up to her and stayed all night. They gave her things to quiet her, and she didn't know much till to'rd morning, and then all of a sudden she woke up just like herself, and looked straight at me out of her big eyes, and said . . . Oh, I don't know why I'm telling you all this," Mrs. Hale broke off, crying. (128)

Like *The House of Mirth*, *Ethan Frome* leaves the incapacitated female body without an authoritative account. As Wharton suggests in *The Fruit of the*

Tree, this silence is ultimately perhaps the most horrifying consequence of lost agency.

The problem of managing Bessy's body, the emblem of social and industrial control, ultimately parallels the status of writing in the novel. Alone at Lynbrook, Justine agonizes over the decision to put Bessy out of her misery. The absence of both Bessy's father and husband compounds the nurse's dilemma: what would they do in her position? Seeking solace in Amherst's personal library, Justine discovers a volume of Bacon. While aimlessly glancing through its pages, she notices Amherst's notes penciled in the margins:

Le vraie morale se moque de la morale . . .
We perish because we follow other men's examples . . .
Socrates used to call the opinions of the many by the name of Lamiae – bugbears to frighten children . . . (429)

The moment becomes a crucial exercise in hermeneutics. "Were they his own thoughts?" Justine asks. "No – her memory recalled some confused association with great names. But at least they must represent his beliefs – must embody deeply-felt convictions – or he would scarcely have taken the trouble to record them" (429). Justine's decision to act upon her own interpretation of Amherst's authorial intent is fateful: true ethics, she decides, transcend the seeming "morality" of the common herd. Indeed, when Amherst eventually learns the truth behind his first wife's death, Justine frantically defends her decision by thrusting the copy of Bacon into his hand. Reading the marginalia, her husband flings the volume aside in disgust. "[She] watched him with panting lips, her knees trembling under her. 'But you wrote it – you wrote it! I thought you meant it!' she cried, as the book spun across the table and dropped to the floor" (524). The wild twirling motion of the book seems to replicate the uncontrollability of the written word itself. Justine's interpretation renders Amherst powerless to exercise authority over his own text. His wife's (mis)reading effectively undermines his authorial control. At stake once again is an anxiety of agency – this time, authorial agency.

In the novel's last chapter, Amherst assembles the Hanaford community in order to announce his plans to build an elaborate gymnasium at Westmore. The idea for the recreation center, he tells the crowd, was inspired by his late wife Bessy. Justine instantly recognizes the blueprint in Amherst's hand: Bessy, estranged from her husband and tired of his self-righteous philanthropy, had commissioned an extravagant gymnasium to be built for her own private use. Her successor is outraged:

> But how was it possible that Amherst knew nothing of the original purpose of the plans, and by what mocking turn of events had a project devised in deliberate defiance of his wishes, and intended to declare his wife's open contempt for them, been transformed into a Utopian vision for the betterment of the Westmore operatives?
>
> A wave of anger swept over Justine at this last derisive stroke of fate. It was grotesque and pitiable that a man like Amherst should create out of his regrets a being who had never existed, and then ascribe to her feelings and actions of which the real woman had again and again proved herself incapable . . .
>
> . . . Why should she not cry out the truth to him, defend herself against the dead who came back to rob her of such wedded peace as was hers? She had only to tell the true story of the plans to lay poor Bessy's ghost forever to rest. (628–9)

Wharton again imagines a text that has escaped its author's original intentions. Reappropriating the blueprint, Amherst reconstructs the persona of an author – "a being who had never existed." For Justine, the moment is a horribly ironic one. As the case of the gymnasium strikingly confirms, the author is indeed "dead" (see Foucault 127–8). An "unreal woman, [a] phantom," invented by the reader, has taken her place (629). Perhaps for Wharton, this anxiety is the most pressing of all. When the author is unable to control the word, her authority is compromised, and her agency disputed.[25] Like the lifeless Lily Bart who falls victim to her lover's romantic hermeneutics and the disfigured Mattie Silver who cannot articulate her own story, Wharton could not regulate the production of "the word which made it all clear" (*House* 329). The author becomes the final prone, incapacitated body in the text.

CHAPTER 4

The Age of Experience: pragmatism, the Titanic *and* The Reef

In the early hours of April 15, 1912, the *H.M.S. Titanic*, making her maiden voyage from Southampton, England to New York, struck an iceberg 400 miles off the coast of Newfoundland, taking 1,503 people to their deaths in the frigid waters of the North Atlantic (Biel 21). Edith Wharton was in the midst of writing a new novel, *The Reef.* She devoted the lion's share of that spring and summer to completing the manuscript. She paused long enough that July, however, to accompany Henry James to Cliveden, the expansive Buckinghamshire estate of Waldorf and Nancy Astor. There, they met 19-year-old Madeline Astor, a *Titanic* survivor and recent widow whose husband, John Jacob Astor IV, had famously gone down with the doomed vessel. Although we do not have a record of what the Cliveden party discussed, it is certain that the recent disaster was on everyone's mind.

Indeed, a number of Wharton's close friends were deeply distressed. James, for one, wrote to Mrs. Francis D. Millet to express his condolences for the death of her husband "in the midst of all the horrors and misery" (H. James, *Letters* 613). Elizabeth Cameron, a Paris hostess, told Wharton that she had received several worrisome letters from Henry Adams, who – as fate would have it – had booked passage aboard the ship's anticipated return voyage to Europe. "This Titanic blow shatters one's nerves," Adams had written. "We can't grapple it" (Adams, *Letters* 535). He had penned a similarly dire letter to Wharton's sister-in-law, Mary Cadwalader Jones: "Society sees for the first time a glimpse of itself running on its ice-berg. . . . Like our friends on board, it can't grasp the idea of sinking. It is so fixed in the habit of thinking itself unsinkable, that it will not listen . . . The whole fabric of the nineteenth century is foundering, and all our friends with it" (Adams, *Letters* 537–8). Alarmed by her 74-year-old friend's agitated state, Jones cabled Wharton, who agreed that the disaster had shaken Adams to the core (R. W. B. Lewis 322).

Like Adams, many contemporary observers saw the wreck as a sign of the times – a dread rebuke against Gilded Age complacency. To the *New York Times*, the calamity was "a terrible warning to bring us back to the moorings of our senses": "We are running mad with the lust of wealth, and of power, and of ambition. We are abandoning the devout and simple lives of our ancestors, and the fabric of our fireside is weakening at the foundation" ("Titanic Verdict is Negligence" 3). By desecrating "the altars of our fathers," America's forces of cultural democratization were under-mining the very genealogical values that served as the ballast to the ship of state. In this respect, the sinking of the *Titanic* was only the tip of the proverbial iceberg. As *The Independent* duly noted, the ship's reckless speed seemed to be an apt metaphor for the breakneck pace of American class mobility. "The causes of our distorted vision and desire are not obscure," the paper's editorial staff intoned:

> The democratic social movement has swept millions of commonplace folk from their old moorings in religion, nationality and industry, and mixed them up indescribably. They are not prepared by education or discipline to value supremely worthy things; but, thrown into the swirl of our material prosperity, they have felt the crass appeal of speed and size, of sense-impression and self-indulgence. ("Realities and Mockeries" 905)

The *Titanic* had foundered on the combined dangers of class mobility, manic materialism and moral decline. Unanchored from the safe moorings of tradition, twentieth-century Americans were intoxicated with finding the fastest, easiest route to material success.

This "love of money and passion for luxury," Dr. Charles H. Parkhurst warned, was precisely the cause of the *Titanic's* ruin ("Religious Views of the 'Titanic'" 939). And while the ship's financiers bore the most obvious responsibility for the calamity, all "arrogant, . . . thoughtlessly pleasure-mad, [. . . and] undisturbed sensualists" shared part of the blame (G. A. Campbell 3). As one critic noted, "Producers and purveyors sell what the market calls for." And while this fact did not "exculpate them . . . it makes millions of consumers their accomplices" ("Realities and Mockeries" 904).

The skewed rates of passenger survival, of course, make the tendency to indict middle-class materialism and working-class mobility seem grimly ironic. Unlike the 60 percent of first-cabin travelers who boarded the limited lifeboats, only 44 percent of second-cabin passengers survived the disaster, while a mere 25 percent of those in steerage lived out the night (Biel 38). Despite such lopsided numbers, the upper classes received most of the credit for acts of selfless heroism. Henry James claimed that the artist Francis Millet had confronted death "asking nothing, round-about him, but giving and suggesting all, irradiating *that* beautiful genius and gallantry and humanity" (H. James, *Letters* 613). The *New York Times* similarly attributed the "heroism displayed on board" to "the willingness of men of action, with everything to live for, to die for duty's sake." Such men – Astor, Harry Elkins Widener, Benjamin Guggenheim and President Taft's military aide, Archibald Butts – were declared strenuous martyrs. Nevertheless, the *Times* was quick to admit that "there would inevitably be men lacking courage among so many of so varied origin and training" ("The Drift of the Testimony").

The caveat was revealing: while the American media was quick to glorify the prosperous Anglo-Saxon hero who had sacrificed his life to save count-less unknown women and children, commentators were at pains to empha-size the counter-Darwinian pathos of these gestures. To Guggenheim's reported vow – "No woman shall be left aboard this ship because Benjamin Guggenheim was a coward!" – reporters responded with lamentation (qtd. in Larabee 10). "Men of Brains and Millions Sacrificed for Lowly Women," one headline declared (Wayne). How could such mighty men have given up their lives to save obscure hoards of working-class women? "Certainly, it was not a case of the survival of the fittest," the Rev. Dr. Leighton Parks remarked in his sermon to parishioners at St. Bartholomew's Church in New York. "There were men lost that the city and the country needed, and there are widows surviving who speak no language that you or I can understand, and who inevitably become public charges" ("Religious Views of the 'Titanic'" 938).

This gendered and class dynamic became something of a set-piece in the days and weeks following the *Titanic*'s demise. Speculating on the ship's final moments, a *Denver Post* reporter, Frances Wayne, imagined the British journalist W. T. Stead, "his helpful messages to the race but half delivered, [stepping] aside [from the lifeboat], as a scrofulous girl, limp with terror, is dragged from below and shoved into the hands of the rescuing crew" (Wayne 18). Archibald Butts is similarly described looking on impassively as "a hollow-chested, blear-eyed woman, gibbering strange sounds, is assigned a place in the boats while the cold waters of Death creep nearer and nearer to him and his friends" (Wayne 18).

Such statements often assumed a curious triangulation between the well-born white man, his affluent wife and the desperate steerage woman. Ann E. Larabee cites an April 17, 1912 drawing that ran in the *St. Louis Post Dispatch* entitled "The Last Seat – Should He Take It?" The sketch depicts a handsome young man poised on the *Titanic*'s gangway; his warmly-clad wife beckons him from a life-raft below, while an attractive young woman, her dress skimpy and head uncovered, appeals desperately from the steps above. The caption asks, "Should the Bridegroom Take the Last Seat With His Bride, or Surrender It to the Unknown Woman Behind Him, and Make His Bride a Widow?" (Larabee 13). Larabee notes that the arrangement of the trio poses an explicitly sexual and moral choice between "the safe haven of domestic bliss" in the lifeboat, "and inevitable destruction through contact with this other woman who is dangerously part of the *Titanic*" (12). Indeed, the maritime habit of referring to the ship as a "she" only underscores the *Titanic*'s dangerous link to the unknown "woman adrift" beckoning from the stairs above. The vessel that the *Washington Post* posthumously christened the "doomed queen of the ocean" seemed to many, in Larabee's words, "a giantess who, putting on her most seductive and opulent clothes, rushed to her ruin" (Larabee 7).

The Reef registers these anxieties. From its first words – "Unexpected obstacle" – the novel echoes with the disaster's reverberant impact. The opening scene, set atop a "windswept platform" amid the waves of an "angry sea," underscores the title's ominous implications (3). At the center of the novel is a love triangle that replays the *Titanic*'s gendered and class anxieties. Like the "Unknown Woman" beckoning from the monstrously feminized vessel, Sophy Viner embodies what her rival Anna Leath calls "that unknown peril lurking in the background of every woman's thoughts about her lover" (270). A naïve but ambitious temptress, Sophy personifies the simultaneous allure and menace of an erotic voyage. She entices *The Reef*'s elite cast aboard a vessel destined for "the cheapest of cheap adventures, the most pitiful of sentimental blunders," plunging everyone into what *Titanic* commentators called "the democracy of humanity" (*Reef* 320; "The Law of the Sea" 901).

It is no surprise that the same generation who saw the *Titanic*'s demise as a cautionary tale on American materialism and class slippage, read *The Reef*, with its casual sexuality, working-class mobility and abundant patrician angst, with similar alarm. A review that Wharton clipped from *The Church Times*, for example, directly addresses itself to a readership transformed by the lessons of the *Titanic*: "The reader will expect shipwreck, and will not be disappointed; but even from a wreck some lives are sometimes saved. There is no salvage here . . . this series of depressing stories . . . are [*sic*] doubtless intended to promote a more earnest utterance of the prayer: 'In all time of our wealth, good Lord, deliver us'" (n.p.). While *The Reef* may not be "depressing," its plot is certainly distressing. The story revolves around the reignited passion of Anna Leath and George Darrow, native New Yorkers who rediscover each other in middle age. Now an expatriate widow, Anna invites Darrow to her mother-in-law's French country estate, only to postpone their highly anticipated rendezvous at the last minute. Irritated and perplexed, Darrow travels on to Paris where he has a brief affair with Sophy, a young American of indeterminate class origin. When ultimately he completes his trip to Givré months later, he discovers that Sophy has become not only the governess of Anna's daughter Effie, but also the fiancée of Anna's stepson, Owen. Realizing the Conradian "horror" of the situation, he struggles to make amends with his desperately disillusioned fiancée, who both despises and covets the illicit sexual attention he once gave to Sophy. The resulting situation is an erotic mess. As a reviewer for the *New-York Tribune* commented, "How is any one to navigate these nominally smiling waters without meeting disaster on the reef? Wreckage of some sort is inevitable" ("A Study by Mrs. Wharton").

Sophy *is*, in a sense, "the reef." Like the "chaos of attractions and repulsions" that Wharton identified "far beneath the ordered surfaces of intercourse," she represents a dangerously democratic impediment to genteel navigation (*Reef* 339). Darrow's regretful insistence that their tryst "seemed such a slight thing – all on the surface" discloses the situation's real menace: they have gone "aground on it because it *was* on the surface" (303). Patrician complacency, coupled with working-class mobility, create a perfect recipe for disaster.

For Anna, the unwonted longing to "be to [Darrow] all that Sophy Viner had been" plunges her into unfamiliar waters. Realizing her sudden kinship with her daughter's governess, a self-styled New Woman, proves increasingly "humiliating to her pride," for it forces her "to recognize kindred impulses in a character which she would have liked to feel completely alien to her."[1] This cross-class commonality among women was, interestingly enough, a frequent *Titanic* trope. In the weeks following the April 15 disaster, journalists rhapsodized, "Mistress and maid were as one, the steerage women as the jeweled and guarded ladies of pampered wealth. All had the same honor and protection" ("The Law of the Sea" 901). As one headline announced: "Women in Silk and Rags Together Await News – Patricians Weep in Peasants' Arms" ("Women in Silk"). Regardless of class, all women were in the same boat, literally and figuratively. "Fashionably gowned women whose friends rode in the de luxe staterooms of the liner are mingling with and confiding their grief to women in shawls and shabby bonnets whose loved ones embarked in the steerage," the *Denver Post* observed ("Women in Silk"). In this respect, the *Titanic* was an unprecedentedly "leveling" disaster, for it brought everyone to a common plain of grief. The "despair in the heart of the coughing peasant woman faded, perhaps, as she found that for her there was a place in the rocking boat by the side of the white-faced lady of the splendid furs" (Wayne).

Such cross-class alignments, however, did not necessarily afford equal "honor and protection" to all. As Anna realizes in *The Reef*, the steerage woman's distinction could be her affluent counterpart's disgrace. By following in Sophy's footsteps, Anna must confront "the deep discords and still deeper complicities between what thought in her and what blindly wanted" (*Reef* 307). Indeed, despite Darrow's warning that "the human problem [. . . is] not always a pleasant thing to look at," Anna is plainly unprepared for what she finds in the brave new world of sexual experience (280). Her decision to surrender to her desires and sleep with Darrow at the end of chapter 36 forces Anna to realize that she has irrevocably forfeited her class-based "reserve of unused power" by casting herself adrift on the uncharted waters of erotic knowledge (84).

THE "WOMAN ADRIFT"

To "be to [Darrow] all that Sophy Viner had been" is obviously a dangerous proposition, for Sophy is a "girl who's had to knock about the world" (183). By straddling "the blurred line between pure and fallen," Sophy titillates and terrifies Darrow and Anna (161). To his fiancée's restless questions "[W]hat *is* she? What are you? It's too horrible!", Darrow can only respond by sheepishly insisting that Sophy cannot be measured by "conventional standards" (280, 281). She is instead an emissary of class, racial and sexual hybridity – the very things that Wharton associated with America itself.

In many ways, Sophy embodies what Joanne Meyerowitz has called the "woman adrift" – the working-class woman who, in the early twentieth century, was "self-supporting . . . headstrong and openly sexual" (Meyerowitz 118). Like the woman adrift, Sophy is at home in the fast-paced environment of the urban metropolis, reveling in the city's "cheap amusements." From nightclubs and vaudeville theaters, to automobiles and dance halls, America's working women were in the vanguard of social experience, spending their independently earned wages on the city's many commercial attractions. In the process, they forged new, sexually revolutionary identities that challenged the nineteenth-century opposition between virgin and prostitute.[2] Indeed, as the social critic William Marion Reedy insisted in 1913, "The working girl is a working girl, not a bawd at large."[3] She set the pace for middle- and upper-class women in the years to come, transforming the American scene. In Reedy's memorable words, the clock had struck "sex o'clock in America" ("Sex" 113).

It seems no accident that Sophy, *The Reef*'s "woman adrift," is at least fleetingly linked to prostitution. When Owen Leath seeks his grandmother's blessing on his engagement to the young secretary-turned-governess, Adelaide Painter, an American family friend, explains her elderly compatriot's reticence: "Madame de Chantelle seems to imagine . . . that a young American girl ought to have a *dossier* – a police-record, or whatever you call it: what those awful women in the streets have here" (207). The comparison is fleeting but significant: while Sophy is not a prostitute and thus has no police dossier, the absence of any record explaining her identity makes her suspect. Like the United States itself, whose origins as we have seen were disrupted by a "sudden uprooting . . . and violent cutting off from all [its] past," Sophy has obscure antecedents (*French Ways* 82). "I've had no history – like the happy countries," she happily tells Darrow (*Reef* 143). Her "vague effusion of goodwill toward unknown fellow-beings," which Wharton considered a hallmark of American political naiveté, helps explain Sophy's adaptive willingness to share Darrow's bed (*French Ways* 91). She has a "loose native quality strained through a closer woof of manners," implying that she is all style without racialized substance (14). As "the composite product of an enquiring and adaptable race," she is difficult to pinpoint (14). Darrow, in fact, finds it impossible "to fit a name to her, for just such instances were perpetually pouring through the London Embassy, and the etched and angular American was becoming rarer than the fluid type" (14). If Sophy's typological ambiguity secures her place in the Galtonian discourse of composite portraiture, it equally reinforces her metonymic association with American pluralism.[4] However charming her "small nose, her clear tints, [and] a kind of sketchy delicacy in her face," her physiognomy indexes America's racial blurring. As Wharton archly insisted in 1908, "We live in the day of little noses: that once stately feature, intrinsically feudal and aristocratic in character . . . has shrunk to democratic insignificance, like many another fine expression of individualism" (*Motor-Flight* 21). Sophy personifies this indistinguishability: she "might be any one of a dozen definable types, or she might – more disconcertingly to her companion and more perilously to herself – be a shifting and uncrystallized mixture of them all" (59–60).

Sophy's "democratic insignificance" comes to play a central part in *The Reef*'s interwoven politics of sex and class. She is nothing less than an envoy from the commonplace world of modern America. Darrow recalls meeting Sophy at Mrs. Murret's Chelsea "dinner-factory" where, as a secretary, she was "one of the shadowy sidling presences in the background" (151–2, 15). Despite her indistinguishability from the "half-dozen fagged 'hands' [. . . who] tend[ed] the machine," Sophy turns out to be more than just a "dumb" appendage to the social engine (152, 15). Indeed, like her predecessor Mrs. Haffen, the blackmailing charwoman in *The House of Mirth*, Sophy is the eyes and ears of a pluralist nation. As she ominously tells Darrow, "We were all invisible to you; but we could see" (18). The former guest is forced to acknowledge that "the blurred tapestry of Mrs. Murrett's background had all the while been alive and full of eyes."[5]

Wharton here transforms Jacob Riis's relatively quiescent "other half" into an ominous "cloud of witnesses" (17). In what Darrow sees as "a queer reversal of perspective," the working class boldly returns the privileged gaze, destabilizing elite power by contesting the downward conventions of visual discipline.[6] Thus when Sophy flirtatiously models a "new dress" by spinning around the room and asking, "Well, what do you think of me?", her companion falls for the coy ruse: "I always adore new dresses," he replies (35). Sophy is triumphant: "I never knew the trick to fail!" As it turns out, she is wearing the same "old rag of yesterday," but has created the illusion of novelty.[7] This self-presentation registers Sophy's double threat: she is both a *femme fatale*, who uses femininity as a subversive masquerade, and a soubrette who can exploit Darrow's smug inattention (Doane 26; Kaplan 90).

If nothing else, Sophy's charades reveal the surprising vulnerability of Darrow's class status. Despite his vaunted pedigree (Madame de Chantelle is said to attach "great importance to the fact that [his] grandmother was an Everard of Albany"), Darrow's initially sanguine view of the "agglutinated humanity" on the Dover dock disappears the instant he receives Anna's disappointing cable (128, 11). Suddenly, he feels "obscurely outraged by these promiscuous contacts" (11). Only with considerable effort can he restore "his usual sense of being a personable young man, with all the privileges pertaining to the state, instead of the anonymous rag of humanity he had felt himself in the crowd on the pier" (17). If mere proximity to the world's "harried wretches" can so easily jeopardize Darrow's fragile class prerogatives, then we are only left to imagine the impact of intimate contact with a "woman who tries to rise above her past" (11, 180). Indeed, Darrow's fleeting assignation with Sophy exposes the frailty of his patrician posture. As he later looks at a photograph of himself, "well-dressed, handsome, self-sufficient – the portrait of a man of the world, confident in his ability to deal adequately with the most delicate situations," he realizes the "huge fatuity" of his class complacency (249).

Darrow vainly tries to offset his vulnerable class position by deploying a stale array of Victorian platitudes. Confronted with the amorphous unpredictability of the crowd, he seeks refuge in a rigid taxonomy of "feminine types." Though women, for Darrow, are either "pronouncedly 'ladies'" or they are not, he is "Grateful to both for ministering to the more complex masculine nature, and disposed to assume that they had been evolved, if not designed, to that end" (25, 26). As a result, "he had instinctively kept the two groups apart in his mind, avoiding that intermediate society which attempts to conciliate both theories of life" (26). Because Darrow likes "his 'ladies' and their rivals to be equally unashamed of showing for exactly what they were," he steers clear of those who try to claim a middle ground (26). Anchored firmly in the double standards of the Victorian past, Darrow's philosophy is blandly chauvinist. He attributes his "more complex masculine nature" to the productive authority of the phallus, and confidently assumes that, were Anna his lover, "he would have put warmth in her veins and light in her eyes: would have made her a woman through and through" (29). It is a self-deifying logic that he applies to Sophy as well: "His caress had restored her to her natural place in the scheme of things, and Darrow felt as if he had clasped a tree and a nymph had bloomed from it."[8] A self-satisfied diplomat, Darrow expresses a condescending interest in women that mirrors his colonial concern for "certain economic and social problems" in South America (113). "[Y]oung, active, stored with strength and energy," he is a self-styled icon of strenuous manhood (327). The world's dependent beings will, no doubt, surrender themselves to his phallocentric control, for he is "tired of experimenting on life; he wanted to 'take a line', to follow things up, to centralize and concentrate, and produce results" (123).

Sophy dramatically challenges Darrow's nineteenth-century model of phallic production. By passionately staking her claim on both Darrow and her own sexual gratification, she shakes the foundations of his "primitive complacency" (250). "I wanted it – I chose it," she boldly declares (274). "I want to keep you all to myself" (48). Only the voracious vocabulary of consumerism, it seems, can fully articulate these avid desires: "'Don't for a minute think I'm sorry!'" she later insists. "'It was worth every penny it cost'" (251). Persistently claiming agency, she insists that hers was a conscious choice: "'I've had you and I mean to keep you . . . To keep you hidden away here,' she ended, and put her hand upon her breast" (251–2). Sophy's forthright assertion unsettles Darrow's unilateral narrative of sexual and rhetorical agency. The circuitous coils of feminine desire undermine the linearity of his phallic plot, and he feels an "instinctive recoil from the thing that no amount of arguing can make 'straight'" (180).

SEXUALITY AND THE STRENUOUS LIFE

While Darrow's smug manliness is a target of Wharton's mordant humor, his class vulnerability is not: Sophy's racial, class and gender plasticity is no laughing matter.[9] Rather, it is her democratic mobility that threatens to lay siege to the genealogical keystones of patrician power and authority. Sophy is like the "average man" in America who is not "lifted up by culture," but instead "[drags it] down to him": in an art gallery, she admires "the worst things" and then lapses into silence, awaiting better entertainment "at a cinematograph show on the Boulevard" (*French Ways* 69; *Reef* 255). She always thinks "it a good sign when people liked Irish stew; it meant that they enjoyed changes and surprises, and taking life as it came" (*Reef* 41).

While such democratic pluralism was alarming to Wharton, she increasingly felt cheated as well, for she sensed that democracy afforded experiences that she had been denied. Hers had been a "numb dumb . . . self . . . that never believed in its chance of having any warm personal life, like other, luckier people," she remarked in 1908 (*Letters* 138). Many of these "luckier people" were average Americans who, like Nettie Struther in *The House of Mirth* and Mattie Silver in *Ethan Frome*, had experienced both the exhilaration of passion and the stimulus of pain. Wharton resented her exclusion from such sensations: "No one can love life as I do, love the beauty & the splendour & the ardour, & find words for them as I can, without having a share in them some day," she insisted ("The Life Apart," May 21 1910]).

It seemed unfair that "other people" were, by contrast, so "alive & active" (*Letters* 55). Wharton's fortieth birthday in January 1902, accompanied by a bout of the "floo," brought these issues to the fore. "I excessively hate to be forty," she wrote Sara Norton (55). "[O]ne longs to go to a hospital & *have something cut out*, & come out minus an organ, but alive & active & like other people, instead of dragging on with this bloodless existence!!" (55). In this strangely surgical birthday wish, Wharton expresses a haunting desire to pierce the body's surface and probe what one critic has called "the secret of fertility and reproduction" (Waid 59). At the same time, the fantasy equally imagines a kind of stylized violence that will cure Wharton's broader anemic complaint. The supposed therapeutic value of violence was, of course, central to what T. J. Jackson Lears has identified as "the antimodern fascination with suffering" (*No Place of Grace* 138). When

Gilbert Warde, Francis Marion Crawford's martial protagonist in his 1898 novel *Via Crucis: A Romance of the Second Crusade*, claims that there is "something far above common desires and passion, dwelling in a temple of the soul [. . . that] must be reached by steps of pain," we are to understand that pain, in Lears's words, brings "freedom, self-worth, a revitalized sense of autonomous identity" (Crawford qtd. in Lears, *No Place of Grace* 121; 122).

Wharton embraced this gospel of pain. "[R]elations between human beings" in the United States had dropped to "a dead level of vapid benevolence, and the whole of life to a small house with modern plumbing and heating, a garage, a motor, a telephone, and a lawn undivided from one's neighbor's," she complained as late as 1927 (*Uncollected* 154). Only a piercing infusion of revitalizing experience could revive the nation's health. To "*have something cut out*" was, in effect, "to move beyond the pleasure principle of a democratic, industrial culture," in Lears's words (118). It was to experience something so violent and visceral that the body could not help but be transformed into a being "active & alive." By 1909, Wharton could conclude that "To have as few numb tracts in one's consciousness as possible – that seems to me, so far, the most desirable thing in life, even though the Furies do dance in hob-nailed shoes on the sensitive tracts at a rate that sometimes makes one wish for any form of anaesthesia" (*Letters* 177). However seductive such panaceas might seem, they were, in reality, a mark of racial and gendered weakness. Pain served as an artistic catalyst, an elite introduction to "real life."[10]

Many Gilded-Age Americans shared Wharton's belief that the country had become soft, self-satisfied and cowardly. Indeed, Wharton openly wondered at "such lassitude in the descendants of the men who first cleared a place for themselves in a new world, and then fought for the right to be masters there. What became of the spirit of pioneers and the revolutionaries?" (*Backward Glance* 55). As her friend Theodore Roosevelt famously insisted in 1899, "it is only through strife, through hard and dangerous endeavor, that we shall ultimately win the goal of true national greatness" (*Strenuous* 21). The virtues of the "strenuous life" were clear: only through self-defining trials of pain could Americans escape the effeminizing weakness of instant gratification and consumerist ease.

It was the bumptious middle class that was blamed for the new climate of consumerism that had compromised both civic virtue and cultural authenticity. In a letter to the Massachusetts senator Henry Cabot Lodge in 1896, Roosevelt complained that "the moneyed and semi-cultivated classes, especially of the Northeast" were "producing a flabby, timid type of character which eats away the great fighting qualities of our race" (qtd. in Mallan 218). In a thinly veiled rhetoric of genteel anti-Semitism, Lodge, Roosevelt, Henry Adams and others perpetuated what Miriam Beard dubbed in 1942 "the myth of Nordic economic innocence" (M. Beard 368). By insisting that the Gentiles of the "pre-Jewish" era had been "swashbuckling D'Artagnans scattering louis d'or without thought of the morrow . . . or hairy-beary Siegfried[s] seizing the Rhinegold in knightly fashion," patrician nativists could blame American Jews for the mushrooming culture of market capitalism (M. Beard 368). And while targeting the upwardly mobile, pleasure-hungry middle class, this "warrior critique" of modern consumerism expressed increasing admiration for the bare-fisted tactics of America's workers (Mallan).

The nation's well-heeled and its down-and-out, it seemed, shared a common enemy: the great, mobile middle class (Higham, "Reorientation" 87). Indeed, the country's more affluent citizens suddenly took a new, somewhat voyeuristic interest in the lives of laboring Americans. "Leave the close air of the office, the library, or the club, and go out into the streets and the highway," an *Atlantic Monthly* writer urged readers in 1897. "Consult the teamster, the farmer, the wood-chopper, the shepherd, the drover. You will find him as healthy in mind, as free from fads, as strong in natural impulses, as he was in Shakespeare's time" (Merwin 846). Heeding the call, a group of prosperous Progressives went undercover, disguising themselves as waitresses, tramps, beggars and steel workers to see how the other half lived. These so-called "down-and-outers" – among them Walter Wyckoff, Frances Donovan and Bessie Van Vorst – "passed" among America's poor, determined to plumb the secrets of those Jack London dubbed the "people of the abyss" (Pittenger 27). In what Mark Pittenger describes as "a peculiar dialectic of attraction and repulsion," sophisticated reporters frequently depicted the poor as simultaneously "more vital and alive than themselves, and as a devolving, degenerating threat to civilized order" (29). Class differences seemed cloudier as "passing" set the down-and-outers adrift in a "region where middle shaded into lower, whiteness into color, and human into subhuman" (Pittenger 41, 29).

The urban patrician's mixed admiration for the vigorous young "man who works with his hands" was matched by an equal ambivalence toward civilization itself. As Henry Childs Merwin announced in 1897, it was possible to be "civilized too much" (Merwin 839). The country's well-to-do citizens had become "over-sophisticated and effete," their "springs of action . . . paralyzed or perverted by the undue predominance of the intellect" (Merwin 839). The essayist Agnes Repplier could only agree. "The early settlers of America, surrounded by hostile Indians, and doubtful each morning whether the coming nightfall would not see their rude homes given to the flames, probably suffered but little from the dullness which seems so oppressive to the peaceful agriculturalist of to-day," she derisively remarked in 1893 ("Ennui" 779). Well-born Americans were losing touch with the rugged world of their pioneering ancestors. Today's Americans wanted only "happiness, without the illusion of pleasure or the reality of pain."[11]

This cowardly aversion to pain appeared to many a symptom of America's overcivilization and decadent decline (Lears, *No Place of Grace* 45). "The modern civilized man is squeamish about pain to a degree which would have seemed effeminate or worse to his great-grandfather," the *Century* complained in 1888 ("Modern Science" 633). The country's transition to a "pleasure-economy" posed a potentially "fatal" threat to educated citizens, who wielded "no powers of defense against its disintegrative influences," William James warned in 1910 ("Moral Equivalent" 1287). Soft and complacent, elite Americans had forgotten that "human life with no use for hardihood" was "contemptible" (1285).

For Roosevelt, such possibilities were particularly ominous. In response to widespread rumor that the old-stock birthrate was declining because genteel women feared the pain associated with childbirth, Roosevelt argued that nervous sensibilities were nothing less than a threat to national security. If well-born women refused to have children, "race suicide" would result – a demographic disaster for United States leadership. When "men fear . . . righteous war, when women fear motherhood," Roosevelt warned, "they tremble on the brink of doom" (*Strenuous* 4).

In April 1910, Roosevelt arrived in Paris to deliver an address at the Sorbonne. In a speech entitled "Citizenship in a Republic," the former President denounced "willful sterility" while extolling the virtues of romantic activism. He called for an end to "ease and self-indulgence, of shrinking from pain and effort and risk, which in the long run Nature punishes more heavily than any other" ("Citizenship in a Republic"). Wharton was in the audience and provided a sympathetic ear. Two days after the speech, she invited Roosevelt to a tea in his honor on the Rue de Varenne. She had invited a number of eminent Frenchmen – including Jules Jusserand, Victor Bérard and André Chevrillon. The afternoon had chiefly been organized, however, to spotlight the talents of one comparatively minor American journalist, W. Morton Fullerton.

Fullerton and Wharton had begun a passionate romance in 1907. In October of that year, she had invited the handsome Connecticut native to her home in Lenox, Massachusetts. Writing Sally Norton that she considered him "very intelligent, but slightly mysterious," Wharton was at once excited and intrigued (*Letters* 113). The two had taken a private walk in the damp Berkshire woods and, pausing to share a cigarette, they had spotted some wild witch-hazel – "the 'old woman's flower'" (qtd. in Benstock 175). The blossom seemed to symbolize all of the belated ardor stored up in Wharton's 45-year-old life. Understanding its charged significance, Fullerton enclosed a single sprig of the flower in his wordless note of thanks. Wharton was elated. As her biographer Shari Benstock has remarked, the momentous weekend ultimately created "an unbridgeable gulf with all that had gone before" (Benstock 175). Their ensuing liaison would shipwreck Wharton on the sexualized reef of "real life," plunging her into the unmediated world of erotic experience.

Fullerton arrived at the Roosevelt tea seemingly prepared to make the most of the professional opportunity that his lover had arranged. As Paris correspondent for *The Times*, he managed to secure ten minutes' private conversation with the former President, to whom he offered a candid critique of the Sorbonne address. Had the speech been delivered by anyone else, Fullerton told Roosevelt, it would easily have been misconstrued as an anti-intellectual indictment of the French literati. Taken with the younger man's forthrightness, Roosevelt told Wharton that he was "greatly struck" by the "able fellow" (Wharton, *Letters* 214, n.1). Wharton was delighted; she wanted nothing more than to please her temperamental amour. Roosevelt's speech, vigorously condemning the "empty phrase-maker," and boldly exalting "the doer of deeds," had surely spoken to her own inner turbulence – the combination of moral hesitance and passionate eagerness she felt in the midst of an adulterous affair. Longing to embrace Roosevelt's ethic and unflinchingly translate romantic abstraction into erotic action, Wharton no doubt appreciated the personal and political message that Roosevelt's speech had delivered.

She was thus entirely mystified when Fullerton seemed to ignore a generous invitation from the President to attend an Embassy affair days later. It seemed incomprehensible to her that he would snub the opportunity to attend an event at which she also would be present. The impassive response seemed less a political insult to Roosevelt than a personal affront to her: "I thought you really wanted to see Mr. Roosevelt, & the opportunity had been 'worked up' admirably," she wrote Fullerton bewilderedly (*Letters* 212). Her mood then quickly turned petulant: "let us regard the Seine as the Atlantic, & ourselves as geographically sundered till some new cataclysm makes things over, & brings us together" (212).

The Fullerton experience was, by turns, exhilarating and shattering: episodes of heated pursuit were followed by weeks of cold, inexplicable silence. Wharton's letters of the period reveal her confused frustration and her pleading desperation. "You write me like a lover, you treat me like a casual acquaintance! Which are you – what am I?" (*Letters* 207). The liaison seemed to raise radical questions about Wharton's own identity. As she asked herself in 1910, "Oh, my free, proud, secure soul, where are you? *What were you*, to escape me like this?" ("The Life Apart," April 25 [1910]). The relationship had brought her face to face with the petty degradations and insecurities of erotic experience. "I, who dominated life, stood aside from it so, how I am humbled, absorbed, without a shred of will or identity left!" she reflected ("The Life Apart," April 20, [1910]).

The surrender to passion had entailed a simultaneous forfeiture of gender and class privilege. The dormant passions that Wharton thought so unique and specific turned out to be prosaic and universal. She was terrified lest her more sexually experienced admirer undervalue her passion. Would the "treasures I long to unpack for you, that have come to me in magic ships from enchanted islands," turn out to be nothing more than "old familiar red calico & beads" to a "clever trader, who has had dealings in every latitude, & knows just what to carry in the hold to please the simple native . . ."? "I'm so afraid of this, that often & often I stuff my shining treasures back into their box, lest I should see you smiling at them!" (*Letters* 135). Her hoarded treasure's magical authenticity had to compete with the lurking possibility of fraud: perhaps her riches were, in fact, ordinary trinkets, the tainted booty of colonialism.

Such anxieties initially overwhelmed Wharton. From the outset, she resisted Fullerton's sexual advances, fearing that consummation would compromise the genteel purity of her passion. "[T]here is a contact of thoughts that seems so much closer than a kiss," she insisted ("The Life Apart," April 20, [1910]). "I thought I could best show my love by refraining – & abstaining" (*Letters* 161). At the same time, Wharton was less alarmed by Fullerton's importunities than she was by her own responsiveness to their appeal. As she admitted after one particularly heated encounter in the summer of 1908, "I feared, if I let you love me too much, I might lose courage when the time came to go away!" (*Letters* 161). Writing served as a refuge from these unruly impulses, creating a "mystic nearness" with Fullerton that avoided the messy complications of contact.[12] The ritual of reading Fullerton's letters thus took on a palpably sexual charge. "[T]here is the delicious moment of postponement," when Fullerton's note would arrive each morning on her breakfast-tray: "one leaves it unopened while

one pours the tea, just in order to 'savourer' longer the joy that is coming!"
After that, the ritual unfolded – from "the slipping of the little silver knife
under the flap" to "the slow lingering again and again over each phrase and
each word, the taking possession, the absorbing of them one by one." The
experience, Wharton insisted, was "an exquisite accompaniment to the dull
prose of life" (qtd. in Benstock 182).

Yet as her relationship with Fullerton intensified, Wharton found such
sublime postures increasingly difficult to maintain. On "tormented days,"
she confessed, "that sense of mystic nearness fails me, [. . . and] in your
absence I long, I ache for you, I feel that what I want is to be in your arms, to
be held fast there – 'like other women!'" ("The Life Apart," April 20, [1910]).
To be Fullerton's lover in body and in spirit, as so many "other women" had
no doubt been before, was to confront the unpredictability and uncertainty
of erotic experience. Like *The Reef*'s Anna Leath, Wharton realized at
midlife that "She had lacked the hard teachings of experience" (*Reef* 269).
Her "instinctive disdain for whatever was less clear and open than her
own conscience had kept her from learning anything of the intricacies
and contradictions of other hearts" (269). No amount of high-minded
rationalization, however, could compensate for direct experience. It was
a realization that would force Wharton to acknowledge her share in the
universal hunger for sexual fulfillment.

Wharton and Fullerton finally consummated their affair in a nondescript
room at London's Charing Cross Hotel in June 1909. Characteristically,
she immediately set about chronicling their night together – this time, in
a startlingly candid fifty-two-line poem entitled "Terminus." "Wonderful
was the long secret night you gave me, my Lover, / Palm to palm, breast to
breast in the gloom," the poem rapturously begins. As the speaker awakens,
she finds her lover asleep beside her. Glancing about the anonymous hotel
room, she thinks about the many people who must have enjoyed similar
nights of passion in this self-same bed:

> [P]erchance [the bed] has also thrilled
> With the pressure of bodies ecstatic, bodies like ours,
> Seeking each other's souls in the depths of unfathomed caresses,
> And through the long windings of passion emerging again to the stars . . .
> ("Terminus" 259)

The room's democratic dinginess – "its dull impersonal furniture" and
"soot-sodden chintz" – seems an appropriate tribute to the "Faces innu-
merous and vague of the endless travelling automata" who have dwelt

within its walls (259). "[F]lagged bodies, dust-stained, averted in sleep, / The hurried, the restless, the aimless" have likewise lain in this "low wide bed, as rutted and worn as a high-road." Sex has brought the speaker face to face with the brute realities of ordinary people. Wharton ponders the matter in empathic detail:

And lying there hushed in your arms, as the waves of rapture receded,
And far down the margin of being we heard the low beat of the soul,
I was glad as I thought of those others, the nameless, the many,
Who perhaps thus had lain and loved for an hour on the brink of the world,
Secret and fast in the heart of the whirlwind of travel,
The shaking and shrieking of trains, the night-long shudder of traffic. (259)

The passage lyrically marks the considerable distance that Wharton herself had traveled from earlier landmarks. If Lily Bart's elite beauty stands in dramatic relief against "the dull tints of the crowd" milling about Grand Central Terminal in *The House of Mirth*, the speaker in "Terminus" experiences something entirely different. She is comforted, not repelled, by her sudden kinship with "the nameless, the many." She is heartened by the possibility that other women have awakened in this very room, and similarly found their lovers dreaming by their side: "Thus may another have thought; thus, as I turned, may have turned / To the sleeping lips at her side, to drink, as I drank there, oblivion" (260).

"Terminus" reveals Wharton's newfound compassion for the everyday experiences of the embodied multitude. Celebrating what Gloria Ehrlich calls "the transcendence of squalor by democratic Whitmanian rapture" (108), Wharton fully acknowledges, for the first time, what William James called "facts in all their crude variety" (*Pragmatism* 12). Consummating her relationship with Fullerton had introduced her to a new, democratic kind of knowledge that rendered abstract theories of human desire null and void. Sexual experience blurred traditional social markers, obscuring the boundaries between bodies, egos, ranks and races. To experience passion, in short, was to experience democracy.

"REAL LIFE" AND THE EROTICS OF PRAGMATISM

On the day of the Roosevelt tea, Wharton received a letter from William James, then visiting his younger brother Henry in Rye, England. James wrote admiringly of Roosevelt's speech, praising the "moral sincerity" of both the message and the messenger:

The beauty of T.R. is that he cares for the matter so much that he forgets the manner; and let us hope that the Parisians, hearing him but this once, will also not have noticed too much the lack of what they call distinction. I myself regard Roosevelt, with all his faults, as a tremendously precious natural asset. (W. James, letter to Edith Wharton, April 25, 1910)

A champion of "concrete personal experience," James was clearly in the position to appreciate "matter" over "manner." His ground-breaking philosophical lectures at Boston's Lowell Institute in 1906 had only amplified his reputation as the country's heir-apparent to Emersonian pragmatism. The purely theoretical world "to which your philosophy professor introduces you is simple, clean and noble," James told his Boston audience; but 'real life,' by contrast, is "multitudinous beyond imagination, tangled, muddy, painful and perplexed" (*Pragmatism* 18, 17–18). The pragmatist "turns away from abstraction and insufficiency, from verbal solutions . . . He turns towards concreteness and adequacy, towards facts, towards action and towards power" (31). Pragmatism was the terrain of the commonplace and the real, for it privileged experiences "to which the street belongs" (17).

This singular attention to "facts in all their crude variety" was ground-breaking. James effectively laid siege to the dignified edifice of nineteenth-century rationalism, that "marble temple shining on a hill" (*Pragmatism* 18). In its place, he proposed to raise a jumbled, plural, democratic structure forged out of the "colossal universe of concrete facts" (22). This icon to the "American Will" would soar over the "American Intellect," a triumphant skyscraper dwarfing its crumbling colonial neighbor. Truth was not a matter of aristocratic prerogative; instead, it was forged by direct engagement with common people in pursuit of their "practical affairs."[13]

It is perhaps no surprise that Wharton initially received Jamesian pragmatism with a mixture of hostility and scorn. Complaining that "William o' the wisp James" was "neurotic, unreliable" and prone to "chronic flares & twitches," she worried that he would have a destabilizing effect on his brother Henry, who, in later years, seemed prone to depression (*Letters* 205). Wharton had little patience for the "psychological-pietistic juggling" of which she thought William "the source & chief distributor," and she thus dismissed *Varieties of Religious Experience* (1902) as "just a Christian Science tract" (*Letters* 101–2; letter to Sara Norton, Sept. 1, [1902]). What were people "so excited about"? "The only interesting people in it are the Catholic mystics, & one can read so much better accounts of them elsewhere" (letter to Sara Norton, Sept. 1, [1902]).

The uncharacteristically shrill tone of Wharton's indictment indicates the troubled nature of her own politics during this period. While applauding Roosevelt's "vigour, clear sightedness, & his immense capacity for taking an interest in things," she condemned similar qualities in William James (letter to Sara Norton, Sept. 1, [1902]). Perhaps his brand of pragmatism hit too close to home. By proposing a genuinely democratic vantage point on meaning and truth, James envisioned a world as politically threatening as it was socially liberating. Twentieth-century Americans, he said, needed to be receptive "to the shocks of the ordinary" (Posnock 324). Young college women, moreover, should work on "the toning-down of their moral tensions," and emulate instead "your relaxed and easy worker" ("Gospel of Relaxation" 507, 504). As his Harvard colleague George Santayana observed in 1913, James was in touch with "the full-blooded irrational movement of life" (*Winds* 23). The newfound hero of "the first self-conscious American cultural avant-garde – the young intellectuals of the generation of 1910," James urged Americans to probe the hidden meanings of their most personal acts, and acknowledge the dynamic pluralism of everyday experience (Posnock 325).

For Wharton, the implications of these ideas were disquieting. A lifetime spent behind the layered curtains of Old New York and within the ancestral walls of Paris and Rome had prepared her less for Jamesian pluralism than for the more self-conscious aestheticism of Santayana. As she told John Jay Chapman in 1917, "whatever Santayana has to say one eternally thanks him for saying it so perfectly" (*Letters* 386). Santayana's elite dismay with James's "prophetic sympathy with the dawning sentiments of the age, with the moods of the dumb majority" struck a chord with Wharton as well (Santayana, "Genteel" 372). Like the native Spaniard, she found James "the friend and helper of those groping, nervous, half-educated, spiritually disinherited, emotionally hungry individuals of which America is full" ("Genteel" 372–3). In the words of Frank Lentricchia, James's "multi-authored book of democracy" could not but threaten the "genteel tradition" to which both Santayana and Wharton remained faithful (807).

Yet as Santayana admitted in 1913, "The shell of Christendom is broken. Our whole life and mind is saturated with the slow upward filtration of a new spirit – that of an emancipated, atheistic, international democracy" (*Winds* 1). The only remedy, as the philosopher saw it, was to embrace the disinterested life of the mind. "[B]y the mind only do we exist as men, and are more than so many storage-batteries for material energy," Santayana told a Berkeley, California audience in 1911. "Let us therefore be frankly human. Let us be content to live in the mind."[14] This abstemious summons to the "inward landscape" had strong appeal for Wharton, whose mistrust of the erratic impulses of the body politic was matched by her wariness of the capricious immediacy of the body human ("Genteel" 380). Consider an anecdote from 1901. Upon returning from a dinner party, Wharton wrote Sally Norton that she had submitted to having her palm read by a "silly woman." "[T]he only true thing she said was: 'What tired hands you have'; but she might have applied it to my whole body!" Wharton exclaimed. "However, one isn't all body, or rather, I should say, one doesn't feel so, & the other side enjoys life more every minute – so there are compensations" (letter, Dec. 29, [1901]). The mind *could* make up for the mean mutability of the body – even if such imaginative escapes were few and far between. Just as it was possible to motor out of Paris "without touching even the fringe of what, were it like other cities, would be called its slums," so it was also feasible to circumvent both the body and the body politic by seeking shelter in the rarified world of the mind (*Motor-Flight* 172).

Circumvention, of course, had been the representative gesture of the genteel tradition. As Santayana put it, "a genteel tradition forbids people to confess that they are unhappy" ("Genteel" 368). This had been precisely the trouble with Old New York. As Wharton recalled in 1937, "The average well-to-do New Yorker of my childhood was . . . starved for a sight of the high gods. Beauty, passion, and danger were automatically excluded from his life." As a result, the "tepid sameness of [New York's] moral atmosphere" encouraged "a prolonged immaturity of the mind" (*Uncollected* 276).

By 1912, such ingenious evasions seemed philosophically, if not practically, untenable. *The Reef*, Wharton's first post-Fullerton novel, reveals that such "miraculous escapes" from modernity's messy pluralism required one to deny the "chaos of attractions and repulsions far beneath the ordered surfaces of intercourse" (*Reef* 339). Those who sought refuge in the "welllit [*sic*] and well-policed suburb to dark places one need never know about," were attempting the impossible, for the world's "dark places" were steadily encroaching on the gated community of patrician privilege (339). As Anna Leath soberly realizes of such places, "henceforth she would always have to traverse them" (339).

Anna acknowledges as much in the opening moments of Book Two. Prior to her erotic entanglement with Darrow, a veil had "hung between herself and life. It had been like the stage gauze which gives an illusive air of reality to the painted scene behind it, yet proves it, after all, to be no more than a painted scene" (82). At midlife, Anna is as much a sexual virgin as

Wharton was at 40, or Lily Bart at 30. A "model of ladylike repression," she has never crossed "the magic bridge between West Fifty-fifth Street and life" (84). Her early romance with George Darrow was thus an exercise in futility: the youthful passion had "swept over her like a wind that shakes the roof of the forest without reaching its still glades or rippling its hidden pools" (29, 84). Like *The Portrait of a Lady*'s Isabel Archer, who rejects two sexually vibrant suitors to marry an effete dilettante, Anna marries Fraser Leath, a snuffbox-collecting widower, whose sexual apathy increases his wife's "belief that 'real life' was neither real nor alive" (92). Even "the irreducible crude fact of childbearing" can teach Anna little about herself or her needs. Like Fraser's first wife, whose lifeless portrait leaves her son Owen "so unaccounted for," Anna seems doomed to go to her grave as an experiential virgin, a victim of the "deadening process of forming a 'lady'" (95, 29).

In this sense, *The House of Mirth* inescapably haunts *The Reef*: Wharton seems to return to her prior novel and to reevaluate its interpretation of race, gender and class. She deliberately restages the desirous tableau that caught Lily and Selden in a Keatsian frieze of thwarted love, but this time "the ghostly lovers on the Grecian Urn, forever pursuing without ever clasping each other," have matured to middle age (*Reef* 29). As a result, the sacred racial achievement that climaxes *The House of Mirth* becomes, in *The Reef*, a sordid parade of human error. Unable to sustain the taxidermic fantasy of permanence and wholeness, *The Reef* rejects the rigid stasis of rationalism for the limpid flexibility of modern pragmatism. The neatly composed tableau that is Lily Bart's spiritualized suicide proves impossible in the chaotic milieu of *The Reef*. As Wharton's friend Walter Lippmann would keenly observe in 1914, "It is far easier to treat life as if it were dead, men as if they were dolls. It is everlastingly difficult to keep the mind flexible and alert" (Lippmann 29).

By 1912, Wharton had lost confidence in the preservationist strategies she had put to such reverent use in *The House of Mirth*. Rejecting the fastidious idealism that Selden had used to justify his own moral cowardice, Darrow instead defends his mistakes in notably pragmatic terms. As he explains to Anna,

"[W]hen you've lived a little longer you'll see what complex blunderers we all are: how we're struck blind sometimes, and mad sometimes – and then, when our sight and our senses come back, how we have to set to work, and build up, little by little, bit by bit, the precious things we'd smashed to atoms without knowing it. Life's just a perpetual piecing together of broken bits." (*Reef* 302–3)

The world that had been safely inoculated against "atrophy and ruin" in *The House of Mirth* is, in *The Reef*, a fragile jigsaw puzzle whose pieces must be perpetually fitted and refitted together. Selden's reliquary reverence for his dead lover proves utterly unviable. When Anna tries to imagine "the hour when she might raise a mournful shrine to the memory of the Darrow she had loved, without fear that his double's shadow would desecrate it," she cannot separate "the real Darrow" from her derisive double: they are inextricably merged (289–90). Similarly, if the "delicate impalpable mask" that Lily wears in death mirrors the interpretive plasticity of their last kiss, wherein Selden ecstatically reads "all that his heart craved to find there," Anna enjoys no such epiphany or closure (*House* 325–6, 329). Instead, Fraser Leath's kiss is an image of deficiency: when his "symmetrical blond mask bent over hers, and his kiss dropped on her like a cold smooth pebble . . . she questioned the completeness of the joys he offered" (*Reef* 89). Like a rigid automaton, Leath plays by the rules: "Life, to Mr. Leath, was like a walk through a carefully classified museum, where, in moments of doubt, one had only to look at the number and refer to one's catalogue" (91). The museum is no longer the iconic house of mourning; instead, Anna feels as though she were groping about in an eerie warehouse "where the exploring ray of curiosity lit up now some shape of breathing beauty and now a mummy's grin" (91). The substitution of the gothic mummy for the taxidermic specimen and the holy relic signifies Wharton's shift from *The House of Mirth*'s aesthetic of death to *The Reef*'s chaotic embrace of life. The Marian sacrifice that climaxes the story of Lily Bart proves too otherworldly for the combative, experiential world of *The Reef*. In the throes of sexual obsession, Anna cannot fathom committing an act of spiritualized martyrdom. Instead, she assumes that "She was his now, his for life: there could never again be any question of sacrificing herself to Effie's welfare, or to any other abstract conception of duty." All that matters is "the tumultuous rumour of her happiness" (331).

For William James, the movement from the unity of the spiritualized museum to the untidy pluralism of the mummy warehouse was salutary and predictable. "[A]cquaintance with reality's diversities is as important as understanding their connexion," he insisted (*Pragmatism* 65). While people thrived on system, unity and order, a competing "human passion of curiosity" for life's practical discontinuities could just as easily interrupt what James imagined as a quasi-electrical path of narrative continuity (65). Like electricity, love relations were an apt metaphor for "the world's *disunion*" (68). As James explains in *Pragmatism*,

[M]en are joined in a vast network of *acquaintanceship*. Brown knows Jones, Jones knows Robinson, etc.; and *by choosing your farther intermediaries rightly* you may carry a message from Jones to the Empress of China, or the Chief of the African Pigmies, or to anyone else in the inhabited world. But you are stopped short, as by a non-conductor, when you choose one man wrong in this experiment. What may be called love-systems are grafted on the acquaintance-system. A loves (or hates) B; B loves (or hates) C, etc. (67)

The possibility of love (or hate) throws a wrench into the orderly "hangings-together of the world's parts," James observed (67). As a result, "there is no species of connexion which will not fail, if, instead of choosing conductors for it, you choose non-conductors. You are then arrested at your very first step and have to write the world down as a pure *many* from that particular point of view" (68).

Wharton's plunge into what James called "the river of experience" had introduced her directly to the "pure many" (*Pragmatism* 63). Her relationship with Fullerton, by turns conductive and non-conductive, gave her a first-hand view of what happened when the pragmatist's unpredictable love-system was grafted on to the rationalist's acquaintance-system. And while Wharton had always been wary of the potentially anarchic demands of this love-system, she increasingly came to think the democratic volatility of pragmatism preferable to the abstemious regulations of rationalism. To prevent potential disorder by banishing sexual ardor from the social economy was, in the end, just as dangerous as capitulating to that disorder altogether. In her 1920 travel narrative, *In Morocco*, Wharton uses the harem as a cautionary example of this phenomenon. Because Moroccan women are forbidden to roam freely in the public domain, they are "imprisoned in a conception of sexual and domestic life based on slave-service and incessant espionage." As a result, they lead "colourless eventless lives depend[ent] on the favour of one fat tyrannical man" (152). The petty and tyrannical logic that encouraged this sort of conspiratorial despotism was at work not only in Morocco but in the United States as well. Americans, like Moroccans, Wharton insisted, were sexual puritans. Women in the United States were often segregated into same-sex activities and clubs where, as "each other's only audience," they missed out on "the checks, the stimulus, and the discipline that comes of contact with the stronger masculine individuality" (*French Ways* 102–3). Similarly, Americans took an equally balkanizing attitude toward sexuality, exiling passion from the mainstream of civic life. "In a society where marriage is supposed to be determined solely by reciprocal inclination, and to bind the contracting parties not only to a social but to a physical lifelong loyalty, love, which never has accepted, and never will accept, such bonds, immediately becomes a pariah and a sinner" (*French Ways* 127). When love is treated like a criminal, it acts like a criminal. A society that "puts love beyond the law," and then proceeds to pay it "such a heavy toll, subjects itself to the most terrible of Camorras," for "except in a world where the claims of the body social are very perfectly balanced against those of the body individual, to give such a place to passion is to risk being submerged by it" (*French Ways* 132).

Wharton's reference to the Camorra, an early nineteenth-century Neopolitan secret society that, like the Mafia, its notorious successor, thrived on racketeering and violence, links the effects of proscribed sexuality to the ravages of organized crime. Because no society can fully reconcile the competing interests of the body social against those of the individual body, the effort to purge the "social economy" of renegade sexuality was pure folly. Alienated impulses, like alienated people, became more dangerous when utterly estranged from the social order. With no purchase on the social order, and with nothing to lose, such impulses tended to congregate in volatile cells of anti-social behavior.[15]

FICTION AND FRICTION

In one of *The Reef*'s most important passages, Anna sees her own sexual awakening as a sort of social revolution. Like a radicalized underclass, her erotic impulses have mounted a subaltern revolt against the ruling elite:

She recalled having read somewhere that in ancient Rome the slaves were not allowed to wear a distinctive dress lest they should recognize each other and learn their numbers and their power. So, in herself, she discerned for the first time instincts and desires, which, mute and unmarked, had gone to and fro in the dim passages of her mind, and now hailed each other with a cry of mutiny.[16]

What Melville had powerfully envisioned in *Benito Cereno* – the arrogant master awakening one day to find himself the servant of his slave – is at the core of Wharton's political vision in *The Reef*. She explores the threat of "mutiny" from below – from one's own sexual urges or from those Madame de Chantelle nervously calls "Anarchists . . . [who] belong to Unions" (130). As "instincts and desires," previously "mute and unmarked," "now [hail] each other with a cry of mutiny," Anna awakens to the revolutionary possibilities of sexual desire. Yet as she quickly discovers, this seeming emancipation from Victorian morality is in fact just another more insidious form of imprisonment. Succumbing to "passionate dependence," Anna experiences "a different feeling from any she had known before: confused and turbid, as if secret shames and rancours stirred in it, yet richer, deeper, more enslaving" (306).

By linking Anna's sexual self-discovery to the painful endeavors of the strenuous life, Wharton simultaneously presents a cure to elite malaise and an uneasy marker of democratic commonality. Like the down-and-outers, Anna covets the raw experiences she has come to associate with the working class. Awed by Sophy's "deep spring of pain," the privileged widow seeks her own share in the erotics of suffering (274). "She had suffered before – yes, but lucidly, reflectively, elegiacally: now she was suffering as a hurt animal must, blindly, furiously, with the single fierce animal longing that the awful pain should stop" (275–6). By rejecting *The House of Mirth*'s mournful distress and exploring instead the "animal anguish" that she had previously said was the exclusive province of the working class, Wharton takes a new activist stance in line with Roosevelt's muscular demand for "vivid and masterful experience" (Higham, "Reorientation" 79). If "the pleasure principle of a democratic, industrial culture" encouraged a life without pain, then "real life" meant something else – the "unmediated experience" of living "at full throttle."[17] Anna's pain is both ennobling and humiliating (275). As an anti-modern antidote to the neurasthenic "weightlessness" of upper-class life, suffering allows her to scale the ecstatic cliffs of affective mysticism. At the same time, though, pain unites Anna to working-class Americans like Sophy Viner, who seems "to have no scruples and a thousand delicacies."[18]

Over the course of the novel, Anna discovers not only what it means to relinquish sexual and class advantage, but more frighteningly still, how seductive such abjection can be. Fascinated with the "intricacies of her [own] suffering," she subjects herself to the kind of mystical torments that Wharton had seen chronicled in Henry Osborn Taylor's *The Mediaeval Mind* (1911).[19] "No 'spiritual exercise' devised by the discipline of piety could have been more torturing; but its very cruelty attracted her. She wanted to wear herself out with new pain" (*Reef* 292–3). Like Taylor's thirteenth-century mystic who "sometimes was seized with ecstasy five-and-twenty times a day, in which state she was motionless, and on returning to herself was so enraptured that she could not keep from displaying her inner joy with movements of the body, like David leaping before the Ark," Anna veers wildly between fits of "demoniac possession" and the *vita contemplativa* (Taylor 478; *Reef* 309). Her romance is both a "fiery initiation from which she had emerged seared and quivering, but clutching to her breast a magic talisman," and a meditative self-examination, which she needs "as she

needed her morning plunge into cold water" (*Reef* 307, 306). In this sense,
Anna mirrors the nun who, according to Taylor, was so "afflicted with the
Lord," that she was sometimes seen "rolling herself in the fire, and in the
winter standing in frozen water" (Taylor 477). If Mary of Ognies could
walk barefoot on ice, and Mechthild of Magdeburg so desperately craved
"the beautiful manhood of her Lord Jesus Christ" that she would fanta-
size about being burned by "The Godhead . . . so fiery hot," then Anna
staggers from "flame and torment into a colourless cold world where everything surrounding her seemed equally indifferent and remote" (Taylor 479;
Reef 282).

This sort of pain is spiritually transfiguring, and to a certain extent
Wharton implies that Anna can inoculate herself against the commonplace
demands of the "individual appetites" by practicing an ascetic aversion to
immanence and ease.[20] This strenuous approach, however, buckles under
its own weight. Though Anna frantically looks to Sophy as a working-
class guide through this experiential quagmire – "It was Sophy Viner only
who could save her – Sophy Viner only who could give her back her lost
serenity" – she ultimately finds herself trapped in the confusing limbo of
democratic mediocrity (346).

Searching for Sophy, Anna wanders into the shabby milieu of Laura
McTarvie-Birch, the young woman's "married, unmarried, remarried" older
sister (23). Anna's quest itself should give us pause: why reopen a closed
case? Owen, jilted by Sophy, is on his way to Spain; Darrow, regaining his
complacency, is planning his wedded future, and even Anna herself seems
newly reconciled to her lover as "the one real fact in the world" (345). Why
then add the novel's unstable and inconclusive final chapter? In the words of
one contemporary reader, how could the closing pages of the novel "thrust
[Anna] back into the underworld from which she was but now escaping?"
(*The Standard*, Dec. 13, 1912).

The novel's conclusion was apparently a conscientious choice. While
finishing the manuscript in August 1912, Wharton wrote Fullerton to stress
that it was "essential that these last chapters should be especially ripe &
homogenous" (*Letters* 275). Yet as Anna ascends "a succession of shabby
landings" to Laura's untidy hotel suite, homogeneity seems to be the last
thing on Wharton's mind. Indeed, Laura's Paris apartment in the *Hôtel
Chicago* brings Anna face to face with the chaotic, Americanized world of
ethnic pluralism, classless anonymity and urban eroticism.

Greeted at the door by Sophy's former acquaintance Jimmy Brance, "a
handsome young man whose . . . general air of creased disorder led her
to conclude that he had just risen from a long-limbed sprawl on a sofa

strewn with tumbled cushions," Anna immediately recognizes in Jimmy's "smooth denationalized English" the slippery charm and careless sensuality of a worldly lothario (348). On the coffee table, a "biscuit-tin and a devastated breakfast tray" add to the atmosphere of unbridled consumerism. When Anna spots "another man, short, swarthy and humble" who peers at her from the corner of the room, she realizes that she is "being minutely catalogued and valued" (348, 349). The anti-Semitic reference links Laura's self-effacing caller to the commodifying gaze of both Simon Rosedale in *The House of Mirth*, and Fleischauer, the "small swarthy" London art dealer in *The Custom of the Country* (*Custom* 298; see Showalter, "Spragg" 93). The furtively observant Jew, the denationalized rake and the half-eaten platter of leftovers together suggest a nightmarish mélange of consumerism and sex. Like the city, state and country for which it is named, everything in the *Hôtel Chicago* is for sale, and nothing is as it seems.

Presiding over this disorientingly libidinal atmosphere is Laura herself, who luxuriates in a "dim untidy scented room," propped up in bed after receiving a massage (350). The massage itself is significant: during that summer of 1912, Wharton had gone to Salsomaggiore, a health spa in north-central Italy. "Here I am," she wrote to her friend Bernard Berenson, "blissfully steeped in ink & iodine – fiction in the morning & friction in the pomeriggio" (*Letters* 269). Despite the delightful compatibility implied by her wry wordplay, Wharton came to associate the "frictional" life with the self-anesthetizing temptations of the body. Such treatments not only encouraged mental atrophy, but they also responded to the body's importunate desires. To succumb to sensual ease was to surrender to the middle-class complacency that blurred the distinction between the inherently vigorous and uncompromising races, and those who yielded easily to languid tolerance.

Massage encourages pleasurable passivity while suppressing mindful self-responsibility. One need only look at the opening moments of *The Custom of the Country* to see why. Leota Spragg, Undine's hapless mother, has sought out the services of New York "'society' manicure and masseuse," Mrs. Heeny (6). Despite her "reassuring look of solidity and reality," the benevolent and affable therapist in fact greases the cogs of social mobility, "manipulat[ing Mrs. Spragg's] imagination as well as her muscles" (5, 9). It is in fact the masseuse who initially instructs Undine on the finer points of social distinction, and it is the masseuse who encourages the young *arriviste* to set her sights on the Knickerbocker bachelor Ralph Marvell. Manipulator of both the body human and the body politic, Mrs. Heeny eases the transition from the old social order to the new.

As Laura McTarvie-Birch apologizes for receiving her visitor *en déshabillé* – "You don't mind, do you? He costs such a frightful lot that I can't afford to send him off" – Anna cannot help but wonder whether Laura is referring to "her *masseur* or her husband" (350). The confusion is symptomatic. Just as Laura vividly incarnates the "dingy distances of family history" that Anna had tried to overlook in Sophy, so Laura's "odd chromo-like resemblance" to her younger sister emphasizes the Viners' mutual place in the democratic discourse of shopping and sham.[21]

Laura's apartment plays out Wharton's worst fears. The "professional expertness" that Anna has detected in Darrow's romantic diplomacy ("He never makes a mistake – he always knows what to do") is mirrored in Jimmy's "long training in all the arts of expediency" (310, 349). Similarly, Laura's lounging pose reproduces Wharton's own writerly habits: indeed, Wharton transforms her own private literary routines into a sensuously public performance. Thus Laura, like her adulterous creator, is a married "artist" who is engaged in a tawdry extra-marital affair. Her languid complaint – "the worst of being an artist" is that "singing takes so much time that I don't get a chance to walk the fat off" – is a vicious self-parody of Wharton's own morning ritual of writing in bed (351). The pedigreed Pekinese accustomed to doze at Wharton's elbow becomes, in *The Reef*, an obscure canine "powder-puff" voraciously assailing Anna in "an outburst of hysterics" from under Laura's profusely pink bed (R. W. B. Lewis 4; *Reef* 352). Disorderly room, excessive body and uncontrollable animal impulse collapse into a democratic mass of sex and sentience.

Chaos of this sort was theoretically anathema to Wharton, whose epigraph to *The Writing of Fiction* (1925) – "Order the beauty even of beauty is," from Thomas Traherne – indicated her deep-seated commitment to the philosophical tenets of rationalism. *The Reef*, however, moves in a different direction. Wharton experiments with a startlingly new and pragmatic vision of life and art. Anna's midlife realization that her own "history" had been "like some grey shadowy tale that she might have read in an old book, one night as she was falling asleep" equally articulates Wharton's verdict on nineteenth-century narrative forms that can no longer communicate the gritty realities of twentieth-century American life (92). It is a conclusion, however, that Wharton can only reach with considerable hesitation. Sophy's struggle to find the right words to express her sexual experience leaves Wharton at a similar loss for words: "It's my fault for not knowing how to say what I want you to hear," the young governess tells Anna. "Your words are different; you know how to choose them. Mine offend you . . . and the dread of it makes me blunder" (295). Anna and Wharton together acknowledge the linguistic lacuna that separates the world of conventional fiction from the discourse of "real life." As Anna stops at a bookshop to buy some "literature" for her fleeing step-son, she realizes that "There was something grotesque and almost mocking in the idea of offering a judicious selection of literature to a man setting out on such a journey." The "newest publications" themselves can be little more than a "mental panacea" for twentieth-century Americans shipwrecked on the shoals of direct, democratic experience (338).

Wharton had embarked on such a journey in the years following 1907. If 1912 marked the "end of American innocence," as Henry F. May has maintained, then Wharton's novel of that year signals her own reluctant immersion in the age of experience. We live in a "tramp and vagrant world, adrift in space," William James remarked in 1906 (*Pragmatism* 260). Ours was a "loose universe" – "a set of stars hurled into heaven without even a centre of gravity to pull against" (261). Inevitably, then, all "finite experience as such is homeless" (260). Perhaps this is why George Darrow, trapped within "the turbid coil of his fears and passions," stares so wistfully at the hoary façade of Givré.[22] Mocked by the "high decorum of its calm lines and soberly massed surfaces," the American can gauge the twentieth-century displacements that James so passionately embraced. As he enters the ancient edifice of European rationalism, Darrow recognizes that he is not an aborigine, but instead an invader from the pluralist present, "a muddy tramp forcing his way into some pure sequestered shrine" (*Reef* 141).

CHAPTER 5

Charity begins at home: Summer *and the erotic tourist*

Edith Wharton recalled writing *Summer* "amid a thousand interruptions and while the rest of my being was steeped in the tragic realities of the war" (*Backward Glance* 356). Yet the story of a backwoods New England woman forced to marry her own step-father after becoming pregnant by a visiting New York architect seems, if anything, a regionalist escape from what Wharton called the "awful ordeal of our race" (letter to Sara Norton, Oct. 15, 1918). The "vision" of a "shortish novel," "about a New England village, rather on the lines of Ethan Frome, but taking place at the height of the hot New England summer," had come to Wharton suddenly in the summer of 1916; by mid-August, she was "putting [it] down as quickly as possible" (*Letters* 385; letter to Charles Scribner, August 16, 1916). She completed the manuscript "known to its author & her familiars as the Hot Ethan" by early 1917 (*Letters* 385). "I don't know how on earth the thing got itself written in the scramble & scuffle of my present life," Wharton told her friend Gaillard Lapsley, "but it *did*" (*Letters* 385).

Despite its isolated setting in the remote hill country of western Massachusetts, *Summer* draws its force from a range of international and domestic concerns that together inform its deeply conservative message. This chapter proposes to account for these diverse cultural sources and their cumulative effect. I will begin by looking at Wharton's experiences in wartime Paris and, in particular, how her war charities fortified her conservative longing for the safety and security encoded in the ancestral home. This impulse emanated from Wharton's own restorative experiences at the Mount, her elegant summer estate in Lenox, Massachusetts. Her former participation in the emerging economy of New England tourism, and her familiarity with the discourse of Yankee decline, of which the racial revitalization of the New England "old home" was to be the cure, inform not only the logic behind her war charities, but also the logic that sustains *Summer*'s central character: "Charity" Royall. As I will suggest in the second half of this chapter, *Summer*'s reification of the Yankee old home corroborates the novel's conservative politics of race and gender. Wharton's severe opinion of Progressive-era reform, women's rights and abortion crucially inform the novel's controversial conclusion. From Wharton's standpoint, *Summer* was not a dark, cautionary tale about incest and sexual repression, but instead an uplifting account of eugenic reproduction, timely legitimization and racial restoration. In short, it was a story with a happy ending.[1]

THE ROOFLESS HOUSE

Wharton was fascinated and horrified by the scene of battle. She rushed back to Paris from Buckinghamshire in September 1914, writing Sara Norton that she "regret[ed] very much not having been in Paris during the week of panic . . . As to the horrors & outrages, I'm afraid they are too often true" (*Letters* 339–40). Six "expeditions" to the front lines with the French Red Cross in 1915 brought these "horrors & outrages" to the fore (*Backward Glance* 352). The "mud-coated military motors & artillery horses, soldiers coming & going," together with the repeated "boom, boom, boom of the guns" made everything seem at once vivid and strange (*Letters* 351). "[O]nce within the military zone *every* moment is interesting," Wharton wrote to Henry James of her experiences in Verdun. "I suddenly refused to believe that *any* of it was true, or happening to *me*" (*Letters* 351, 353). The journeys were galvanizing: Wharton quickly proposed to write a series of eye-witness accounts of life on the front for *Scribner's*. "We were given opportunities *no one else* has had of seeing things at the front," she told Robert Bridges, a Scribner's editor. "I was in the first line trenches, in 2 bombarded towns, &c &c – don't proclaim it too soon, for I don't want to be indiscreet" (letter, May 27, [19]15, qtd. in Price 56).

If this first-hand perspective was oddly thrilling, it was shocking as well. Horrified by the vision of so many quiet French villages reduced to riotous rubble, Wharton told James that the experience was overwhelming. She had seen a makeshift field hospital near Verdun that had been improvised from the bombed-out remains of a local church. The wounded soldiers, she reported,

sleep on straw, in queer little compartments a dozen or so are crammed, in their trench clothes (no undressing possible) – with nothing that I could see to be thankful for but the fact that they were out of the mud, & in a sort of fetid stable-heat . . .

. . . In other places, of course, we saw things better done – but for a Horror-of-War picture, that one won't soon be superseded. (*Letters* 352)

The sordid spectacle of these "poor devils," packed into pews themselves desecrated by dirt and disorder, crystallized for Wharton the war's abomination (*Letters* 352). To see this famously home-loving "artist [race]," who were accustomed to living in some of Europe's most "noble monuments of architecture," suffer the foul vagrancy of the trenches was almost unbearable (*French Ways* 53, 43).

Wharton's reaction to these scenes was formative. The war, as she came to understand it, was less an international military conflict than a systematic attack on the rites and rituals of that most conservative of sanctuaries, the ancestral home. "It is not in the mud and jokes and everyday activities of the trenches that one most feels the damnable insanity of war," she remarked in 1915; "it is where it lurks like a mythical monster in the scene to which the mind has always turned for rest" (*Fighting France* 200). Alarmed by "the separate terrors, anguishes, uprootings and rendings apart involved in the [war's] destruction of the obscurest of human communities," Wharton came to associate the military conflict with the painful publicity of the roofless house.[2] The bombed-out remains of countless French villages, she thought, bore brutal testimony to the defacement of tradition and privacy. Warfare publicized the private, making the confidential painfully accessible.[3] Amid the "squalid revelation of caved-in floors, smashed wardrobes, dangling bedsteads, heaped-up blankets, topsy-turvy chairs and stoves and wash-stands . . . the poor little house reminded one of some shy humdrum person suddenly exposed in the glare of a great misfortune" (*Fighting France* 174). The roofless house betrayed national and familial secrets: within such "exposed interiors, the poor little household gods shiver and blink like owls surprised in a hollow tree" (*Fighting France* 153).

For someone who had devoted entire volumes to the merits of architectural structure and the sanctity of privacy, the roofless house was nothing less than a stark profanity. While the civilized home preserved a "quality of aloofness, of almost classic reserve . . . [that] defends it from the inroads of the throng," judiciously allocating spaces "according to the varied requirements of its inmates," the bombed-out dwelling obliterated all distinctions between peoples, classes and races (*Motor-Flight* 143; *Italian Villas* 47). In the blasted interior, "Everything was cold and bare and blank: like a mind from which memory has gone" (*Fighting France* 156). Domestic traditions disappeared, and so too did "all the thousand and one bits of the past that give meaning and continuity to the present" (*Fighting France* 58). Helplessly exposed to the elements, the domestic ruin became a powerful symbol of the war's assault on ancestral memory itself.

The Belgian refugee at the center of Wharton's 1916 poem, "The Tryst," speaks to this sense of familial and domestic loss:

> My house is ill to find, she said,
> For it has no roof but the sky;
> The tongue is torn from the steeple-head,
> And all the rivers run poison-red
> With the bodies drifting by.
> (*The Book of the Homeless* 41)

With "no roof but the sky," all of life's private rituals – the "hundred signs of intimate and humble tastes, of humdrum pursuits, of family association" – are vulnerable to public scrutiny (*Fighting France* 153). Corpses floating by in a blood-red river reveal the enormity of privacy's demise. As Wharton had earlier acknowledged in 1902, a "vast system of moral sewage" lay "honey-combed" beneath the "fair surface of life" (*Sanctuary* 110). When unearthed, "unsuspected similarities and disagreements, deep common attractions and repulsions declare themselves" (*French Ways* xvii–xviii). In *Fighting France*, she summarized this traumatic sense of exposure: "The world since 1914 has been like a house on fire. All the lodgers are on the stairs, in disha-bille. Their doors are swinging wide, and one gets . . . revelations of their habits . . . that a life-time of ordinary intercourse would not offer" (200).

Despite her confessed "luke-warmness in regard to organized benefi-cence," Wharton responded to the immediate "necessities of the hour" by launching a series of wartime charities (*Backward Glance* 356–7). One way or another, each was designed to aid the region's harried refugees by sur-rounding them with the domestic comforts of the French home. In 1914, at the request of the Comtesse d'Haussonville, who was then president of a local branch of the French Red Cross, Wharton opened an *ouvroir* for jobless seamstresses and *lingères* in "a big empty flat" on the Rue de l'Université, just a short walk from her own home on the Rue de Varenne (*Backward Glance* 341). The workroom was an instant success: at its peak, it employed nearly a hundred lingerie makers who sewed dainty items for affluent clients. And despite her scorn for the "silly idiot women" who were busy transforming their own Faubourg St. Germain "drawing-rooms into hospitals (at great expense), & are now making shirts for the wounded . . . robbing the poor stranded ouvrières of their only means of living," the *ouvroir*'s location was central to Wharton's logic (*Letters* 334). Situated in one of the most fashionable districts in Paris, the workroom restored domestic civility and the fruit of domestic labor to a land frayed by war.

The workroom's unexpected success convinced Wharton to found the American Hostels for Refugees in 1914, a network of houses and apartments which eventually accommodated nearly 9,300 war evacuees. Though it was "appalling [to undertake] to do good unremittingly for eight months when you've had no previous experience or training," Wharton made sure that her hostels offered a variety of settlement house services, from health clinics and day nurseries, to clothing, grocery and coal distribution (letter to Bernard Berenson, May 4, 1915). By 1916, she had founded the Children of Flanders Rescue Committee, a group organized to house parentless Flemish children in handsome accommodations from Paris to Normandy, and the *Maisons Américaines de Convalescence*, a system of sanatoria for tubercular soldiers. "It is awful to be quiet a minute, [and] think of the crashing ruins all around one," Wharton told friend and co-worker Elisina Tyler. "I'm so glad to be absorbed in the price of sweaters & the cut of flannel shirts" (letter, Oct. 11, [1914]). If the comforts afforded by such age-old domestic practices were palpable, the benefits were equally so. "Who can long be rough and slatternly and indifferent in a pretty, well-kept house?" Wharton had asked in an 1897 article on schoolroom decoration. "If a little of the prettiness and order is allowed to overflow into each room, each member of the family will come to regard himself as holding a share in the capital of beauty, and as vitally interested in preserving and increasing that capital" (*Uncollected* 59). Like Catherine Beecher before her, Wharton saw the aesthetic and efficient household as both a stimulant to citizenship, and a catalyst for the conservative principles of capitalist order.

To help finance these philanthropic endeavors, Wharton put together an anthology of original poetry, fiction and artwork by "literary and artistic celebrities" of the day including André Gide, Joseph Conrad, Igor Stravinsky, Sarah Bernhardt, William Butler Yeats, Henry James, Claude Monet and Theodore Roosevelt (*Backward Glance* 349). *The Book of the Homeless* (1916), according to Wharton, was a collective enterprise. It had been the brainchild of "a small group of French and American friends moved to pity by the thousands of fugitives wandering through the streets of Paris and sleeping on straw in the railway station" (*Book* xx). Not only would the proceeds of the book give succor to these weary refugees, but the volume itself would also offer a kind of artistic shelter all its own. As Wharton proudly declares in the introduction, "You will see from the names of the builders what a gallant piece of architecture it is, what delightful pictures hang on its walls, and what noble music echoes through them" (xxiv).

The metaphor is a suggestive one. Like the civilized French estate, this "gallant piece of architecture" promises to restore artistic decorum and elite well-being to a world profaned by war. Elsewhere in the introduction, Wharton describes herself awaiting a group of refugees at the elegant Villa Béthanie. "The day was beautiful, the borders of the drive were glowing with roses, the lawns were fragrant with miniature hay-cocks, and the flower-beds about the court had been edged with garlands of little Belgian flags" (xxi–xxii). The arrival of a ragtag group of war-weary boys, nuns and old men throws the villa's refined ground into even more vivid relief. "[I]n pitiful contrast to the summer day and the bright flowers," the hapless cluster of refugees appear "a lamentable collection of human beings" (xxii). Beleaguered by exhaustion, home-sickness and fear, the weary wanderers gaze at "the wide house-front with all its windows smiling in the sun" and are overcome with relief (xxii). Like the reader who finds aesthetic solace in the "delightful pictures" and "noble music" of *The Book of the Homeless*, modernity's "piteous waifs" are comforted within the elite villa's hallowed walls (xxiv). As the grateful refugees begin to sing the Belgian national anthem, the Villa Béthanie, like the anthology itself, becomes a model for the frail but orderly state, a conservative bulwark against the senseless ravages of modern warfare and warlike modernity.

For Wharton, the war was the decisive, if catastrophic climax of a long-standing battle between the champions of tradition and privacy on the one hand, and the forces of barbarism and publicity on the other. The Great War dramatized America's own domestic turmoil, but on a geopolitical scale. In this sense, the assassination of Archduke Ferdinand in Yugoslavia simply recapitulated the United States's own reckless assaults on racial entitlement, class privilege and genealogical advantage. In both Sarajevo and New York, distinctions between races, classes and nations collapsed into the cultural maelstrom of the modern.

In the war's forlorn soldier, Wharton saw America itself – a vulnerable youth wrested from the security of its ancient ancestral home and flung pell-mell into a muddy, senseless wasteland where "irreverence, impatience . . . all sorts of rash and contemptuous short-cuts" replaced "routine, precedent, tradition, the beaten path" (*French Ways* 32). Germany was merely another more violent version of the American invader – the immigrant, *arriviste* or worker who had, over the past twenty years, besieged the bastions of Knickerbocker and Yankee sovereignty. A guileful opponent who concealed his "stern and bullying" nature beneath a flourish of fakery and sham, the "fearless Teuton" was the adaptable American invader writ large (*Fighting*

France 90; *French Ways* 13). Like *The Custom of the Country*'s rapacious anti-heroine Undine Spragg, the German was the consummate impostor, a master of disguise who dissociated himself from what Nancy Bentley calls the normative "demand for authentic identity" by capitalizing on any number of "inexhaustible self-representations" (Bentley 196). If Undine can incarnate "new paths of desire, social energy, technology, and capital" by ignoring conventional markers of realist ontology, then the German foe was just as tricky and unscrupulous (Bentley 197). Like his materialistic American counterpart, "The German does not care to be free as long as he is well fed, well amused and making money" (*French Ways* 14–15). "[T]he essential difference between the Germans and ourselves" was clear (14). Despite their ability to pass for "native citizens . . . *in our home*" where they quietly assimilated into the American melting pot, German citizens could not fool their neighbors in Europe (10). Europeans recognized Germany for what it was – a country of bogus democrats who disguised "their statues of Bismarck as 'Liberty Enlightening the World' when democratic visitors [were] expected" (10–11). Germans were the masters of "camouflage" – the consummate wolves in sheeps' clothing. Wharton recalled how she had nearly being taken in by the average German's "extraordinary politeness" on a 1913 trip to Berlin (11). She soon discovered the error of her ways when, one night, she refused to relinquish her silk cloak to an usher before entering the chilly Royal and Imperial Opera House. The erstwhile courteous attendant became suddenly irate: "*Es ist verboten*," he barked. "Take off your cloak" (12, 13). Though Wharton succeeded in retaining her wrap, she nonetheless saw the writing on the wall. German civility was a ruse – a mantle of false benevolence that concealed a deep reservoir of native despotism.

Fighting France (1915), Wharton's collected essays on her six wartime expeditions to the front, rotates around this tense semiotics of camouflage and visibility. Despite her first-hand knowledge of the trenches, Wharton found her attempts to visualize the war's "all-pervading, invisible power of evil" frustrated (*Fighting France* 167). To "the bewildered looker-on," she remarked, "[t]he contradictory scenes of war . . . bring home . . . the utter impossibility of picturing how the thing *really happens*" (*Fighting France* 208–9). *Fighting France* turns on this tantalizing prospect. Knowing the Germans "*are there*" transforms an otherwise "innocent vignette" of "bucolic peace" into a hazy "human mask of hate" (110). When sniper fire interrupts a tour of the battle lines near Lorraine, Wharton is therefore eager to pinpoint the hidden German gunner. Following her guide's pointed finger, she peers breathlessly into the surrounding woods only to realize the futility of the effort:

The longer one looked, the more oppressive and menacing the invisibility of the foe became. "*There* they are – and *there* – and *there*." We strained our eyes obediently, but saw only calm hillsides, dozing farms. It was as if the earth itself were the enemy, as if the hordes of evil were in the clods and grass-blades. (109–10)

Camouflaged in the woods, the armed antagonist is simultaneously everywhere and nowhere. Days later, when Wharton at last spies a "grey uniform huddled in a dead heap," she is relieved "to find it was after all a tangible enemy hidden over there across the meadow" (134).

Although she had toyed with the erotic possibilities of such mimetic and visual ambiguity in *The Reef*, these episodes brought Wharton back to her conservative roots.[4] Like Jacob Riis, the New York tenement reformer, Wharton came to believe that "where the home imposes no barrier," "it is one of two things, a gun on the shoulder or stripes on the back" (Riis 137–8). Her biblical gloss on the "life-drained" condition of wartime France spoke with equal force to her own native land: "Your country is desolate; your cities are burned with fire; your land, strangers devour it in your presence, and it is desolate, as overthrown by strangers" (*Fighting France* 158). Confronted with "the queer rootless life" that she identified both with the trenches of the western front and with the streets of "ugly, patchy, scrappy New York," Wharton sought to restore modernity's hapless waif to the safety and security of the racially hermetic ancestral home (*Letters* 312, 313). As indebted to the material realities of early twentieth-century popular culture as it was to the narrower demands of her own patrician politics, *Summer* poses a series of conservative alternatives to the menacing vagrancy of no man's land. Drawing on a confluence of discursive elements – from elite philanthropy and New England tourism to French abortion debates and the historic preservation movement in the United States, *Summer* answers the chaotic multiplicity of war with a conservative paean to the racial uniformity of the old home.

NEW ENGLAND, RACIAL RENEWAL AND THE MOUNT

Wharton's appreciation for the tonic effects of the well-appointed house stemmed from her own experiences at the Mount, her Lenox estate which she built with her husband Teddy in 1901. Modeled after Sir Christopher Wren's Belton House in Lincolnshire, England, the house was christened "the Mount" in honor of the Long Island country home of Wharton's great-grandfather, Ebenezer Stevens. The reasons behind Wharton's "secret partiality" for this maternal ancestor, the "only marked figure among my forbears," were clear (*Backward Glance* 12). Not only had Stevens served as a major-general in the Revolutionary War, commanding artillery divisions at Ticonderoga, Stillwater and Saratoga, but if legend was correct, he had also served as a pall-bearer at George Washington's funeral. As a child visiting the Capital rotunda in Washington, DC, Wharton had seen her ancestor figured prominently in John Trumball's painting, "The Surrender of Burgoyne." From his descendant's admiring perspective, Stevens was a kindred spirit: his good taste in "classical mantelpieces imported from Italy" and "fine gilt andirons crowned with Napoleonic eagles" revealed his aesthetic affinity with the mistress of the new, latter-day Mount.[5]

Indeed, Wharton's elegant home effected an implicit protest against the "wild, disheveled backwoods" of the American scene (*Letters* 84). A new house designed to look like an old home, the Mount self-consciously traced its origins from Lenox back to Long Island and Lincolnshire. To borrow Eric Hobsbawm's phrase, the Lenox house was a monument to "invented tradition."[6] Its orderly spaces, its patterned gardens and its Arcadian views all embodied a utopian alternative to modern America. Like Central Park, Frederick Law Olmstead's green oasis in the heart of messy Manhattan, the Mount was designed to be an "enchanting . . . country" in the midst of an otherwise heterogeneous nation.[7] To sojourn at the Mount was, in Wharton's words, to escape the "watering-place trivialities" of Newport and Bar Harbor and instead "plunge into congenial ways of thinking and enjoying" (*Backward Glance* 124; letter to Sara Norton, July 15, 1901). Monumentalizing Wharton's longing for "the real country," that mythical "patrie" where "everything speaks of long familiar intercourse between the earth and its inhabitants, every field has a name, a history, a distinct place of its own," the Mount served as an anti-modern refuge from the transitory terrain of modern America (*Letters* 380; *Motor-Flight* 5).

The Mount gave antiquarian refuge to the seasonal connoisseur who longed for a simpler time when earnest Yankees pursued honest crafts. Wharton had nothing but praise for the Mount's "devoted and admirable head gardener," who declined a more lucrative offer to remain on Wharton's estate. As she told Morton Fullerton in July 1911,

[H]e loved too much the work of our hands . . . I never saw a more *mouvant* example of devotion to one's calling. He *couldn't* miss the first long walk with me yesterday afternoon, the going over every detail . . . every tiniest little bulb and root we had planted together! It is the sort of emotion a good gardener very rarely gets in this country where so few people and places care about them intelligently, and really work on them; and he sacrificed for it the prospect of a secure future and unlimited sway over some millionaire's orchids! (*Letters* 242)

For Wharton, the Mount's gardener was an ideal laborer. Like the medieval craftsmen of yore, he worked "Not for greed of gold, but simply from the ambition to excel in [his] own craft" (*French Ways* 56). His indifference to pecuniary gain and his absence of class consciousness testify to his genuine "enthusiasm for his work" – what the Arts and Crafts proponent Gustav Stickley called a "contentment with his lot, in gaining pleasure with the small things" (qtd. in Lears, *No Place of Grace* 86). Like the happy villagers whom Wharton had admired while traveling through France in 1906, the head gardener at the Mount occupied an "established niche in life" and took pleasure "in the frankly avowed interests and preoccupations of [his] order" (*Motor-Flight* 28; see Lears 70–1).

Wharton considered the Mount, in all of its feudal civility, her "first real home" (*Backward Glance* 125). Like the "individual [French] garden," with its "insistence on civic dignity . . . so miraculously maintained, through every torment of political passion, every change of social conviction," the "stillness . . . greenness . . . sylvan sweetnesses, of the Mount . . . reconcile[d] me to America" (*Motor-Flight* 29; *Letters* 251–2). This may be the most important "secret" in Wharton's "secret garden" (*Backward Glance* 198). A conservative landscape, impervious to "every torment of political passion," the Mount was a haven in an otherwise hostile world. Long after the property was sold in September 1911, the memories of "long days at the Mount, in the deep summer glow or the crisp glitter of autumn, the walks in the woods, motor-flights over hill and dale . . . and . . . the figures of our most beloved guests" filled Wharton with nostalgia (*Backward Glance* 192). Remembering the "inexhaustible delight" of motoring with friends through the surrounding "slumbrous mountain valleys," Wharton cherished these trips to "the remoter parts of Massachusetts and New Hampshire," where she discovered "villages still bedrowsed in a decaying rural existence" in which "sad slow-speaking people [lived] in conditions hardly changed since their forbears held those villages against the Indians" (*Backward Glance* 153–4). Such daytrips to "derelict villages with Georgian churches and balustraded house-fronts" only enhanced the Mount's well-appointed charm (153). After a long day of antiquarian sightseeing, one could return to the estate to enjoy "evening talks on the moonlit terrace and readings around the library fire" (192).

The Whartons' arrival fortified Lenox's growing reputation as the "social capital" of the Berkshires (Amory 10). By 1900, the area's count of so-called "cottages" had more than doubled: Anson Phelps Stokes's 100-room granite castle and Wharton's 128-acre estate were only two of a new generation of opulent properties that ornamented the Massachusetts landscape

(Amory 21; R. W. B. Lewis 93). Lenox, however, continued to advertise itself as a quaint rural retreat – a "civilized . . . old country" of "ancient houses" nestled into the sleepy New England hillsides (Hibbard 4). "Lenox in some mysterious way has gathered up something of the old life, and has carried it on and made it part of the new," travel writer George A. Hibbard insisted in 1894. "[T]his feeling of continuation certainly tends to make it the reposeful abiding place it is" (3).

Wharton found this combination of ambiance and abjection appealing. As Veronica Makowsky and Lynn Z. Bloom have noted, Wharton clearly had a vested hope that New England would remain in "picturesque, fantastically feudal decrepitude" (224). Unlike multifarious Manhattan, New England was an abiding sanctuary for the real thing – a place where "solid" Yankees could boast even "more homogenous, Colonial-stock roots" than their affluent summer visitors (Baltzell 118). Indeed, Wharton was delighted after visiting the Farmington, Connecticut home of Theodore Roosevelt's older sister, Anna Cowles. "I didn't know there was any village in the country so pure pre-Revolutionary," she told Sara Norton in 1907. "The Cowles family has always lived there, & the house is full of old faded letters, diaries, samplers, silhouettes &c. What a flavour the least little thing of the kind has in our insipid surroundings!" (letter, Oct. 26, [1907]).

By the turn of the twentieth century, the New England colonial village had come to represent "a new Eden or second Zion" – what Lawrence Buell calls the "utopian model of millennial promise" (Wood 34; Buell 312). The region's charming "eighteenth-century atmosphere" captured the imagination of far-flung Yankee descendants (Lodge 18). Indeed, like so many "imperialists seeking solace for their souls among the 'natives' of Lenox, Bar Harbor or Kennebunkport," early twentieth-century tourists turned to New England as the last outpost of Anglo-American purity, a place where "homogenous, peaceful people [still] lived in sturdy two-story, white-painted dwellings."[8] As Barrett Wendell fondly observed in 1900, only in New England was "the frank recognition of certain social classes as superior to others" still a matter of "deeply rooted [tradition]."[9] "[N]either Irishman nor Negro ever [set] foot" in towns like Petersham, Massachusetts, John Fiske, a turn-of-the-century historian, insisted (qtd. in Kammen 239). The small towns of New England offered a welcome bulwark against what Henry Cabot Lodge, senator of Massachusetts, called "the featureless, characterless masses" of America's cities (18). Unlike the rest of the country, New England had preserved that "note of the aristocratic in the air," according to Henry James (*American Scene* 34). As William A. Giles, the president of Chicago's New England Society, optimistically averred in 1905, New England's "Puritan ideals, strength and character" were "leavening the life of a continent" (995).

In singing the praises of "*the* New England village of fiction, with its old houses almost intact, & their old fences & gates also," Wharton was participating in an ideologically charged contest over the changing face of America itself (letter to Sara Norton, Oct. 26, [1907]). As Morton Keller has acknowledged, by the century's turn, the effort to "encase the New England town in amber" was well under way (441). The region's transformation into a national fetish came in response to the perceived threat of Anglo-American decline. Alarmed that the country's "native stock" were leaving the "historic towns founded by the Puritans" in the hands of a "foreign element . . . not qualified to strengthen or perpetuate the old New England type of character and spirit," University of Iowa dean Amos N. Currier spoke for a generation of elite Americans when he warned that New England was lapsing into decadence (388).

Indeed, by the mid-1890s, the subject of New England decline had created a full-blown panic among the Eastern establishment. "One by one, family by family, [small-town] inhabitants slip away in search of other homes," Henry U. Fletcher fretted in *The Forum* in 1895. They took with them "the young, the hopeful, the ambitious," and left "the superannuated, the feeble, [and] the dull" (214). Dysgenic racial dissolution hung ominously on the horizon. As Andrew Carnegie warned in 1903, "New England may lose her position as the dominant strain in this Republic" (New England Society 56–7). In the words of education professor Ellwood P. Cubberly, America was about to be overrun by an "Illiterate, docile [strain] lacking in self-reliance and initiative, and not possessing the Anglo-Teutonic conceptions of law, order, and government" (qtd. in Bowers 36).

Although commentators like MIT's Francis Amasa Walker and Thomas N. Carver, an economist at Harvard, blamed federal immigration policies for compelling "old [New England] families" to shrink in size in order to protect their higher standard of living, others pointed at the debased Yankee population itself (Carver 24; see Solomon, *Ancestors* 76–7). Tracing the unfortunate descendants of one "roving Dutchman" who had spawned several generations of "ignorant, unintelligent, indolent, and alcoholic" New Englanders, Arthur H. Estabrook and Charles B. Davenport claimed to have pinpointed the biological origins of the "illegitimacy, inbreeding, and their attending evils of pauperism and dulness" that were in the process of overtaking the region (Estabrook and Davenport 2). As Ruth Moxcey Martin told the Second International Congress of Eugenics in 1921, New England's home-loving pioneer stock had intermarried with such frequency that insanity and suicide were now rampant. In the town of "Z," she alleged, the population had become "an almost inextricable group of 'by marriage' relatives" who were tending toward "actual degeneracy" (283, 284).

The idea that New England's own provincialism was at the root of its social and economic decline hit a raw nerve among the region's well-to-do diasporants. Identifying their native heath as an exigent site of race suicide, historic preservationists and Country Life reformers found a new rallying cry in New England. If the area's "stately old buildings" had foreign tenants and "pigs running about the door," Wallace Nutting, a Colonial Revival entrepreneur, admonished in 1923, then New Englanders had only themselves to blame. "We hear indignation expressed . . . but if the owners . . . had not the pride or energy to keep up their places someone must own them. Certainly unless a critic himself has redeemed such country places his mouth is stopped" (225). Wharton herself wrote a letter to the *Newport Daily News* in 1896 criticizing the posh community's neglect of its own historic buildings. If "we Newporters" really admire "our old houses," she charged, "why have so many been demolished, and so many ruthlessly mutilated?" (*Uncollected* 56–7). Mary Bronson Hartt agreed. "Old New England is passing away," Hartt warned in 1912. "Why not bestir ourselves before it is too late?" (Hartt 920). Increasingly, historic preservationists like William Sumner Appleton responded to these challenges by urging old-stock Americans to mobilize in defense of their "old hereditary homesteads." Such ancestral relics represented "not only the single individual . . . ," he insisted, "but . . . the whole race, generation after generation" (Appleton 177).

Country Life reformers applied these arguments with particular force to the New England farm. Fearful that the sturdy Yankee farmer was losing his position as the racial cornerstone of American citizenship, conservative activists devoted great energy to extolling the virtues of rural life (Bowers 36–7). Where the New England farmer went, they argued, so went the nation. As Theodore Roosevelt told a Lansing, Michigan crowd in 1907, the old New England homestead must be kept from falling into the wrong hands:

It would be a calamity to have our farms occupied by a lower type of people than the hard-working, self-respecting, independent, and essentially manly and womanly men and women who have hitherto constituted the most typically American, and on the whole the most valuable, element of our entire nation. Ambitious native-born young men and women who now tend away from the farm must be brought back to it. ("The Man" 134–5)

John M. Thomas, the president of Middlebury College, agreed. Speaking to the Class of 1913, Thomas urged Middlebury graduates to come to the aid of Vermont's languishing hill towns. "The old stock is here still, in greater proportion . . . than in any other commonwealth of the north," he insisted. "The old spirit is by no means dead. All we need is organization, the power and the habit of working together and holding together for a fixed and determined purpose" (18). By saving the Yankee farmer, Americans would preserve their "fixed and limited nationality" (Keller 441). Former New Englanders did heed the call, but they did so in ways that neither Thomas nor Roosevelt anticipated. They returned to the region not as farmers, but as tourists.

"SONS AND DAUGHTERS . . . COME BACK, COME BACK!"

In 1897, New Hampshire governor Frank West Rollins launched a highly effective public relations campaign in which he declared New England America's newest vacation destination. By fashioning a self-styled "East Cure," Rollins strategically exploited not only the urban preoccupation with neurasthenia, but also the broader national nostalgia for "the old New England idea of home, with its cheerful simplicity, quiet atmosphere, strong ties of affection and ruggedness of virtue" (Gleason 678). "[I]n our valleys [the city-dweller] will . . . find a tonic for his mind," Rollins insisted, "and our lakes will draw him from the struggle for wealth and existence to the contemplation of the greater problems of life."[10] New England's vacant homesteads, which were to be "found on every roadway," Clifton Johnson agreed, would make "ideal places for summer residents" (219–20). Once they had been "rebuilt or refitted, the walls and fences straightened up, the lands enriched," the region's "old homes" would be just what the doctor ordered.[11] A vacation in New England would mean "plain country fare . . . served by as pretty a girl, a farmer's daughter, . . . neatly and prettily dressed" as the visitor could imagine (Rollins, "New" 539). In the words of Philip Morgan, the "true mountain-bred girl," with her "flushed face, large wild eyes, and slightly disheveled hair," might easily be mistaken for "Aphrodite herself."[12]

Rollins and his colleagues aggressively marketed a revitalized version of the mythic colonial village, a place where upright Protestants lived in rural simplicity, unmolested by the complicating demands of ethnic and racial pluralism.[13] In cozy clapboard dwellings, shaded by "a typical New England Colonial roof-tree," playful children cavorted amid the "autumn wood-flora" (Chandler 35). These "household[s] which we wish, for the good of the country . . . we might call *average*," Joseph Everett Chandler, an architect, remarked in 1924, bore vivid testimony to the "strength of moral fiber which we look back upon with pride as the consummation of the desires of our forefathers" (Chandler 35–6). In a polyglot nation where historical amnesia seemed to be consigning America's venerable Yankees to the forgotten past, architectural restoration and historic preservation became an upper-class fetish. The "old home," the focus of this antiquarian tumult, became the reified expression of "the genteel elite's confidence in the vitality and picturesqueness of its own Anglo-American Protestant history and customs" (Glassberg, *American* 34).

The effort to reclaim the old New England homestead enacted a stylized contest over America itself. When Appleton, founder of the Society for the Preservation of New England Antiquities, tried to evict an Italian family from Lynn's historic Bennett-Boardman house in 1913, a group of local Massachusetts residents pelted the structure with stones, shattering lights and windows. Alarmed, Appleton called for increased security around houses that represented "what there is left of our artistic and historic heritage" (Appleton 181). For Rollins, the solution was clear: entice New England's far-flung descendants back to the "old home" by organizing an annual festival of picnics, patriotism and pageantry. In 1897, the resourceful New Hampshire governor created "Old Home Week," a civic celebration designed to lure prodigal New Englanders back to their ancestral soil. "Sons and daughters of New Hampshire, wherever you are listen to the call of the old Granite State!" he majestically urged in 1897. "Come back, come back! Do you not hear the call? What has become of the old home where you were born? Is it still in your family? If not, why not? Why do you not go and buy it this summer?" ("New" 542).

A paean to small-town values, Old Home Week was first and foremost to be a family affair. "Civic officials," David Glassberg notes, "touted each familiar face returning home for the holiday as a reminder of the continuity between the town of the past and the present" (*American* 18). Proudly provincial, the week-long pageant was designed to be incestuously seductive as well – a combination that Robert Frost aptly captured in his 1915 poem "The Generations of Men." Describing a flirtatious encounter between two young cousins who have just met at an Old Home Week family reunion, Frost explores new possibilities within the familiar family romance. "What will we come to / With all this pride of ancestry, we Yankees?" the poem's young speaker flirtatiously asks his kinswoman (77). Wryly channeling the

voices of their mutual ancestors, he foresees a house among the raspberries
that he and his cousin will share:

> "And come and make your summer dwelling here,
> And perhaps she will come, still unafraid,
> And sit before you in the open door
> With flowers in her lap until they fade,
> But not come in across the sacred sill–"
>
> "I wonder where your oracle is tending."   (80)

The young woman's coy but knowing response underscores her interlocu-
tor's suggestive message. Thanks to Old Home Week, Frost's two cousins
have discovered their shared interest in the old home and in each other as
well.

The rhetoric of Old Home Week invited this sexually charged interpretation. Festival promoters frequently portrayed the old home as a fireside
sweetheart who had long sat, patiently awaiting the return of her long-lost
lover. In the words of one provincial bard,

> Come rally, boys! Awake! Awake!
>   Hear old affection on you calling;
> Your Childhood's Home appeal doth make,
>   On willing ears may it be falling;
> It calls you from your busy care,
>   To meet here in her pleasant places,
> Her old regard again to share,
>   'Mid smiles from "old familiar faces."
>   (qtd. in T. Anderson 685)

Like a winsome Penelope beckoning her prodigal Odysseus, New England
urged its errant "boys" to heed the seductive call of the old home.

At its base, of course, Old Home Week was an elaborate promotional
stunt designed to stimulate the region's sagging economy. Not only were
"[a]nnual home-comers" invited to patronize local businesses, but they were
equally expected to replenish the region's needy coffers (T. Anderson 676).
As one festival promoter cheerfully noted in 1906, visitors often "signif[ied]
their appreciation of the friendly . . . invitation by sending here and there a
substantial check for a new drinking fountain, a statue or memorial window
in honor of some deceased worthy, a public park, a tablet for some historic
landmark, or the liquidation of a burdensome church debt" (T. Anderson
676). A catalyst for investment, philanthropy and incestuous nativism,

Old Home Week appealed frankly to its own. Charity, it seemed, began at home.

CHARITY BEGINS AT HOME

This is, of course, precisely where the opening moments of *Summer* find Wharton's heroine, Charity Royall. Charity literally begins at home – on the doorstep of "lawyer Royall's house" (3). "Cheerless and untended," the faded red façade indicates the town's "desolate" role in the larger drama of Yankee decline (14, 10). Though there must be "a history of the place," North Dormer's colonial record seems to have dwindled into obscurity. The town is a depressed, "weather-beaten sunburnt village of the hills, abandoned of men, left apart by railway, trolley, telegraph, and all the forces that link life to life in modern communities" (5). Its remaining georgic charms, moreover, are lost on Charity, whose opening cry – "How I hate everything!" – sets a tone of apathy and despair (4).

By situating the novel in one of the "derelict mountain villages" near the Mount, where "insanity, incest and slow mental and moral starvation were hidden away behind paintless wooden house-fronts . . . or in the isolated farm-houses on the neighbouring hills," Wharton unflinchingly locates *Summer* within the discourse of Yankee decline. The novel's at times brutal presentation of its vulnerable heroine, whom we find teetering on the cusp of "slow mental and moral starvation," bears out those who, like Rhonda Skillern, read *Summer* as the tale of "the resisting feminine, [who] is drawn into the symbolic order of North Dormer and pressed into becoming a 'good girl'" (119). Trapped in a claustrophobic small town with a dissolute step-father who tries to rape her and an opportunistic lover who leaves her pregnant and with no recourse other than abortion, prostitution or retreat to the backwater squalor from which she came, Charity seems to be Wharton's most abject heroine. As Carol Singley remarks, Charity's "joyous adventure toward self-discovery and love is at best a compromise with, and at worst a capitulation to, social and biological forces beyond her control" (150).

This grim scenario, moreover, seems to corroborate what many critics have identified as Wharton's realist efforts to distinguish herself from the sentimental "rose-and-lavender pages" of New England local color writers like Mary Wilkins Freeman and Sarah Orne Jewett.[14] In this respect, we might read *Summer* as an unrelenting narrative of *Ethan Frome*ian doom in which Charity revives Mattie Silver's romantic hopes only to have them similarly dashed on the cold grate of New England's decline. Wharton, however, did not reject local color out of hand: what she objected to was its superficiality, not its sanguinity. Local colorists, she felt, had exploited the effects of regional decline while remaining oblivious to the root causes of what was fundamentally a *racial* predicament. In a 1902 review essay entitled "The Three Francescas," Wharton faults the British playwright Stephen Phillips for "his neglect of local colour" in his 1897 drama *Paolo and Francesca* (*Uncollected* 82). Local color, she insists, must convey an implicit "historic truth and racial psychology" (92). It is not a matter of mere "sentimental fatalism" (84).

Local colour of the external sort is, on the whole, an overrated pigment; but there is a subtle way of suggesting the atmosphere of a period and country, of indicating, allusively, the racial point of view and the natural environment. In a general – a very general – sense, it may be said that such primary passions as love and jealousy are the same in all races and ages; but this generalization will not stand the test of specific application . . . It is still broadly true that *la morale est purement géographique*, and that, in an Italian and an Anglo-Saxon temperament, love and jealousy do not operate in the same way. (82–3)

By arguing that "colour" transcends "external . . . pigment," and expresses instead an innate "racial point of view," Wharton plays with the phenotypic connotations of color only to reject them as ultimately too limiting. "Race" transcends the superficiality of mere skin, speaking more specifically to considerations of historical period, environmental stimulus, "local habitation" and national identity (82).

This alignment between local color and race informs Wharton's dissatisfaction with the New England regionalists' cozy treatment of Yankee decadence. The region's disorder could not be remedied by folksy homeopathic cures:[15] New England required a dramatic and actively interventionist approach to what was essentially a racial problem. Wharton thus takes Phillips to task for his wan interpretation of Dante's fiery Giovanni Malatesta. High-stakes situations call for electrifying actions. Malatesta would not have "behaved like a gentlemanly Englishman with a tendency to introspection and melancholia." He would have "kill[ed] an unfaithful wife with his own hands" (83). Stepping into the self-perceived void of regionalist reform, Wharton acknowledged New England's decadence only to propose a similarly radical remedy.

Consider North Dormer itself. Despite the menacing events that take place behind closed doors, Wharton endows the town with rich antiquarian meaning. The Royall house, for example, with "its scrubbed floor and dresser full of china" and its "high-backed horsehair chair, the faded rag carpet, the row of books on the shelf, the engraving of 'The Surrender of Burgoyne' over the stove, and the mat with a brown and white spaniel on a moss-green border" seems, on many counts, "the very symbol of household order" – "a vision of peace and plenty."[16] If "The Surrender of Burgoyne" invokes the patriotic memory of Ebenezer Stevens, then the room's antiquarian appointments recall the broader contours of America's Puritan past. Indeed, the faded red dwelling as a whole bears a strong resemblance to Lenox's most famous landmark – the "old red farm-house" of Nathaniel Hawthorne (Wolfe 178). Though a "ragged remnant of an abode" by the century's turn, Hawthorne's house was nonetheless "one of the 'show places' of Lenox," George Hibbard, a travel writer, boasted in 1894 (Hibbard 24). "[I]n this place where materialism may be said to offer one of its finest and most luxurious displays, the remains of the 'small red house' are, and long will be, distinguishable and distinguished" (23–4). Wharton associated Hawthorne with America's "sedentary days . . . long since past" when "Old New York and old New England sat chiefly at home" (*Uncollected* 156). This homespun image of "Hawthorne coloring his [tales] with the prismatic hues of a largely imaginary historic past" mirrors Royall's comparably cozy antiquarianism (*Uncollected* 156). Sequestered in his study with the works of Daniel Webster and George Bancroft, Charity's step-father wistfully recalls "the vague legend" of his own "ruined and unforgotten past" (45, 44).

In "New England," an unfinished predecessor to *Summer*, Wharton gives added meaning to these antiquarian details. After scratching out the name "Charity Royall" in favor of "Alida Gage," Wharton proceeds to tell the story of a young woman returning from Europe who develops a new appreciation for the colonial architecture of her old New England home. Though she is embarrassed by the shabby chromolithographs that formerly adorned her bedroom walls, Alida sees her "heavy old-fashioned furniture" with new eyes.

A young architect in Boston had taught her to admire the solid lines & deep lustre of old mahogany, & she saw now how her brass-handled chest-of-drawers, her claw-foot table, & the carved chairs with clustered feathers forming the centre of their backs, harmonized with the plain rectangular room, with its freshly-starched dimity curtains, its rag carpet, & delicately-fluted mantelpiece. She understood why occasional sight-seers, in driving through Highfield, paused before her grand-father's door, & sent in to ask if this were the old "Governor Royall" house. ("New England")

Trained by a "young architect" to value the "pure pre-Revolutionary" significance of the "old 'Governor Royall' house," Alida suddenly recognizes
her old home for the antiquarian prize that it is.[17]

Thus, when Lucius Harney, *Summer*'s "young architect," arrives in town
at the novel's beginning, he is quick to observe that "This place must have
had a past – it must have been more of a place once" (10). A straw-hatted
visitor from the industrialized twentieth century, Harney is precisely the
kind of seasonal tourist that Governor Rollins hoped to lure to the region. As
Charity recognizes, the young architect represents the "people with holiday
faces" who temporarily stop over in the area. With a native's distain, she
bluntly tells him, "you don't live here, and you don't know anything about
any of us" (4, 30).

As pithy as this characterization is, however, it is not altogether accurate:
Harney is in fact an insider passing as an outsider. He is kin to the town's
most prominent family, spending his "limited holiday" at the "remarkable"
if aging home of his elderly cousin, Miss Hatchard (78, 10). Though adorned
with "ancestral daguerrotypes and didactic samplers," the house, however,
is nonetheless as sexually charged as it is erotically restricted (16). When
Charity eavesdrops on Harney one evening, she is aroused by the spectacle
of the young man in an unbuttoned shirt that exposes "the vigorous lines of
his young throat, and the root of the muscles where they joined the chest."
Sitting amid the room's old-fashioned furnishings – a "mahogany bed, an
engraving on the wall, . . . [and a] green-covered table" – Harney is the
sexualized descendant of the daguerrotyped Hatchards featured on the wall
(66–7). He gives his colonial environs new, erotic appeal.

Indeed, *Summer* is consumed with the tempting erotics of "home." By
merging the ancestral and the sexual, Wharton lures Charity into a powerful romance both with and within the "old home." Harney, despite his
transient status in North Dormer, is Wharton's agent of familial seduction. He first meets Charity in the "Honorius Hatchard Memorial Library,
1832" – the "queer little brick temple" in the center of town built to
commemorate the literary contributions of the Hatchards' distinguished
great-uncle Honorius, the "sole link between North Dormer and literature" (7). Reputed to have been an "acquaintance of Washington Irving
and Fitz-Greene Halleck," Hatchard achieved a modicum of local celebrity
when he published "a series of papers called 'The Recluse of Eagle Range'"
(7). Daisy Miller-like, however, Miss Hatchard's uncle was unfortunately
"cut off in his flower by a fever contracted in Italy" (7). In his wake, he
left a legacy of culture, a firm link between familial descent and literary
accomplishment (7).

Harney is interested in the library from the beginning. "[F]ond of old books," he startles Charity one day by criticizing the old building's dilapidated condition and its consequently moldering volumes (31). Fearful that Harney's comments will jeopardize her position as the town's apathetic librarian, Charity protests that she "wanted [the job] more'n anyone in the village, because I haven't got anybody belonging to me, the way other folks have" (31). If the library compensates Charity for familial loss, it equally serves as the town trysting spot. "Do you suppose anybody ever comes here for books?" Charity incredulously asks her visitor. "What they'd like to come for is to meet the fellows they're going with – if I'd let 'em" (30). Within this context, Harney's attraction for the young librarian seems only appropriate. Stimulated by the library's potent combination of lineage and libido, he volunteers to ventilate the otherwise "ridiculous mausoleum" (31). By circulating a restorative breeze through the building's musty aisles, Harney intends to revive and revitalize the past.[18] Like Charity, who opens the library's shutters each morning "to see if there were any eggs in the swallow's nest above one of the windows," Harney's housekeeping blends the ancestral, the sexual and the bibliophilic.[19]

The young architect's interest in "books on the old houses about here" and his quest for "a book or pamphlet about [North Dormer's] first settlement" culminate in what is simultaneously a sexual and structural passion for the region's old homes. As he tours the area's crumbling houses, Harney finds himself increasingly attracted to his sensuous guide. Like the decaying structures "found on every roadway," Charity is accessible and supine – "as passive and sunwarmed as the slope on which she lay" (24, 35). It is no accident, then, that the two lovers dramatically consummate their affair in "a little deserted house . . . said to be haunted" – an "abandoned house" on which Wharton lavishes loving antiquarian detail (105).

The little old house – its wooden walls sun-bleached to a ghostly grey – stood in the orchard above the road. The garden palings had fallen, but the broken gate dangled between its posts, and the path to the house was marked by rose-bushes run wild and hanging their small pale blossoms above the crowding grasses. Slender pilasters and an intricate fan-light framed the opening where the door had hung; and the door itself lay rotting in the grass, with an old apple-tree fallen across it.

Inside, also, wind and weather had blanched everything to the same wan silvery tint; the house was as dry and pure as the interior of a long-empty shell. But it must have been exceptionally well-built, for the little rooms had kept something of their human aspect: the wooden mantels with their neat classic ornaments were in place, and the corners of one ceiling retained a light film of plaster tracery. (107–8)

A "frail shell dried and washed by many seasons," the house resembles Charity herself, whose face, when framed by a fetching new hat, "glow[ed] like the inside of the shell on the parlour mantelpiece" (115, 80). Both Charity and the old home are "dry and pure" interiors awaiting patrician revitalization. It is only within this distinctly reliquery context that Harney can fulfill his passion for "primitive New England."[20] Taking Charity in his arms, he "[pushes] her hair back as if to draw her whole face up into his kiss" (109). Old home and young woman collide in a palimpsest of erotic antiquarianism: "all the rest of life had become a mere cloudy rim about the central glory of their passion."[21]

The location of the deserted dwelling, midway between North Dormer and the Mountain, figures crucially into the novel's political geography. Mediating the backwoods promontory where "poor swamp-people lived like vermin in their lair," and the rigid, upright village where "all the blessings of the most refined civilization" were to be had, the abandoned house reveals the interdependence of these two seemingly divergent communities (5, 55). As Royall himself readily admits, "The Mountain belongs to this township, and it's North Dormer's fault if there's a gang of thieves and outlaws living over there, in sight of us, defying the laws of their country" (46). The valley folk can, in fact, secretly identify with "savage misery of the Mountain farmers" (170). Royall, his own law practice dwindling, is himself "poorer than people knew" (45). Like his Mountain counterparts, he relies on "the scant produce of his farm," and poverty and depression have taken their toll (45). His sole consolations – the alienating compensations of liquor and prostitutes – make his self-righteous characterization of Charity's birthmother, "a woman of the town from Nettleton, that followed one those Mountain fellows up to his place and lived there with him like a heathen," a hypocritical diversion from his own "obscure debaucheries" (135, 113). Like Liff Hyatt, the doltish Mountain man who, despite his probable kinship to Charity, flirts with her nonetheless, Royall obscures relational boundaries, attempting to seduce a young woman whom he raised as a daughter.

Royall's ambiguously paternal relationship to his ward only intensifies this confusion. Although she recognizes that "Mr. Royall was her guardian," Charity also knows "that he had not legally adopted her, though everybody spoke of her as Charity Royall" (14). At once father and not-father, Royall presides over a household that mirrors the genealogical confusion atop the Mountain, where one "could not even make out what relationship these people bore to each other" (170). In this sense, Royall's proto-legal relationship to Charity underscores the valley's complicity with the Mountain's extra-legal sovereignty. Charity's real father was a Mountain outlaw whom Royall convicted on charges of manslaughter, but who nevertheless implored the prosecutor to rescue his infant daughter from the heathen hilltop and raise her as a Christian in the town below.[22] Royall's indeterminate paternity thus springs precisely from an extra-legal contract between lawyer and criminal – an arrangement that the prosecutor himself calls a "queer thing" (47). In effect, Charity passes from the custody of a "drunken convict" to the guardianship of a lapsed lawyer who speaks through "the tremulous majesty of drunkenness" (47, 98).

The by-product of a gentleman's agreement between two non-gentlemen, Charity embodies the conflation of town and Mountain, legal and illegal, daughter and lover – blurrings that curiously serve Wharton's conservative purposes. Despite Charity's "tainted [Mountain] origin," *Summer* insists on the value of her biosocial inheritance (39). While the Mountain people are "rough customers," in Harney's words, "they must have a good deal of character" (41). Like their ramshackle dwellings which have "traces of real architecture," the Mountain folk can claim an obscure but notable genealogy (40). "Down at Creston they told me that the first colonists are supposed to have been men who worked on the railway that was built forty or fifty years ago between Springfield and Nettleton," Harney reports. "Some of them took to drink, or got into trouble with the police, and went off – disappeared into the woods. A year or two later there was a report that they were living up on the Mountain" (42). Singley's observation that "the mountaintop is a version of John Winthrop's 'Citty upon a Hill' – insular and fiercely independent" is not far from the mark (153). Though hardly the heroes of Puritan lore, these "first colonists" *are* in fact consistent with Wharton's own legend of national origins. In *French Ways and Their Meaning* (1919), Wharton identifies America's original European settlers as outlaws schooled by their "English forbears . . . to flout tradition and break away from their own great inheritance" (*French Ways* 97). These "new people" were "a pioneer people, a people destined by fate to break up new continents and experiment in new social conditions" (*French Ways* 18–19). The Mountain community has inherited this revolutionary and defiant legacy. Like their renegade forebears, the Mountain's "queer colony" of "outlaws" forms "a little independent kingdom" (*Summer* 41).

By connecting the Mountain's unruly citizens to America's pioneer stock, Wharton betrays her own urgent fears of Anglo-Saxon atavism. The Mountain's degraded state delivers a graphic warning: without immediate action, America's old stock would suffer a similarly degenerate fate.

As Rollin Lynde Hartt cautioned in 1900, if "people descended from the Puritans" could spawn "'a brood of deformed and even idiot children,'" then clearly the nation's Anglo-Saxon population was on the brink of 'race suicide' (577, 578). Although Country Life reformers disputed such dire warnings, they agreed that "whole families [were] sunk in a slough of vice and poverty" and that "men, brutalized by liquor . . . inflict torture upon their wives and horses." Nevertheless, they insisted, the racial "stock" was still essentially "good" (Morgan 583). As one native son, Philip Morgan, insisted in 1897, "it is our boast that Americans of pure English descent are found only in remote New England towns like ours. There is not an Irishman, nor a German, nor an Italian, nor a negro in the village; until lately there was not a foreigner of any description" (583). Despite such claims, however, alarmists continued to warn that New England's noble origins alone could not protect the region from what Josiah Strong called the "heathenish degradation" of its "mountain whites." Attributing this decline "not to antecedents, but primarily to . . . isolation," Strong cautioned that if "*no new preventative measures are devised*," there was no reason why "isolation, irreligion, ignorance, vice and degradation should not increase in the country until we have a rural American peasantry, illiterate and immoral, possessing the rights of citizenship, but utterly incapable of performing or comprehending its duties" (*New Era* 173–4).

Despite such dire premonitions, *Summer* confounds this racial pessimism. Through a strategy of genteel acculturation, patrician insemination and patrimonial restoration, the novel brings generative and financial renewal to Anglo-America's depressed and stagnant origins. Lucius Harney is, in this sense, the novel's erotic tourist; a New Yorker with a New England past, he instills the region with "new life." Making good on Rollins's optimistic prediction that visitors to New England would "rebuild and revivify the old blood, the old stock, somewhat depleted, perhaps" by rekindling "[t]he old fires of reverence and respect and energy and self-sacrifice," Harney has an electrifying effect on both Charity and North Dormer (Rollins, "Renaissance" 70). As Wharton's heroine quickly realizes, "beneath the visible incidents resulting from . . . Harney's arrival, there ran an undercurrent as mysterious and potent as the influence that makes the forest break into leaf before the ice is off the pools" (48).

A seasonal vacationer with "the air of power that the experience of cities probably gave," Harney is one of the rejuvenating "summer people" who held New England's future in their hands (32). By converting his sentimental attachment to the "old home" into the potent currency of regional and racial renewal, Harney catalyzes both economic and erotic revitalization. Not only does he supply Charity's lonely step-father with "a man's companionship," but he equally furnishes the downtrodden lawyer with hard cash. While boarding at the Royall home, Harney hires out the lawyer's buggy "at a dollar and a half a day" – an economic arrangement that helps keep the insolvent attorney afloat (45). Flush with "satisfaction" over "the bargain," Royall "unexpectedly enough [. . . tosses] a ten-dollar bill into Charity's lap," urging her to buy "a Sunday bonnet that'll make all the other girls mad" (45). The gesture neatly summarizes Harney's dual impact: like the currency, which falls suggestively into Charity's lap, Harvey stimulates both fiscal and sexual renewal.

FOUNDING FATHERS

Charity does in fact spend the money on a new hat. "[D]etermined to assert her independence" she purchases a new bonnet to wear to Nettleton, where she secretly plans to spend the Fourth of July with Harney (81). Just as the nation's Independence Day conservatively commemorates the brave actions of the Founding Fathers, however, so Charity's renegade holiday winds up reinforcing her step-father's authority. Nowhere is this more evident than at the lakeside fireworks display. Seated on the bleachers in front of Harney, her head leaning against his knee, Charity watches breathlessly as the fiery display climaxes in a "set piece" that depicts "Washington crossing the Delaware." The glittering tableau of the Father of her Country, "erect, solemn and gigantic," astride a "golden boat," proves overwhelmingly arousing (96). As a voice in the crowd cries "Now – now!"

Charity, grasping the hat on her knee, crushed it tight in the effort to restrain her rapture.

   For a moment the night seemed to grow more impenetrably black; then a great picture stood out against it like a constellation . . . [A]cross a flood of motionless golden ripples the National Hero passed . . .

   . . . "Oh-h-h," Charity gasped: she had forgotten where she was, had at last forgotten even Harney's nearness. She seemed to have been caught up into the stars . . . (96)

The couple's patriotic ecstasy merges with their libidinous longings: pulling Charity's head back "[w]ith sudden vehemence," Harney passionately kisses her, as his lover "gave him back his kisses" (97).

As Charity's orgasmic response to George Washington seamlessly gives way to sexual surrender, the new hat proves to be a central prop. With the fireworks display drawing to a close, Charity gets up to leave, only to confront her inebriated stepfather in the company of several dissolute young "secret society" men and North Dormer's hometown prostitute, Julia Hawes. Royall's appearance is one of "lamentable ruin": from his modishly narrow tie, to his rumpled shirt and "new Panama hat," he looks the picture of a "pitiable" old man desperately grasping at his lost youth. Embarrassed, Royall immediately takes the offensive: "'You whore – you damn – bare-headed whore, you!'" he curses (98). "[H]atless, dishevelled, with a man's arm around her," Charity feels suddenly ashamed and exposed (98). Unchecked by the "pure and dry" architecture of the shell-like hat, her "rumpled hair" is a graphic symbol of female sexuality unfettered by familial restraint (24).

Charity's hair continues to be a charged signifier when Royall later discovers the couple's secret trysting house. He opens the door to find his stepdaughter in sensuous dishabille awaiting her lover's arrival: "The combs had slipped from her hair, and it trailed in a rough dark rope across her breast" (132). Shocked and flustered, Charity quickly "[gropes] for her combs, and [tries] to fasten up the coil. Mr. Royall silently watched her" (132–3). If the Mountain girl's willingness to 'let her hair down' reveals both her sexual accessibility and her newfound independence from familial restraint, her impulse to repin her hair is equally significant. Within the domestic architecture of the hat or braid, Charity's "loose" fertility is constrained, and her sexual independence is redomesticated within the patriarchal "home." Later smoothing "back the locks that had escaped from her braid" in response to Royall's observation that "'[y]our hair's got kinder loose with the wind'" on their wedding day, Charity resigns herself to the safe limitations of patriarchal domesticity (181).

To do this, *Summer* must develop a conservative politics of incest. As Wharton famously indicated in her unfinished pornographic manuscript, "Beatrice Palmato" (1918–19), the power of incest lay not so much in its abhorrence as in its titillating appeal. Unlike her historic namesake, Beatrice Cenci, who was indicted and executed for parricide in 1599, Beatrice Palmato seeks not retribution but continued incestuous pleasure.[23] It is only after discovering her husband and daughter in an innocent embrace that Beatrice violently brings her own father–daughter liaison to an end. Screaming "Don't kiss my child. Put her down! How dare you kiss her?" Beatrice snaps. Her stunned husband suddenly understands the "hidden power . . . perpetually coming between them . . . some strange initiation, some profound moral perversion of which he had always been afraid to face the thought" (R. W. B. Lewis 546). Horrified by her self-betrayal, Beatrice rushes upstairs and shoots herself. The donnée's tragic outline, as striking as it is, hardly prepares us, however, for the still more controversial quality of the "Palmato" fragment itself. In this graphic exploration of the "new abysses of bliss" that Beatrice experiences under her father's knowing touch, Wharton transforms incest into a pleasurable threat. Beatrice feels "a sensation . . . so exquisite that she could have asked to have it indefinitely prolonged . . . [A]lready lightnings of heat shot from that palpitating centre all over her surrendered body, to the tips of her fingers, and the ends of her loosened hair" (548).

For Wharton, the appeal of incest was both visceral and political.[24] As an ancient strategy for the preservation of aristocratic dominion, elite inbreeding had traditionally perpetuated oligarchic insularity by guaranteeing the mutually reinforcing relationship between blood and power. Indeed, Wharton went so far as to insist that such endogamous practices were the source of French racial continuity. The Gaul's traditional aversion to "Adventure" and "Risk," she argued, made the French "the most conservative of western races" and preserved the nation's tradition as "an old and excessively self-contained civilisation" (*French Ways* 84, xxii). A "dogged resistance to invasion" and a habit of "clinging to the same valley and the same river-cliff" over countless generations enabled the French to preserve "a plan of life which is as settled, ruled off and barricaded as their carefully-measured and bounded acres" (*French Ways* 84, 91). Individualism has no place in such an insular culture, where society has always served "the interests of the family, and of that larger family formed by the commune or the state" (*French Ways* 143). At once racially homogenous and culturally parochial, the French constituted, in effect, one national family. In a country where everyone was related to everyone else, all alliances were necessarily (and beneficially) incestuous.

Wharton's glorification of French insularity finds its fictional counterpart in *Summer's* extended treatment of Old Home Week. Cementing the link between Wharton's conservative agenda and the incestuous family, the town pageant opens, appropriately enough, with a rousing chorus of "Home, Sweet Home." Despite the song's homely message, however, Charity performs the anthem with new, erotic force:

It was a joy to Charity to sing: it seemed as though, for the first time, her secret rapture might burst from her and flash its defiance at the world. All the glow in her blood, the breath of the summer earth, the rustle of the forest, the fresh call of the birds at sunrise, and the brooding midday languors, seemed to pass into her untrained voice, lifted and led by the sustaining chorus. (123–4)

As she exults in the knowledge of her clandestine romance with Harney, Charity's domestic homage takes on sensuous new meaning. Home is "sweet" because it serves as the site of sexual awakening. The same antiquarian interests that brought Harney to North Dormer now set the stage for their erotic fulfillment.

Mr. Royall's keynote address underscores this fusion of the ancestral and erotic. Using the Puritan jeremiad formula of "jeopardy and renewal," Royall calls on the town's "young men who are perhaps planning even now to leave these quiet hills and go down into the struggle" to come back to the old home "for *good*" (Glassberg, "History" 967; Wharton, *Summer* 125, 126). Despite the public forum, however, Royall's summons speaks directly to Charity. Anyone who seeks fulfillment outside of the town's old homes, he says, "must keep on loving them while you're away from them," for events one "cannot foresee may send you back some day to the little township and the old homestead . . . [E]ven if you come back against your will – and thinking it's all a bitter mistake of Fate or Providence – you must try to make the best of it, and to make the best of your old town" (125–6). The incestuous message is clear: by returning to the old home "for good," Charity will renew and regenerate the New England regional family. As Royall reminds his rapt listeners, "Our very experiments in larger places, even if they were unsuccessful, ought to have helped us make North Dormer a larger place" (126).

Despite or perhaps *because* of this incestuous message, the narrative endows Royall with renewed sexual potency. As her guardian addresses the crowd, Charity acknowledges that "nothing in his grave and impressive demeanour revealed a trace of the lamentable figure on the [Nettleton] wharf" (124). The "magnificent monument of a man" she had seen as a child when refusing to go to boarding school, and the "suddenly tall and strong . . . towering and powerful" man who had proposed to her for the second time, summons here a comparable "air of majesty" that vivifies his regal name.[25] As the town pastor Mr. Miles appreciatively remarks, "That was a *man* talking."[26]

The narrative gradually augments Royall's erotic appeal. The dirty old man we see at the novel's beginning is gradually transformed into a revitalized symbol of hometown success. Wharton thus prepares us for the novel's incestuous outcome by coordinating Charity's romance, point by point, with her maturing relationship with Royall. The night after she and Harney first meet, Charity imagines herself as a sensuous bride. Alone in her bedroom, she lets her nightgown slip from her bare shoulders and captures a fantasized kiss in her hands. Suddenly, she hears her step-father's footfall on the stairs, and experiences "a fierce revulsion of feeling . . . Until then she had merely despised him; now deep hatred of him filled her heart. He became to her a horrible old man" (24). Freshly recognizing her own sexual desires, Charity suddenly sees her guardian in a new light. Next to the "sunburnt and sinewy" Harney, Royall is "a horrible old man," an inferior specimen on a newly discovered manly continuum (13).

Her visceral antipathy for her guardian only piques Charity's interest in Harney. "[I]nstinctively aware that few things concerning her escaped the eyes of the silent man under whose roof she lived," she fears her step-father's intervention (40). Her anxieties, however, only give "sharpened joy to the hours she spent with young Harney" (40). An invisible but ubiquitous mediator, Royall triangulates the young couple's romance, intensifying its illicit charge. When the suspicious attorney abruptly bars Harney from his regular round of meals at the Royall home, Charity's response is thus swift and passionate:

> The tone which Mr. Royall had said "He's not coming" seemed to her full of ominous satisfaction. She saw that he had suddenly begun to hate Lucius Harney, and guessed herself to be the cause of this change of feeling . . .
> After supper she went up to her room . . . She seated herself on her bed and began to struggle against the desire to go down and ask him what had happened. "I'd rather die than to do it," she muttered to herself. With a word he could have relieved her uncertainty: but never would she gratify him by saying it. (63–4)

Realizing that her step-father is no longer "the dull-witted enemy with whom she had supposed herself to be living" but now a calculating suitor, Charity greets Harney's dismissal with sexual force (180). "Struggling" against her "desire" to plumb her step-father's motives, she is willing to "die" rather than "gratify" his interests and thus "relieve" her own frustration.

Despite her stated aversion, Charity finds the very qualities that most mystify her in Harney fully comprehensible in Royall. Her step-father's attitudes, habits and philosophies are deeply familiar to her; she has witnessed everything from his drunken exploits with local prostitutes to his most casual conversations with neighboring selectmen. Yet when Charity spots Harney sitting next to the fashionable Annabel Balch at Old Home Week, she realizes that "Behind the frail screen of her lover's caresses was the whole inscrutable mystery of his life: his relations with other people – with other women – his opinions, his prejudices, his principles, the net of influences and interests and ambitions in which every man's life is entangled. Of all these she knew nothing" (127). Disabused of her mistaken conviction that she "was the only being on earth who really knew him, knew him from the soles of his feet to the rumpled crest of his hair," Charity ultimately acknowledges that the only person she truly knows is her own step-father (114).

This familiarity is central to the narrative's evolving treatment of Royall. When we first encounter the shabby attorney, he is the "dreadfully 'lonesome' man" knocking on Charity's bedroom door, pleading with her to "'let me in . . . I'm a lonesome man'" (15, 17). Speaking "in the deep voice that sometimes moved her," Royall's plea vaguely stirs Charity, "because she was so 'lonesome' herself" (15). Wharton's use of quotation marks only highlights the couple's shared sexual frustration (itself encoded in the rhetorical frustration of euphemism). At once disgusted and sympathetic, Charity temporarily fends off her own ambivalence. As she nears the consummation of her romance with Harney, however, she obsessively revisits her conflicted feelings for Royall:

[S]uddenly she understood that, until then, she had never really noticed him or thought about him. Except on the occasion of his one offense he had been to her merely the person who is always there, the unquestioned central fact of life . . . Even then she had regarded him only in relation to herself, and had never speculated as to his own feelings, beyond instinctively concluding that he would not trouble her again in the same way. But now she began to wonder what he was really like. (71)

Charity's burgeoning awareness of her own sexuality compels her to re-examine her step-father, for "Everything that in any way affected her was alive and vivid: even the hateful things had grown interesting because they were part of herself" (38). As odious as Royall initially appears, he is nonetheless a "part of herself," a kindred spirit whose "sudden rages probably made him understand the uselessness of reasoning with hers" (27). Confronting each other "eye to eye," the Royalls stare at each other "for a long moment . . . with the terrible equality of courage that sometimes made her feel as if she had his blood in her veins" (76). The familial and sexual curiously overlap, as "blood" converges into an amalgam of kinship and erotic attraction. We can recall Charity's sensual pose early in the novel:

[T]o all that was light and air, perfume and colour, *every drop of blood in her responded*. She loved the roughness of the dry mountain grass under her palms, the smell of the thyme into which she crushed her face, the fingering of the wind in her hair and through her cotton blouse, and the creak of the larches as they swayed to it. (12, *emphasis mine*)

Blending the ancestral and the erotic into a complex semiotics of blood, Wharton transforms Royall into the novel's agent of racial continuity.

Though ostensibly a rival, Harney in fact corroborates Royall's incestuous claim. His status as both an enthusiastic antiquarian and a seductive patrician enhances the erotic appeal of the old home. According to Wharton's conservative political calculus, both the spirited tourist and the stoic local are needed to solve New England's decadent, racial equation. To bring racial vitality back to the region, the erotic and the domestic must coexist in separate but equally powerful domains.

Here again, Wharton grounds her logic in her reverence for French culture. In contrast to America's sexually puerile population, the French grounded marriage in "parenthood, not . . . passion." They realized that marriage "is designed not to make two people individually happy . . . but to secure their permanent well-being as associates in the foundation of a home and the procreation of a family" and thus that wedlock ought to be "a kind of superior business association, based on community and class, of political and religious opinion, and on a fair exchange of advantages" (*French Ways* 128, 130). Love had nothing to do with matrimony – "not because love is thought unimportant, but on account of its very importance" (130). Unlike the temperate moderation required to sustain a family, passion "moves to a different rhythm, and keeps different seasons" (130). Unlike the Anglo-Saxons, who insisted on a puritanical distinction between love ("purity and poetry") and sex ("pruriency and prose"), the French considered love and eros to be deeply and inextricably interconnected (125). "It is because the French have refused to cut love in two that they have not attempted to subordinate it to the organisation of the family," Wharton insists. "They have left it out because there is no room for it" (130).

Summer plots Charity's progress toward this mature realization. The impulsive Mountain girl must come to understand that sexual desire is not compatible with domestic permanence. As Wharton had indicated through Anna Leath's experience in *The Reef*, "to give a place to passion is to risk being submerged by it" (*French Ways* 132). Thus, if Lucius Harney embodies the momentary flash of sexual desire – "the melting of palm into palm and mouth on mouth, and the long flame burning her from head to foot" – then Royall stands for the steady glow of the domestic hearth – "the way a man loves a decent woman" (68, 75). This distinction becomes clear when Royall discovers the lovers' secret hideout and demands to know from Harney, "Is this your house?" The latter's ambiguous reply – "Well – as much as it's anybody's" – gives the former prosecutor a bitter advantage. "Is this the home you propose to bring her to when you get married?" he asks (134). The moment of truth has arrived, and Wharton draws a clear distinction between house and home. If a house offers temporary sanctuary to erotic love, then a home gives permanent shelter to the committed family. What Harney is to the fleeting days of summer; Royall is to life's autumn and winter. As Wharton remarked in *French Ways*, passion "moves to a different rhythm, and keeps different seasons." In *Summer*, Wharton tries to reconcile the passionate and domestic impulses that threatened to dissolve the family in *The Reef*. Charity's movement between Harney and Royall signifies the interdependence of sexual liberalism and ancestral conservatism. Both ideas are mutually, if serially, necessary to the other. If Harney ignites the passions that produce a child, then Royall furnishes the "old home" that will nurture what Robert Frost called future "generations of men." As Charity ultimately realizes, only her step-father will provide "warmth, rest, silence" (179).

THE VILE BODY AND THE GLORIOUS BODY

Charity's thwarted quest to find her birth-mother on the Mountain reveals the striking extent of Wharton's conservative vision. Frustrated that within "the established order of things as she knew them she saw no place for her individual adventure," the young pregnant woman turns to her mother for help: "She supposed it was something in her blood that made the Mountain the only answer to her questioning, the inevitable escape from all that hemmed her in and beset her" (153, 154). Once on top of the mountain, however, Charity discovers something very different. Rather than a zone of counter-patriarchal transcendence, the Mountain is a squalid sty of material immanence. Far from a spiritualized savior, Mary Hyatt is a grossly embodied corpse. As she looks down at her mother's dead body, Charity shudders to find that "There was no sign in it of anything human: she lay there like a dead dog in a ditch" (163). Hyatt's atavistic appearance dramatically confirms at once the inaccessibility of a pre-oedipal past and the inevitability of the masculine, patriarchal future. The dead woman's feral presence weirdly corroborates Royall's earlier claim that Charity's "mother . . . wasn't 'half human'" (47). Unregulated by the abstract law of the father, Mary Hyatt is a degenerate example of grotesque corporeality. Like Mary Johnson, her prolific predecessor in Stephen Crane's *Maggie: A Girl of the Streets* (1893), Hyatt's unregulated body has spawned a "miserable herd" of children (*Summer* 171). When Charity introduces herself as Mary's daughter, a nearby Mountain girl can only sneer, "What? Her too?" (163).

A sexual renegade unfettered by patriarchal law (even Charity's father, we remember, was an outlaw), Hyatt is abjectly alienated from God the

Father. This is nowhere more evident than in *Summer*'s brilliant funeral scene. As Mr. Miles reads the Lord's Prayer over the dead woman's "vile body" and invokes "Our Father which art in Heaven," Charity is struck by a sudden sense of paradox: "Up there somewhere, she supposed, the God whom Mr. Miles had invoked was waiting for Mary Hyatt to appear. What a long flight it was! And what would she have to say when she reached Him?" (167, 169). Hovering in a matriarchal netherworld that stands outside of patriarchal law, Charity's mother is speechless before the Eternal Father.

Wharton's critical assessment of Progressive-era gender politics informs her treatment of Mary Hyatt. "No matter how intelligent women are individually," she remarked in 1919, "they tend, collectively, to narrow down their interests, and take a feminine, or even female, rather than a broadly human view of things" (*French Ways* 119). The Mountain's anti-patriarchal profile aligns it with the unregulated dynamics of women's reform. "[S]hut up together" in situations where they were "each other's only audience, and to a great extent each other's only companions," reform-minded women wasted their time "developing ['their individuality'] in the void" (*French Ways* 102–3). Wharton had nothing but contempt for the "independent and resonant activities" that preoccupied the Progressive-era woman: "her 'boards' and clubs and sororities, her public investigation of everything under the heavens from 'the social evil' to baking-powder" (*French Ways* 101). Progressive activism was itself just another patronizing palliative – a new way of accomplishing the old goal of segregating American women into the undisciplined "baby world" of feminine endeavor (*French Ways* 101). Indeed, while American women were mollifying themselves in the feminized nursery of Progressive reform, "[r]eal living" was going on elsewhere – in "[r]eal civilization[s]" that encouraged "close and constant and interesting and important relations between men and women."[27]

In this respect, the Paris *salon* embodied an ideal alternative to the homosocial world of reform. By assembling an enlightened class of aristocrats, artists and intellectuals, the *salon* encouraged "frank and free social relations between men and women" (*French Ways* 112). Those unqualified by either education or class (and usually both) were not included – a fate the uninvited complacently accepted. Wharton had nothing but praise for the average Frenchman's "admirable *fitting into the pattern*," that "led the race to the happy . . . discovery that good manners . . . lubricate the wheels of life instead of obstructing them."[28]

Like the segregated female reformers whom Wharton condemns, Hyatt cannot subordinate her so-called "individuality" to the vital needs of either the patriarchal family or the patriarchal God. Without "the checks and the stimulus, and the discipline that comes with contact with the stronger masculine individuality," she remains mired in the petty, the immanent and the material (*French Ways* 102–3). Her bestial embodiment, the monstrous by-product of profligate, mass-culture reproduction and mindless, feminist individualism, isolates her in a separate sphere writ large.

Charity must reject her mother's sordid fate. Encumbered with "the weight of reality . . . the bodily burden of her child," she must transcend maternal immanence and recognize the transcendent advantages of the patriarchal order (173). Unlike her mother, she must subordinate her own sexualized individuality and manifest corporeality to a greater abstraction – God the Father, "who shall change our vile body that it may be like unto His glorious body" (166). Her unborn child is central to this endeavor: "But for it she would have felt as rootless as the whiffs of thistledown the wind blew past her" (173). By domesticating the wild erotic impulses that formerly engulfed her, pregnancy transforms Charity's spirited sexuality into a passion for parenthood. Her body is now the site of anamnesis and history, and she must therefore relinquish her former indifference to genealogy and precedent. Although "Speculations concerning the past [formerly] could not hold her long when the present was so rich, the future so rosy," the past is now "hers; [her memories] had passed into her blood, and become a part of her, they were building the child in her womb; it was impossible to tear asunder strands of life so interwoven" (38, 150).

Charity's tender acknowledgment of Harney's role in her new, conservative family begins to explain why abortion plays such a crucial role in *Summer*'s overall political agenda. Charity's visit to the ominous Dr. Merkle, Nettleton's menacingly maternal abortionist, crucially resembles her journey to the Mountain. Both the Mountain and the abortionist's office house the deathly mother. Merkle's very name – from the Latin root "marc-," *to decay*, links her to racial decline (*American Heritage Dictionary* 1529). An agent of race suicide, Dr. Merkle perverts the generative process: she is a pseudo-mother whose "false hair . . . false teeth, [and] false murderous smile" betray the specious immunity she offers from the "unthinkable crime" (145, 146). Not only does she blur the distinction between the real and the artificial, but her office also deconstructs the difference between black and white. When a "mulatto girl with a bushy head and a frilled apron" answers the abortionist's door, Wharton reinforces the associative pairing between spurious identity and racial mixing. As Anne MacMaster observes, the mulatto servant in Wharton's fiction frequently "braces her mistress's stand against convention," in this case disturbingly so.[29]

As Dale Bauer has observed, moreover, Dr. Merkle's own "vague for-
eignness – her pronunciation of 'noospaper' [–] provides just a hint of
her (perhaps German) difference."[30] Although Bauer does not pursue this
connection, I find it extremely important in light of Wharton's wartime
sensibilities. In February 1915, Wharton wrote to her friend Robert Grant
to thank him for joining the Boston Committee of her American Hostels.
His efforts, she assured him, would not be for naught:

Of course you know that all the wild rumours of "atrocities" are *true, & understated*,
& that the question of abolishing the penalty for abortion & infanticide is to be
considered in the French Senate! The assination [*sic*] of countless priests is fully
established, & there are mutilated soldiers here in the hospitals now. At first we
none of us believed these stories, but now we know, alas, how true they are. And
half the horrors are yet untold, because no Belgians still in Belgium dare speak of
what they have seen, for fear of reprisals. (Letter, Feb. 13, [19]15)

Wharton's source for these claims was a January 1915 report by the *Commission instituée en vue de constater les actes commis par l'ennemi en violation
du droit du genes*, headed by the prominent French jurist, Georges Payelle
(Read 66). Serialized in the *Journal officiel*, the report was cited in all of
the leading French dailies, and published in both a cheap brochure edi-
tion as *Le Livre Rouge: les atrocités allemandes* and in English translation as
The Black Book of the War: German Atrocities in France and Belgium (1915)
(Read 150–1). Despite its relatively muted account of German assaults on
French and Belgian civilians, property and homes, the *Commission* showed
no similar restraint when describing the enemy's sexual crimes. The report,
in fact, described these offenses in such graphic detail that even *Le Matin*
felt obligated to apologize to its readers for the verbatim account. "[T]his
is no time for prudery," the editors explained (qtd. in Read 152).

French readers were shocked by the lurid revelations. The report
described mothers being raped in front of their small children, daughters
assaulted in plain view of their "half-maddened" mothers, aging grand-
mothers sexually molested, and young girls – 13, 11, and even 4 years old –
raped and brutalized (*Black Book* 6, 8). Gang rapes and sexual dismemberment were common. Several French women had been executed after
having their breasts severed, and in one case a pregnant woman was shot in
front of her fellow villagers. The "appalling frequency" of "[c]rimes against
women and young girls," the report concluded, could "only be considered
as the individual and spontaneous acts of uncaged beasts" (2).

Feeding a long-standing controversy over France's declining fertility, *Le
Livre Rouge* excited unprecedented outrage. Wharton's evident alarm that

"the question of abolishing the penalty for abortion & infanticide is to be considered in the French Senate!" suggests as much. In a country where depopulation had, by the late nineteenth century, become a "master pathology," abortion was declared tantamount to treachery (Nye). Defeat at the hands of the Prussians in 1870 had only compounded French fears that their nation was withering on the vine. Unlike the united German population which had grown exponentially since the close of the nineteenth century, the French populace was shrinking. As Paul Leroy-Beaulieu warned in 1911, "The children of our families, one or two in number, surrounded by indulgent tenderness, with debilitating care . . . do not but exceptionally manifest the spirit of enterprise and adventure, of endurance and perseverance that characterized their ancient ancestors and which the sons of prolific German families possess today" (qtd. in Nye 142). Captain E. de Blic, a spokesman for the pro-natalist *Alliance nationale contre dépopulation*, went so far as to blame French women who practiced birth control and abortion for the German invasion. By dramatically depleting French strength, these women, de Blic charged, had practically invited German aggression. Anyone who was "consciously or unconsciously responsible for national weakness" was probably a secret German agent (qtd. in McLaren 178). For pro-natalists, abortion was the obvious source of French decadence and military weakness. The government's willingness to authorize abortion in light of reported German atrocities only highlighted the urgency of the matter. Germany's sexual and geopolitical aggression had made abortion a bellwether for racially beleaguered times.[31]

Charity's decision to keep her baby underscores two sides of Wharton's wartime logic. If abortion remedied the dysgenic consequences of the invader's vicious penetration, then proactive reproduction, timely legitimization and incestuous isolation represented a weirdly eugenic alternative – the patriotic nexus of family, sexuality and national defense.[32] Wharton explores these possibilities in both *French Ways and Their Meaning* and *Summer*. In the former, France is a legendary heroine who doggedly resists the "invasions of savage hordes" but wisely welcomes "the ancient Mediterranean culture which penetrated her by the Rhone and Spain and the Alps" (80, 81). Such strategic geosexual decisions, Wharton reasons, "would explain the ripeness and the continuity of her social life. By her geographic position she seemed destined to centralise and cherish the scattered fires of these old societies" (81–2). Wharton's generative imagery invites an evocative comparison between Charity and France. Both have descended from an "astounding race" which has undergone "a period of retrogression" when "savage hordes" tried to sweep it away. Both, however, have ultimately (and strategically) surrendered to a penetrating element "from the south" which has injected "ripeness and continuity" into a dormant culture (*French Ways* 80). Pregnant with new life, both France and Charity can fruitfully "centralise and cherish the scattered fires" of a revitalized racial past.

If Charity's capitulation to her guardian seems a Faustian bargain at best, her decision nonetheless embodies Wharton's conservative response to the social upheavals of her day – "the violent convulsions of a world in the making" (*French Ways* 80). What begins as an inarticulate longing for a place that can accommodate Charity's "individual adventure" gives way, at the novel's end, to a conservative desire "to centralise and cherish" the racially rejuvenated, patriarchal clan (*Summer* 153). As Royall brings Charity down from the Mountain, his paternalistic logic sharply forecloses the manifold possibilities encoded in her speechless stutter, "I want you to know . . . I want . . .":

"Do you know what you really want? I'll tell you. You want to be took home and took care of. And I guess that's all there is to say."
"No . . . it's not all. . . ."
"Ain't it?" He looked at his watch. "Well, I'll tell you another thing. All *I* want is to know if you'll marry me. If there was anything else, I'd tell you so; but there ain't. Come to my age, a man knows the things that matter and the things that don't . . ."
His tone was so strong and resolute that it was like a supporting arm about her. She felt her resistance melting . . . (177)

Like the "New Frenchwoman" in *French Ways and Their Meaning*, Charity realizes that parenthood, not passion, is the proper arbiter of matrimonial choice. Despite the Kate Chopin-like image of the "broken wing" that hinders her final fugitive "impulse of flight," Charity's commitment to generational continuity trumps her desire for feminist individualism (182–3). As she follows her guardian into the Nettleton chapel, "as passively as a tired child," Charity resigns herself to her new, compliant position within the old home (180).

In contrast to the irresponsible individualism cultivated atop the Mountain and within the duplicitous precincts of Dr. Merkle's office, Royall offers legitimacy and stability. He detaches himself "with rocky firmness from this elusive background," supplanting both unmanageable spaces (180). Recalling the "fugitive impression" of her guardian's "startling distinctness" at Old Home Week – a distinctness that "made her see why he had always struck her as such a lonely man" – Charity has "a sudden sense of their nearness to each other" (180–1). The source of their mutual 'lonesomeness' becomes clear: it is erotic individualism, in all of its democratic unruliness, alienated from the racial stability of the ancestral home.

By enclosing the erotic within the domestic, Wharton translates incest from the summertime domain of sexual perversion into the autumnal realm of conservative calm. On the night after their wedding, Royall sleeps in a rocking-chair, as his frightened bride lies alone in their bed. With "ineffable relief," Charity realizes that her new husband has decided to subordinate his sexual desires to the primacy of her gestating child: "He knew, then . . . he knew . . . it was because he knew that he had married her, and that he sat there in the darkness to show her she was safe with him" (186 [ellipses in original]). Unlike "Beatrice Palmato," *Summer* incarnates a vision of father–daughter incest that is neither erotic nor tragic: it is beneficent and familial. For Wharton, this distinction is crucial. In seeking to transcend the more sensational implications of incest, *Summer* probes its political possibilities. Rather than dodging the incestuous bullet by letting the Royalls' marriage off on a technicality, Wharton mines a more complex and conservative possibility. As reviewer H. W. Boynton recognized in 1917, marriage gives Charity a "foothold of safety and of real, if wintery [*sic*] sunshine" (qtd. in Benstock 328). In this sense, Wharton's representation of incest is even more shocking than it is in the work of Herman Melville, Pauline Hopkins or William Faulkner. Incest need not be an act of perversion, she implies; rather, it can be an aristocratic, recuperative response to racial emergency, a way of repopulating the elite home.

The novel's final business transaction seals this resolution. As Charity returns to Dr. Merkle's office, determined to redeem the blue brooch that Harney had given her on the Fourth of July, the new Mrs. Royall effectively closes the loop between her husband/guardian and her tourist/lover. By paying off the "evil" abortionist, whose pseudo-motherly beneficence ("I just put it to you as your own mother might") masks a scurrilous intent to blackmail, Charity conclusively aligns herself with the transactional domain of men (188). If the blue brooch, like the Fourth of July hat, represents the genealogical and financial continuity between New York's upper classes and New England's decadent gentry, then her redemption of the souvenir formalizes this link. "She wanted [the brooch] for her baby: she meant it, in some mysterious way, to be a link between Harney's child and its unknown father. Trembling and hating herself while she did it, she laid Mr. Royall's money on the table, and catching up the brooch fled out of the room and the house" (188). By using Royall's forty dollars to redeem her pin, Charity completes the financial triangle, forging a symbolic link between her child, its biological father and the economic renewal he has brought to the community. The tourist's fiscal and sexual "investment" accomplishes its goal – ensuring patriarchal continuity by replenishing Royall's diminished store, and reviving paternal authority by stimulating a new generation of Royall-ty. Like the Mountain girl herself, the brooch – as "blue as a mountain lake" – is acquired by a tourist and redeemed through the dividends of tourism (87).

THE EMPIRE OF CHARITY

It is important to recognize that this transactional model is not one of exchange, but one of "charity." As the mission statement of the New England Society of Cincinnati declared in 1845, members should not only "cherish the memory and perpetuate the principles of the original settlers of New England," but also "extend charity to the needy of New England descent'" (qtd. in Westbrook 201). These philanthropic expectations, and their attendant class assumptions, dominate *Summer*. For Wharton, true philanthropy required the presence of a leisured class. New York, she complained, had lost its "municipal conscience" (*Backward Glance* 57). Despite her own father's role as "a director on the principal charitable boards of New York," and her mother's annual participation in a "ladies' 'sewing class'" that stitched garments for the poor, Wharton recalled that "none of my friends rendered the public services that a more enlightened social system would have exacted of them" (*Backward Glance* 95). By her lights, the blame for this sorry state of affairs lay with American democracy. In "every society there is the room, and the need, for a cultivated leisure class; but from the first the spirit of our institutions has caused us to waste this class instead of using it" (*Backward Glance* 95–6). By putting an end to the genteel practice of *noblesse oblige*, moreover, Progressive-era reformers had deprived America of its most high-minded and benevolent class of philanthropic activists.[33] John Oppenheim, a social worker-turned-poet, summarized the new Progressive ethos in 1916:

> Understanding – not faith.
> Will – not hope.
> Service – not charity.
> (qtd. in Burnham 214)

As Robert H. Wiebe has observed, by 1900 the charitable "panacea of the patrician" had given way to "the administrative tool of the expert, with efficiency rather than moral purity its objective" (171). Elite philanthropists watched as their exclusive "Empire of Charity" increasingly became the public province of the professional social worker (Paine). Brahmin reformers like Joseph Lee could only warn that this "passing of control of the destiny of social work from the few choice spirits who created and lovingly fostered it, to the great and merciless democracy" would tarnish the moral splendor of traditional benevolence. "Public relief," he insisted, "will never replace the expression of the nearer loyalties" (qtd. in Saveth 87, 88). While activists like Jane Addams and Lillian Wald preferred organized reform to individual beneficence, and charitable foundations to private philanthropy, traditionalists like Wharton and Lee lamented a bygone era when charity had been a matter of personal inclination rather than professional occupation. As one of Sinclair Lewis's haughty small-town matrons insists in his 1920 novel, *Main Street*, "'[T]here never can be anything to these so-called scientific schemes for abolishing charity, never! . . . I should hate to think of a world in which we were deprived of all the pleasures of giving. Besides, if these shiftless folks realize they're getting charity, and not something to which they have a right, they're so much more grateful.'"[34]

Despite his professed admiration for Wharton, to whom he dedicated his 1922 novel *Babbitt*, Lewis's satirical tone could not have stood in sharper opposition to the older, pre-Progressive model of Christian charity that Wharton espouses in *Summer*. While the latter's heroine acknowledges "that she had been christened Charity . . . to commemorate Mr. Royall's disinterestedness in 'bringing her down,' and to keep alive in her a becoming sense of her dependence," she initially resents what Josephine Shaw Lowell called "the redeeming features of private charity" (*Summer* 14; Lowell qtd. in Saveth 80). Mortified when Harney attempts to donate a dollar to the impoverished Bash Hyatt family, she tearfully insists, "I ain't – I ain't ashamed. They're my people, and I ain't ashamed of them" (57). In attempting to liberate Charity from such shame, *Summer* seeks not only to teach her the advantages of private benevolence but also to revive in her "a becoming sense of her dependence."[35]

In his composite role as prosperous tourist, patrician patriot and sexual gadfly, Harney imbues New England's old homes with "Charity." By contributing life and livelihood to the white elite's depressed origin, he galvanizes regional renewal through a kind of libidinous and incestuous tourism.[36] If Rollin Lynde Hartt was right to point out that "many a family [could] be lifted out of squalor and degradation" by "something like what the 'organized charity' people call 'friendly visiting,'" then Harney personifies this distinctly patrician form of traveling beneficence (581). As social worker Marian C. Putnam had explained to a convention of colleagues in 1887, the role of the "friendly visitor" was that of "seeing and knowing people in their homes, and trying, by means of personal influence and practical suggestion, to improve their conditions."[37] Like Royall, who hires the "doddering and shiftless" Verena Marsh, a "deaf pauper" from the Creston Almshouse, to cook in exchange for room and board, Harney "organizes Charity," saving her from a lifetime of degradation and potential prostitution.[38]

In this sense, Harney is the novel's agent of sexual "radicalism" in the deeply conservative sense of the term. As Brahmin philanthropist Joseph Lee noted in 1922, social workers "are our radicals in the true sense – not of those obsessed with the desire to pull things up by the roots, useful where destruction is the need, but of those whose passion is to make the flower grow, essential in the more difficult process of development" (Lee 142). The true social worker, Lee maintained, "recognizes in every man not a static problem but a process, a flame, the possibility of a divine fire, and seeks that combination of which the inducement of this flame depends" (141). Harney's "friendly visit" ignites this flame in Charity – "the long flame burning her from head to foot." Impregnating "charity" with the conservative values of kin, he accomplishes what Wharton herself strived to achieve in her own war work. He returns the confused refugee to her conservative point of Yankee origin. Charity begins – and ends – at home.

CHAPTER 6

Coda: The Age of Innocence *and the Cesnola controversy*

Near the end of *The Age of Innocence* (1920), would-be lovers Newland Archer and Ellen Olenska seek a private colloquy in the new Metropolitan Museum of Art. "It's odd . . . I never came here before," Ellen remarks, as the couple stroll through "the queer wilderness of cast-iron and encaustic tiles." "Ah well –," Archer replies. "Some day, I suppose, it will be a great Museum" (258). In a city where "there are no churches . . . no monuments," the Metropolitan seems to offer the adulterous pair temporary refuge from the prying eyes of Old New Yorkers for whom "any less systematized and affluent existence" than their own seems "unreal and precarious" (257, 183). Archer, who has grown to feel increasingly alienated from this "hieroglyphic world, where the real thing was never said or done or even thought, but only represented by a set of arbitrary signs," seeks out the new museum as a haven of authenticity – a place where his "real life" with Ellen can supplant his "sham one" as May Welland's respectable husband (41, 220, 203).

Indeed, Archer's illicit passion for May's cousin Ellen, the estranged wife of a corrupt European count, has dangerously unsettled his own precarious relationship to the real. "The things that had filled his days seemed now like a nursery parody of life, or like the wrangles of medieval schoolmen over metaphysical terms that nobody had ever understood" (153). Seizing hold of the forbidden ardor that has come to dominate his inner life, Archer protests that "The only reality to me is this" (242). His more realistic lover, however, demurs. Archer's "trusting" belief in their future is, from Ellen's point of view, little more than a whimsical "vision" (241). "[W]e'll not look at visions," she insists, "but at realities" (242). Despite Archer's profession that theirs will not be "an ordinary hole-and-corner love-affair," Ellen sees the situation plainly for what it is. "Is it your idea, then, that I should live with you as your mistress – since I can't be your wife?" she asks (242). Startled by "[t]he crudeness of the question," Archer can only assert his imperviousness to "the love that is fed on caresses and feeds them" (241, 204). A "stolen kiss isn't what I want," he insists, for he is "conscious of a curious indifference

153

to her bodily presence" (241, 204). Rather, he prefers to worship Ellen from afar, in a mental "sanctuary," "built up within himself," where "she [thrones] among his secret thoughts and longings" (204, 220). The museum, in this respect, represents a perfect site for the lovers' clandestine rendezvous. In the hushed corridors of New York's aesthetic sanctuary, Archer discovers a purified alternative to adultery's "hackneyed vocabulary," a place "where words like that – categories like that – won't exist" (257, 242).

As they enter the Metropolitan, the lovers bypass "the popular 'Wolfe collection', whose anecdotic canvases filled one of the main galleries," and instead seek out a more "melancholy retreat" among "the 'Cesnola antiquities'" which molder "in unvisited loneliness" (258). The trove of ancient Cypriot artifacts had been the gift of the museum's first director, Luigi Palma di Cesnola, who had personally excavated the collection, and donated his discoveries to the museum in March 1880. Next to the delineative European canvases that Catharine Lorillard Wolfe, a wealthy patron of the arts, eventually contributed in 1887, the Cypriot objects appeared esoteric indeed. As John L. Myers, professor of ancient history at Oxford, admitted in the Metropolitan's *Handbook of the Cesnola Collection of Antiquities from Cyprus* (1914), "Many objects in the Cesnola Collection are still hard to explain fully; a few, for want of exact record at the first, have lost the meaning they had, perhaps permanently" (xxi). Ellen recognizes as much. Gazing at the "the recovered fragments of Ilium" amassed on the gallery's shelves, she is struck by the number of "small broken objects – hardly recognizable domestic utensils, ornaments and personal trifles – made of glass, of clay, of discoloured bronze and other time-blurred substances" (258). "It seems cruel," she wistfully remarks, "... that after a while nothing matters ... any more than these little things, that used to be necessary and important to forgotten people, and now have to be guessed at under a magnifying glass and labeled: 'Use unknown'" (258).

This pensive observation signals Wharton's own preoccupation with the anthropology of cultural extinction in *The Age of Innocence*. In the wake of the Great War, the seemingly "unalterable rules of conduct" that had governed Old New York had become "observances as quaintly arbitrary as the domestic rites of the Pharaohs" (*Backward Glance* 6). As Wharton would acknowledge in *A Backward Glance*, "The compact world of my youth has receded into a past from which it can only be dug up in bits by the assiduous relic-hunter, and its smallest fragments begin to be worth collecting and putting together before the last of those who knew the live structure are swept away with it" (7). Saturated in the rhetoric of archaeology, anthropology and antiquarianism, *The Age of Innocence* builds a sustained comparison between New York City in the 1880s and such ancient civilizations as Pompeii or Troy. Like the reliquary inhabitants of these famously lost cities, Manhattan's elite are "rather gruesomely preserved in the airless atmosphere of a perfectly irreproachable existence as bodies caught in glaciers keep for years a rosy life-in-death" (*Age of Innocence* 47). By placing the reader at two removes from the story – the remove of time and the "objective remove of the social sciences" – Wharton frames a present that is not only some thirty years after the central action of the story, but also some twenty years earlier than the novel's publication and thus a world war away (Trumpener and Nyce 162). The museum reifies this distance by marking off what David Lowenthal calls "a special past" – a past distinct from the "unremarked present" and thus reliable in a way that current events can never be (Lowenthal 360).

For Wharton, the modern museum trod a fine line. Because she felt that art was the province of the private collector who could shield his treasures from the indiscriminate crowd, she deplored the movement to make galleries more democratically accessible. In Dijon, France, for example, she praised a palace that housed "a number of small collections, the spoils of local dilettanti," because "many of the rooms exhibit a charming habitable mingling of old furniture, old porcelain and the small unobtrusive pictures that are painted to be lived with, not glanced up at from a catalogue" (*Motor-Flight* 155). If anything, the museum should emulate the patrician home. By contrast, the tombs of Burgundy's dukes had been "so cruelly torn from the hallowed twilight of Chartreuse, and exposed to the cold illumination of museum windows," that they no longer served their hallowed purpose (*Motor-Flight* 153). Transformed from "a guard-room" into a gallery for gawking spectators, the vaunted medieval hall had been effectively desecrated, its dukes ceasing "to be [the castle's] lords" (153). "[T]he trail of label and number, of velvet cord and iron rail, is everywhere in their democratised palace" (153, 154). Like *The Valley of Decision*'s deposed but resistant duke, Odo Valsecca, however, the palace refuses to submit: it yields "as little as might be of its private character to the encroachments of publicity" (154). Wharton is relieved to note that a visitor can still drift "from one bright room to another" and sense herself in "the house of a great collector who still lives among his treasures" (155).

If Wharton criticized the "secularised, museumised aspect" of contemporary art venues, then she was equally unstinting in her condemnation of the overzealous art restorer (*Motor-Flight* 150). When a "too-highly treasured relic" was "fenced about, restored, and converted into a dry little museum," it lost the "colour and pathos of extreme age" (89). As Wharton humorously

remarked in 1908 (109): "It has been the fate of too many venerable architectural relics to sacrifice their bloom of *vetusté* to the scrupulous care which
makes them look like conscious cosseted old ladies, of whom their admiring
relatives say, 'Should you ever suspect her age?'" The artifacts of the past
were meant to fill us with "the sense of undisguised antiquity, of a long
stolid existence exposed to every elemental influence." Only in their visibly
antiquated condition could these pieces communicate the "impression of
rugged, taciturn strength, and of mysterious memories striking back" (109).

These ideas reached a critical mass for Wharton in 1903, when she discovered a set of misidentified terracotta statuettes in an obscure church
in San Vivaldo, Italy. Although the figurines were attributed to the
seventeenth-century sculptor Giovanni Gonnelli, a blind student of the
artist Pietro Tacca, Wharton was convinced that the statuettes were in fact
much older examples of the turn-of-the-sixteenth-century Robbias school.
"[C]ircumvent[ing] the compiler of [her] guide-book" and "eluding [her]
cicerone," she independently sought "expert confirmation" of her theory
from Enrico Ridolfi, then the director of the Royal Museum in Florence
(*Italian Backgrounds* 105). To her considerable elation, she found that she
"had not overestimated the importance of the discovery" (105). The statuettes *were*, in fact, products of the Robbias school. Her delight was palpable; she had experienced that "rare sensation of an artistic discovery made in
the heart of the most carefully-explored artistic hunting-ground of Europe"
(85, 87).

Wharton's reaction to this discovery supports Dean MacCannell's observation that "The rhetoric of tourism is full of manifestations of the importance of the authenticity of the relationship between tourists and what they
see" (14). Her anxious desire to discover "a few miles unmeasured by the
guide-book," and thereby experience "the thrill of explorers sighting a new
continent," reveals not only her share in the anti-modern quest for the real
more generally, but also her contempt for those who failed to appreciate
the true, the authentic and the original (*Italian Backgrounds* 86). Wharton
thus increasingly sought to distinguish herself from her fellow "tourists" –
a term that, as MacCannell observes, had begun to serve as a "derisive
label for someone who seems content with his obviously inauthentic experiences" (MacCannell 94). In 1915, after stopping at a wartime hospital for
shell-shocked soldiers, Wharton criticized other visitors who had called
on the wounded out of mere ghoulish curiosity. "I don't know anything
ghastlier & more idiotic than 'doing' hospitals en touriste, like museums!'"
she remarked to Mary Berenson (*Letters* 346). When she urged Mary's husband, Bernard Berenson, to see North Africa "before the Teuton hordes

do," she cited her own experiences in Naples. The German tourists "are here in their might . . . Ach-gotting over everything, & in the museum I heard a beefy bridegroom point out Silenus to his Gretchen with the instructive note: 'Der Erzieher des Bacchus' ['The Tutor of Bacchus']" (*Letters* 322). The growing affordability of international travel had opened the world's museums to the gaze of the sundry hoards. Despite her best efforts to see the paintings that Berenson had recommended to her in London's National Gallery, Wharton reported that "a weak-voiced lady with a rabbit chin was 'lecturing' . . . to fifty of her sex, whose serried hats completely shut out the uncultured from the least glimpse of the picture!" (letter to Bernard Berenson, Dec. 16, 1911). Unlike her own dramatic discovery in San Vivaldo, where she had stumbled upon "the center of an unexplored continent," the modern museum was a place of promiscuous contact, sham revelation and derivative knowledge (*Italian Backgrounds* 104).

In this context, Newland Archer's decision to bypass the Metropolitan's popular Wolfe Collection in favor of the neglected Cesnola antiquities seems strategic. Next to the stylish, representational canvases of such French painters as Adolphe-William Bouguereau and Alexandre Cabanel, the cracked Cypriot artifacts seemed obscure and arcane. For Ellen, however, the Cesnola collection's antiquarian disrepair confirms its value. Attracted by the damaged and the old, rather than the new and the fashionable, the Countess sees these ancient shards as graphic testimony to both social transience and cultural stamina. Archer's refusal to believe that a woman as beautiful as Ellen "should ever suffer the stupid law of change" bears out this paradoxical logic (*Age of Innocence* 259). Inasmuch as the artifacts themselves bear witness to the ravages of historical change, they equally mark the survival of something rare and true. To the secret lovers, whose future seems as doomed as their shared patrician past, these disintegrating fragments metonymically commemorate at once ancient Cyprus and Old New York – both civilizations destroyed by modern philistines. As John Taylor Johnson, the President of the Metropolitan, remarked in 1877, General di Cesnola had, "by his researches, rescued these treasures from time and an unappreciative race" (Cesnola 455). He had preserved vestiges of "the central meeting-point of the old races" – Phoenicians, Greeks and Romans – from what Cesnola regarded as the "impractical and monstrous government" of the Ottoman empire (Cesnola 454, 40). And just as the Turks had conquered Cyprus, so "the bosses and the emigrant" had overtaken Dutch Manhattan, replacing the chromatic consistency of America's "remote ancestral authority" with a "huge kaleidoscope where all the social atoms spun around on the same plane" (*Age of Innocence* 294, 49, 294). As

Wharton looked about New York, she found that "old landmarks" had disappeared, "and with them the signposts and the danger-signal" (294, 298).

Suspended in their glass cases, however, the Cypriot artifacts have, by contrast, transcended time. Even in their fragmented condition, they bear mute testimony to a bygone culture whose value they poignantly commemorate. For Newland and Ellen, the shattered artifacts eloquently speak to their own sense of doom. Despite their head-on collision with "the embodied image of the Family" – realized palpably in May's pregnancy – Archer seeks to preserve his passion for Ellen in the museum of the mind (277). Indeed, when he has the opportunity to visit the Countess many years later, after May's death, the potency of this museum logic becomes clear. Because Ellen is "more real to me here than if I went up," Archer refuses to accompany his son Dallas to her Paris apartment. Instead, the widower sits on a park bench and gazes up at Madame Olenska's windows, fearful "lest that last shadow of reality should lose its edge" (301). As is the case in the museum, where the object is made precious by its mysterious inaccessibility, so Ellen retains the edge of reality by escaping the visible ravages of time. Her authenticity, like the Metropolitan's Cypriot antiquities, rests with her ability to transcend use. The "domestic utensils, ornaments and personal trifles" that comprise the Cesnola Collection gesture at Ellen's potential serviceability (as mistress, social rebel, divorcee). At the same time, however, they pointedly underscore their own impracticality. For Archer, this impracticality is precisely the source of Ellen's erotic appeal: like the encased implements, her body remains for Archer unconsummated and her use unknown.

To read *The Age of Innocence* as a requiem for American authenticity, however, is to miss Wharton's ironic point. The Cesnola antiquities were, in fact, thought to be fakes. In August 1880, a French antiquarian and third-generation proprietor of a highly regarded numismatic house in Paris, Gaston L. Feuardent, published an explosive series of accusations in *The Art Amateur* charging that "certain deceptive alterations and unintelligent restorations of some of the antiquities of the Cesnola collection" cast doubt on their authenticity (Feuardent, "Tampering" 48). The allegation that these alterations had been "made . . . under the supervision of General di Cesnola himself," moreover, added personal venom to the accusations ("Tampering" 50). According to Feuardent, several statues had been altered or enhanced under Cesnola's own direction in order to augment their supposed historical value. In particular, one female figurine had been doctored with the addition of a "brand new" stone mirror that made the piece falsely appear to be a seventh-century Greek Aphrodite (McFadden 194; see also Feuardent, "Tampering" 48). "[T]o amalgamate various pieces, strangers to each other, in order to complete an object, and not publicly to indicate it," Feuardent charged, "is not only bad faith, but positive vandalism" ("Tampering" 50).

The charges provoked a three-year furore. The ensuing legal battle became, in the words of Cesnola's biographer Elizabeth McFadden, "one of the great diversions of the decade . . . It was a sensation" (McFadden 209, 210). Outraged by Feuardent's accusations, Cesnola publicly and insistently denied any tampering. This "dastardly attack by the French Jew dealer in an obscure monthly paper edited by a Jew" was, he insisted, "an absurdity" (qtd. in McFadden 195; "The Charges against Cesnola"). All restorations, where they had been needed at all, had been done "conscientiously and properly." It was "ludicrous," moreover, "for a mere dealer to bring such charges when the best archaeologists of both hemispheres have fully recognized that no one is more competent than the discoverer himself to make the proper restorations" ("The Charges"). Feuardent was "thoroughly dishonest, ignorant, and reckless," Cesnola concluded, and the coin-collector's archeological appraisals would soon be recognized for what they were: "charlatanism" ("Di Cesnola's Statuettes").

Feuardent angrily responded by stepping up his attack. Not only had the statues been suspiciously reassembled, but the collection's bronzes had also been smeared with a "false patina" which made them "appear at first sight to be forgeries" (Feuardent, Letter). It was indeed "curious," Feuardent sarcastically added, "for a museum to try to make antiques appear as if they were imitations" (Feuardent, Letter). Cesnola's repeated claims that the Frenchman's charges had been "maliciously made, and [were] absolutely without foundation in fact" only served to pique the public's interest, however. When the *Art Amateur* demanded an immediate and thorough investigation, the Metropolitan, heretofore silent about the controversy, was forced to respond ("Feuardent–Cesnola Controversy"). The museum organized a panel of Cesnola allies and non-specialists to study the matter. It was a move that only fed the controversy. Criticism came from all sides. As the *New York Times* editorialized, "The Trustees of the Metropolitan Museum may rest assured that, whatever may be the actual state of their Cyprus collection, the verdict of their committee will add little to its reputation for authenticity. On such a subject, the opinion of one accomplished expert is worth a hundred times that of a hundred doctors of laws who are not experts" ("The Cesnola Investigation"). Cesnola, the *Times* continued, was neither qualified nor prepared to authenticate the artifacts. "Gen.

DI CESNOLA was not known as an authority in art, nor even, we believe, as a student of art, before his appointment, a few years ago, as Consul at Cyprus" ("The Cesnola Investigation"). The protean museum director found himself increasingly at the center of the controversy. Did "Col. Di Cesnola" have "the right . . . to assume half a dozen of his titles, among those of General, Count, Doctor of Laws, and Cavalier," the *Times* wanted to know ("Another Title for Di Cesnola"). Was not Cesnola's initial attempt to sell part of the collection to finance the excavation a conflict of interest? "A man may have to be at the same time a dealer and an archæologist," *The Nation* agreed, "but just in so far as his collections become wares must his judgment of their scientific or artistic value be disturbed or impaired" (Godkin, "Trial" 113). If Feuardent's tampering charges were true, then, the *Times* averred, "it must place DI CESNOLA in the category of impostors, and must discredit every enterprise with which he is prominently identified."[1]

The controversy culminated in 1883, when Feuardent sued Cesnola for libel and defamation of character (McFadden 208). The trial became a *cause célèbre*. In an effort to bolster Cesnola's case (and to profit, perhaps, from pre-trial publicity), the Metropolitan's Executive Committee ordered that two of the most disputed statues be put on public display under "ample light" in the Grand Hall. Next to the statues, Feuardent's charges were printed in bold type and categorically refuted. "Members of the Museum, the public and especially Editors of Public Journals, Sculptors, Workers in Stone, Scholars and all persons interested in the truthfulness of archaeological objects" were invited to "make careful examination of the Statues" (qtd. in McFadden 210). In the ensuing fortnight, the museum was inundated with visitors: several thousand poured into the Grand Hall to see the disputed artifacts.

The trial began in October 1883. Expert witnesses took the stand, among them the sculptor Augustus Saint-Gaudens, who testified on December 6 that several of the antiquities had, in his opinion, been altered. Noting the "remarkable uniformity of color, which he found to be due to the use of a wash," Saint-Gaudens said that one figure holding a cow's head looked as if it had new feet that had been retooled to resemble "the original stone" ("Columbia's President"). While Cesnola conceded that some of the figures had been repaired and restored, he denied that the artifacts had been manufactured out of whole cloth. In closing arguments, Cesnola's lawyer, Joseph H. Choate, repeated the instructions that his client had supposedly given to the museum's staff: "there is to be no restoration . . . these statues must be exhibited to the world as they came into the hands of the

discoverers in Cyprus . . . Don't put together any pieces unless you are absolutely sure that they are parts of the original" ("Mr. Choate's Argument").
Ultimately, the jury acquitted Cesnola, bringing "a very brilliant and excit-
ing 'art' episode" to "a melancholy close" ("The Feuardent–Cesnola Trial"
114).

The Age of Innocence is, of course, preoccupied with such questions of
authenticity: to Archer's mind, the Wellands' "sham Buhl tables and gilt
vitrines" cannot compare with his own family's "'sincere' Eastlake furniture" (63). Similarly, Archer's mother insistently differentiates those who
are merely wealthy from those "who can claim an aristocratic origin in the
real sense of the word" (45). The disputed status of the Cesnola antiquities
adds a new dimension to these concerns. Even artifacts that were themselves supposed to build an allusive bridge between the disappearing world
of Old New York and similar lost civilizations of the past, prove unreliable.
Indeed, the novel bears out Ellen's complaint that New Yorkers are bound
by a "blind conformity to tradition – somebody else's tradition." As the
Countess mildly observes, "It seems stupid to have discovered America only
to make it into a copy of another country" (201).

America, though, cannot even aspire to be a "copy of another country,"
for the referents by which Americans know those countries are themselves
untrustworthy. As benchmarks of identity and cultural meaning, the artifacts of the past prove to be tainted. The novel's opening sequence at the
Academy of Music prepares us for this conclusion: like the opera diva
Christine Nilsson, who presses a crushed daisy to her lips while looking
into the eyes of "the little brown Faust-Capoul, who was vainly trying . . . to
look as pure and true as his artless victim," Wharton's Old New Yorkers live
in a factitious "age of innocence" (8–9). The past is no more innocent than
the performance is an authentic encounter between real lovers. As Archer
acknowledges, "Untrained human nature was not frank and innocent, it
was full of the twists and defences [*sic*] of an instinctive guile" (42).

Despite this prescient realization, however, *The Age of Innocence* hinges
on its hero's fundamental misconception of his seemingly naive wife. Like
Ralph Marvell before him, Newland Archer mistakes his dewy bride for a
chaste Diana, goddess of the hunt. Because he believes so completely in
his own chauvinistic fantasy of May's impenetrable and "abysmal purity,"
Archer is reliable neither as a narrator nor as the phallic "archer" that his
name would suggest (10). Instead, it is May who, returning "flushed and
calm from her final bull's eye" at the Newport Archery Club, hits the
mark by strategically revealing her pregnancy just before her husband and
cousin consummate their forbidden affair. In this respect, May's athletic

vitality clearly poses a castrating threat to her ultimately powerless husband. She is the Moby Dick to Archer's Ahab: just as the dismasted captain is tormented by the white whale's impenetrable mask, so Archer fears the possibility that May's "'niceness'" is "only a negation, the curtain dropped before an emptiness" (178). His sharp-shooting wife exacerbates his anxieties by embodying the fearful prospect of castrated absence. Fearful that May could turn out to be just like "the Kentucky cave-fish, which had ceased to develop eyes because they had no use for them," Archer frantically wonders, "What if, when he had bidden May Welland to open hers, they could only look out blankly at blankness?" (72)

This blankness is, of course, simultaneously the source of May's power and Archer's dread. Like the potentially sham Cesnola antiquities, innocence represents both a point of pure historical origin and its possible contamination – the real thing and its menacing twin, the conniving impostor. For Wharton, this was a central liability of American identity. To be an American was to be denied the privilege of racial innocence. It was instead to trace one's beginnings back to the democratic, the hybrid, the plural and the indefinite. Indeed, if Wharton sought refuge in poiesis, that process by which, in Dana D. Nelson's words, "a self-directed emphasis on form is substituted for the uncertainties of a more open-ended interpersonal praxis," then her own changeful nation taught her otherwise (Nelson, "Representative/Democracy" 221). Wharton could no more tame the Leviathan than the Metropolitan Museum could authenticate, police or preserve the past.[2]

In her pained recognition that America lacked a stable source of genealogical, racial or national origin, Wharton confronted "the messy, ongoing political work of democracy" (Nelson and Castronovo, "Introduction" 10). The democratic texture of American life was, for Wharton, a repressed but dynamic source of literary creativity. Democracy disputed the orderly mandates of aesthetic theory by insisting instead on its own ungainly diversity. Henry Adams observed as much in 1918: "Society in America [is] always trying, almost as blindly as an earthworm, to realize and understand itself; to catch up with its own head, and to twist about in search of its tail" (*Education* 237). Such circuitous ambiguity became readily apparent to Wharton in the wake of her extra-marital affair with Morton Fullerton. A sexual liaison that was as common as it was unmanageable, the affair gave Wharton a newfound appreciation for the variable, the unexpected and the mundane. As Chris Castiglia has argued in another context, adulterous passion not only can disrupt domestic tranquility, but also can, in certain circumstances, pose a challenge to the notion of "abstract national allegiance" (Castiglia 209). "In putting our trust in a government that promises us the unity and harmony that actual people challenge," Castiglia asserts, "we become increasingly willing to sacrifice our local loyalties to abstract national allegiance. Looked at in this way, commitments are the death not just of trust but of democracy" (211). In defying such commitments for the first time in her life, Wharton experienced, with new immediacy, both the promise and the peril of American democracy, a finding that found its fullest expression in *The Reef.*

In the years following World War I, the stylized virginal aesthetics that had been at the core of Wharton's first big literary success, *The House of Mirth*, came to seem impractical at best, and dangerous at worst. By the 1930s, the combination of decadence, aestheticism and eugenics that had so captivated turn-of-the-century elites had begun to bear poisonous fruit.[3] The rise of Hitler in Germany and Mussolini in Italy amazed an aging Wharton, who found it hard to believe that the world could suddenly find itself "at the mercy of two madmen" (qtd. in Bauer 202, n.7). From her point of observation in southern France, it was increasingly clear that the world's precarious future was no longer contingent on unkempt electorates, but was instead at the whim of powerful new dictators. Her 1920 travel narrative, *In Morocco*, begins to register this shift. Here as elsewhere, she criticizes the "disconcertingly free and familiar" exchanges between "prince and beggar, vizier and serf" (130). Wharton, however, is less concerned with these alliances *per se*, than she is with their obvious disingenuousness. "[N]othing is as democratic in appearance," she comments, "as a society of which the whole structure hangs on the whim of one man" (130).

Indeed, as Wharton watched the turbulent blood-rite of the Hamadchas, a religious sect in Moulay Idriss whose members ritually flagellated themselves to commemorate the death of a seventeenth-century saint, she focused her attention on one man: a "tall grave personage in a doge-like cap . . . the only calm figure in the tumult" (*In Morocco* 55). As his frenzied followers dance about in pools of their own blood, the mysterious central leader remains impassive, quietly "regulating the dance, stimulating the frenzy, or calming some devotee who had broken the ranks and lay tossing and foaming on the stones" (55). Despite or perhaps *because* of his sober appearance, this man was, for Wharton, the most menacing of all: "There was something far more sinister in this passionless figure, holding his hand on the key that let loose such crazy forces, than in the poor central whirligig who merely set the rhythm of the convulsions" (55–6). The power to produce this wild state of "cataleptic anæsthesia," or numbed consciousness, struck Wharton as particularly sinister (54). The passionless figure was, in effect, a provocateur who could inspire brutality while himself remaining unmoved by the violence he stimulated.[4]

Wharton's uneasiness with the stoic priest registers her growing mistrust of disinterestedness as a response to political trauma. As Susan Buck-Morss has observed in her analysis of the complex relationship between "aesthetics and anaesthetics" in the work of Walter Benjamin, by the late nineteenth century aesthetics had begun to shift "from a cognitive mode of being 'in touch' with reality to a way of blocking out reality" (18). The phantasmagoria of modern "technoaesthetics," evidenced in the visually dazzling displays at the World Fairs and the glittering shopping arcades of Paris and New York, had begun to "alter consciousness, much like a drug" (Buck-Morss 22). Sensory surfeit, Buck-Morss remarks, anesthetized "the organism, not through numbing, but through flooding the senses," making a "narcotic out of reality itself" (22). When a population is anesthetized against physical and moral pain, "Sensory addiction to a compensatory reality becomes a means of social control" (23).

Despite her early compassion for Lily Bart, the chloral-addicted heroine of *The House of Mirth*, Wharton grew increasingly disillusioned with anesthesia as a response to modern experience. In *Twilight Sleep*, her 1927 novel, she begins to correlate medical anesthesia with political apathy. Unlike Lily, whose narcotic habit becomes its own form of political agency, connecting her to the "mighty sum of human striving" (319), *Twilight Sleep*'s insouciant flapper, Lita Wyant, is as indifferent to global suffering as she is to the doomed fish she keeps in her huge aquarium: "'Why shouldn't the Bolivians have earthquakes if they chose to live in Bolivia?'" she flippantly asks (*Twilight Sleep* 7). This casual disregard, Wharton implies, is of a piece with Lita's personal aversion to pain and consequent reliance on anesthetics. The novel, in fact, takes its title from the analgesic, Twilight Sleep, whose use enables Lita to drift "into motherhood as lightly and unperceivingly as if the wax doll which suddenly appeared in the cradle had been brought there in one of the big bunches of hot-houses roses that she found every morning on her pillow" (14). Unlike Lily, the singular hothouse specimen who dies with a hallucinated working-class infant in her arms, Lita's experience of parturition is so alienating that her own child seems to her little more than an artificial doll, and childbirth itself, like the perfunctory gift of roses, "something to be turned out in series like Fords" (15).

Lita's experience seems to support Walter Benjamin's claim that "Comfort isolates . . . it brings those enjoying it closer to mechanization" (Benjamin 174). "[H]alf-dancing, half-drifting," she is a member of a volatile generation who demands "a more personal outlet" for its impulsive energies – "drinking and drugging," or other, more "insidious form[s] of time killing" (32, 5, 14). The novel's repeated attacks on "popular ways of reducing cultural conflict and contradiction – Freud, drugs, Oriental thought . . . alcohol, twilight sleep, golf" that Dale Bauer has observed (Bauer 101), underscore Wharton's well-placed fear that intellectual indolence will lead the lost generation to accept the irrational answers of despots and dictators.

By the mid-1930s, tranquilizing modes of escapism seemed to pose a menacing alternative to the passionate rigors of direct, democratic engagement. Ultimately, Wharton became convinced that in democracy's inconclusiveness lay the promise of America's future. Although her own early accounts of high-minded aristocrats, martyred debutantes and dormant Yankees had explored any number of ways to master the colossus of American democracy, she recognized that such strategies were ultimately unsustainable. "The world is a welter and has always been one," she wrote in 1934, "but though all the cranks and the theorists cannot master the old floundering monster, or force it for long into any of their neat plans of readjustment, here and there a saint or genius suddenly sends a little ray through the fog, and helps humanity to stumble on, and perhaps up" (*Backward Glance* 379).

Notes

INTRODUCTION

1. Michaels, *Our America* 8. For recent exceptions to this trend, see my discussion of the work of Wegener, Elizabeth Ammons, Judith Sensibar and Hildegard Hoeller in chapter 2.
2. See Eliot's 1918 review of *Summer* and Pound's correspondence with Margaret Anderson.

1 INVADERS AND ABORIGINES

1. New York City's slave population grew nearly 25 percent in the wake of the economic boom of the 1790s. The number of white households that relied on some form of black labor tripled over the course of the late eighteenth century (Burrows and Wallace 347). Those who prospered most (merchants, professionals and investors) devoted a significant proportion of their newfound wealth to the purchase of slaves (S. White 35). As William Strickland, an English traveler, casually remarked after a 1794 visit to New York, "Most of the inferior labor of the town is performed by Blacks" (qtd. in Burrows and Wallace 347).
2. Rumors about Wharton's own paternity may have contributed to her persistent fascination with American origins. Some speculated that Edith Jones was actually the child of an adulterous liaison between Lucretia Rhinelander Jones and her sons' English tutor. Others whispered that the youngest Jones child was the result of an illicit dalliance between Wharton's mother and a Scottish lord. Although Wharton only learned of these rumors later in her life, she took them seriously enough to conduct an abortive search for the tutor who, by that time, was long since dead (Benstock 11). Ogden Codman Jr., Wharton's co-author for *The Decoration of Houses* (1897), added a dash of frontier romance to these well-circulated rumors by suggesting that the Jones tutor had been killed fighting at Little Bighorn (Benstock 8). While Shari Benstock, Wharton's most recent biographer, reads these rumors as intentional slights to the "haughty Mrs. Jones" (10), R. W. B. Lewis dismisses these legends as both apocryphal and trivial. Wharton's "troubled moments had to do with her *role* rather than her *origins*," Lewis insists; "at no time does she strike one as in the least

troubled about the very sources of her existence" (537). Wharton did, in fact, have profound questions about her origins. The rumors' potent blend of paternal mystery and frontier violence may have contributed substantially to Wharton's sense of her own share in American hybridity.

3. *Letters* 57–8. As Shirley E. Thompson acknowledges, "Creole" is, at best, "a chameleon of a term." In antebellum New Orleans, only those with Revolutionary-period French ancestors were considered Creoles. After an influx of Haitian immigrants in the early nineteenth century, however, the category expanded to include immigrants from the French colonies, including Haiti. Despite the fact that "writers and historians of New Orleans racialized the term" after the Civil War, claiming "that only 'pure whites' could be called 'Creoles,'" Wharton evidently had the earlier, more racially diverse meaning in mind (see Thompson 259, n.2).

4. *Valley* 2: 298. Odo is the first in a long line of Wharton's weak male protagonists who fail to live up to the standards of her otherwise strong women. Elizabeth Ammons points out that Wharton "always had difficulty granting anything approaching full humanity to her male characters, and only a few achieve empathetic complexity" (*Edith Wharton's Argument* 14). Curiously, Ammons singles out Odo as an exception to the rule: he is, for her, "a male protagonist for whom we can feel sympathy and admiration" (18).

5. For a full discussion of the relationship between sexuality and democratic politics, see chapter 4.

6. *Valley* 1: 30. Dana D. Nelson is one of several scholars who have analyzed the correlation between homosexuality and radical democracy. Drawing on the work of Michael Moon, Christopher Newfield and Julie Ellison, she explains that "'homosexuality' was conceptualized [in the early American republic] as a kind of radical equality, a mob equivalent, a de-individualizing sameness, a dangerous construction of democracy that threatened to emerge from the ranks of the citizens" (*National Manhood* 187).

7. Wharton struggled to avoid this worrisome individualism in the form of the novel as well. Fearing that some readers would be put off by *The Valley*'s bookish antiquarianism, she told Sally Norton that she had wanted the narrative "to be a picture of a social phase, not of two people's individual history" (*Letters* 57).

8. *Valley* 2: 216. Fulvia's martyrdom crucially prefigures the sacrificial pose of Lily Bart in *The House of Mirth*. See chapter 2.

9. *Valley* 2: 279. By performing an overdetermined tableau of national uniformity, militarism unites the disparate classes into a common brotherhood. Wharton applauded the average Frenchman's willingness to put private interests aside in order to serve the national good during World War I. At a wartime rally in Paris, she rapturously observed how

> [t]hese people, only two days ago, had been leading a thousand different lives, in indifference or in antagonism to each other, as alien as enemies across a frontier: now workers and idlers, thieves, beggars, saints, poets, drabs and sharpers, genuine people and showy shams, were all bumping up against each other in an instinctive community of emotion.

The "people," luckily, predominated; the faces of workers look best in such a crowd, and there were thousands of them, each illuminated and singled out by its magnesium-flash of passion. (*Fighting France* 16–17)

Divested of their individual needs, the people become a homogenous corps committed to serving the French cause.

10. Herman 180. Norton and Wharton, of course, were not alone in this opinion. According to Henry Seidel Canby, Old New York's decadent torpor signaled "the decline and fall of [the] second American aristocracy" (6). While late nineteenth-century Yankees "remembered the responsibility of [their] American ancestors," they nevertheless "accepted none for [themselves]" (6). The Civil War's pluralist transformations had stripped them of their belief that "the American had the same springs of civilization as the European" (Hugh Smith). "Too many of the old stock were killed in the Civil War," Wharton's friend, John Hugh Smith, speculated in 1936. "[I]n the years of the great economic development which followed, the American working class was smothered by the peasants of Eastern Europe and the middle class poisoned by a plague of Jews." Wharton had been wise to abandon a country so dramatically transformed, Hugh Smith concluded. In her adopted land, Wharton was "one of the last, perhaps the last, of the American emigres" (Hugh Smith).

11. *Valley* 2: 303. From their hotel window in central Paris in 1848, Wharton's parents witnessed "the flight of Louis Philippe and Queen Marie Amélie across the Tuileries gardens" (*Backward Glance* 19). Their royalist sympathies were clear. As George Frederic Jones, Wharton's father, wrote in a travel journal that Wharton later had transcribed into a typescript, "a change in the appearance of things" had taken place: "not as much refinement as before – everything too democratic and republican" (Jones 65).

12. The term "Knickerbocker" refers to the descendents of New York's Dutch settlers. The name was derived from Diedrich Knickerbocker, the fictitious Dutch "author" of Washington Irving's 1809 *History of New York*. Knickerbockers were knee breeches worn by Dutch settlers.

13. On the turn-of-the-century ethnographic display of Native Americans, see Fogelson, Corbey, Meyn and D. H. Thomas.

14. On the Woodcraft Indians, see Deloria and Mechling. For an analysis of Indian play in secret societies, see Dilworth. Wharton's maternal great-grandfather, Ebenezer Stevens, was supposed to have taken part in the famous incident in Boston harbor. Although he later claimed that "'none of the party was painted as Indians, nor, that I know of, disguised,'" he later admitted "(. . . a trifle casuistically)" that "'some of them stopped at a paint-shop on the way and daubed their faces with paint'" (*Backward Glance* 12).

15. Nelson, *National Manhood* 67. For an interesting example of Indian play in the service of oppositional or counter-hegemonic politics, see George Lipsitz's discussion of the Mardi Gras Indians in New Orleans.

16. Deloria 100–1; see also R. Green 30. As the new nation's only source of aboriginality and its simultaneous obstacle on the road to conquest, Native Americans were a site of considerable ambivalence. For a discussion of this anxiety, see Scheckel and Bergland.

17. *Custom* 88. The Pure Water Move represents a curious inversion of ancestral logic. While Ralph associates his highest aspirations with the seaside cave that he once explored as a boy – "a secret inaccessible place with glaucous lights, mysterious murmurs, and a single shaft of communication with the sky" that inspires him "to know what the great people had thought, think about their thinking, and then launch his own boat" – water, for the Spraggs, is a sign of duplicity (*Custom* 46). Undine's family grows wealthy at the expense of their antecedents. After losing two children to typhoid fever, Abner E. Spragg vows "on his children's graves that no Apex child should ever again drink poisoned water" (49). He then proceeds to swindle his own father-in-law out of a valuable piece of land, however, thereby cementing "the occult connection between [his] domestic misfortunes and his business triumph" (49). In the next generation, Elmer Moffatt repeats the process, blackmailing Spragg into betraying his former Pure Water Move partner. The ex-son-in-law's actions underscore the corrupt nature of the original deal: both the "Pure" Water Move and Undine's prior elopement are evidence of a virginal site that has turned out to be impure.

18. *French Ways* 80. Wharton was not insensible to the potential excesses of national insularity. In "The Last Asset," a 1908 short story, she describes a Faubourg St. Germain clan whose members are each "stamped with the same air of somewhat dowdy distinction, the air of having had their thinking done for them for so long that they could no longer perform the act individually" (*The Hermit and the Wild Woman* 101). Similarly, in *The Custom of the Country*, Ralph rejects the socially appropriate Harriet Ray, who is "sealed up tight in the vacuum of inherited opinion, where not a breath of fresh sensation could get at her" (*Custom* 50).

19. On this point, Wharton disagreed with Theodore Roosevelt, who saw the frontier as the crucible of racial awareness. Roosevelt considered the Indian so entirely "alien and antipathetic by 'blood'" to white Americans that he thought frontier interbreeding impossible (Slotkin 622). Emulation, not amalgamation, the center of the President's model. In America, white people had to learn to fight "less like the over-civilized British regulars" than like "their deadly [aboriginal] foes" (Slotkin 623). Combat would not 'Indianize' the settlers; on the contrary, frontier skirmishes would reconnect the pioneer with his own ancestral bellicosity. "[T]he Indians' strengths brought out the full measure of white power" (Slotkin 623).

20. *French Ways* 81. Similar ambivalence informs Wharton's theory of landscape architecture. Although she famously modeled her own western Massachusetts gardens on European outdoor designs, she criticizes the Englishmen who "have colonized in such numbers the slopes above the Arno" for altering Florence's "old [Italian] gardens" and introducing "alien vegetation in those which have been partly preserved" (*Italian Villas and Their Gardens* 21, 22). The English had effectively robbed the Florentine landscape of its indigenous glory.

21. *House* 71. Lawrence W. Levine's claim that turn-of-the-century upper-class Americans wanted a "culture free of intrusion, free of dilution, free of the insistent demands of the people and the marketplace; culture that would

ennoble, elevate, purify; culture that would provide refuge from the turmoil," supports not only Selden's vision in *The House of Mirth*, but also Wharton's vision of the Land of Letters (Levine 206).

22. *Backward Glance* 210. Despite its French origins, Wharton had little patience with broad patriotic monuments like the Statue of Liberty. Compared with the intimate beauty of an ancestral villa near La Panne, where "dead faiths have come to life," America's "statue of a goddess with a torch, designated as 'Liberty enlightening the World,'" was "pompous." "It seems as though the title on her pedestal might well, for the time, be transferred to the lintel of that villa in the dunes" (*Fighting France* 177–8).

23. Conn 8. Wharton's fetish for order is well known: in a scribbled list of her "ruling passions," she ranked "Justice – Order" first ("My ruling passions"). R. W. B. Lewis, citing Wharton's notebooks, slightly misquotes this item in his elegant 1975 biography. Rather than "Justice – Order," Lewis has "Justice *and* Order" (see Lewis, *Edith Wharton* 160, *my italics*). While this is a minor discrepancy, Lewis's version implies that Wharton saw justice and order as two separate ideas. By eliding "Justice – Order," however, Wharton implies that the two concepts are, in fact, interchangeable. Just as justice has little meaning outside of a pre-existing system of order, so order enables genealogically competent citizens to demonstrate their own civility and thus lead by example. By contrast, disorderly societies, according to Wharton, are always inherently unjust.

24. See chapter 2.

25. Wallace Nutting, a Colonial Revival entrepreneur, similarly associated architectural ornamentation with national decline. Without a "sense of permanence and strength," Nutting insisted, there was no way to avoid "the shingled candle extinguishers and the gimcrack ornaments, which are placed on dwellings." Domestic gewgaws were agitating distractions that interfered with the larger project of "blending of color, form and material." "Unless there is repose in a man's nature," Nutting remarked, "reposeful architecture will not result" (288–9).

26. Wharton, *Letters* 45; *Uncollected* 155. For an excellent analysis of Wharton's imperialism, see Wegener, "Rabid."

2 "THE REAL LILY BART"

1. The Progressive era bears out Thomas Gossett's observation that the ambiguity of the notion of race "made it a powerful tool for the most diverse purposes" (117–18). While nativists, nationalists and racists grounded campaigns for immigration restriction, segregation and imperialism in the spurious claims of eugenicists, the Supreme Court's "separate but equal" ruling in *Plessy v. Ferguson* (1896) vested hermeneutic authority in the vagaries of local "custom," forcing New Negro intellectuals to formalize, however problematically, a "representative" African American (see Higham; Solomon, "The Intellectual Background"; Sundquist 233–49; Gates).

2. These concerns were by no means confined to the upper classes. Fearing immigrant competition, Populists descried "imported pauperized labor" in their 1892 platform, and deplored the horrors of mob rule in Ignatius Donneley's *Caesar's Column* (1891; Hofstadter 66–70). The rhetoric of race suicide, moreover, pitted native middle- and working-class Americans against their seemingly more prolific immigrant peers (Gordon 136–58).

3. What Wharton and Taine saw as matters of racial inheritance now seem to be little more than questions of literary influence. Taine's explication of Chaucer's "racial heritage," for example, turns on nothing more than traces of French courtly romance and the English tradition of common sense (Gossett 200). For an alternative consideration of Taine's impact on Wharton, see Joslin, *Edith Wharton* 40–2.

4. While conceding that dark complexions often presage "something 'bad'" in Wharton's writings (Rohrbach 102), both MacMaster and Rohrbach are sanguine about Wharton's treatment of race. MacMaster defends the "fine sense of irony and . . . good eye for the cultural construction of identity" that enable Wharton to "record some of the complexities of American identity where race, gender, and class intersect" (202). Rohrbach, in turn, finds Wharton in quest of a new mode of identity, "not one defined by an ideology of race legislating sameness, but one that accommodates difference" (113).

5. Despairing of America's "gros public," Wharton in 1903 located the patriciate's evolutionary dilemma in the hothouse: "We are the wretched exotics produced in a European glass-house, the most déplacé & useless class on earth!" (*Letters* 84). While clearly overstating the elite's socio-economic vulnerability, Wharton nonetheless imagined the glasshouse as a Europeanized alternative to the United States – at once patrician breeding ground and decadent refuge from the country's emerging identity as the "house of mirth."

6. I have confined my analysis to writers most pertinent to the formation of Wharton's intellectual perspectives. For further discussion of American decadence, see Auchard, Herman, Hoopes and S. Williams.

7. Qtd. in Ellis 26. For Wharton on Gautier, see "The Eyes" 338, *Uncollected* 191 and *Backward Glance* 330.

8. Wharton champions this "artificial–natural" aesthetic in *Italian Villas and Their Gardens* (1904), where Italy's "frank artifice" outstrips England's "laboured naturalism" by unabashedly replacing nature's "deficiencies . . . repetitions . . . meannesses and profusions" with a "fixed smile of perennial loveliness" (205, 206).

9. Such concerns have a long history in Wharton criticism. Recent examples include Michaels (*Gold Standard*), Dimock, Showalter and Kaplan.

10. The notion of a pristine Knickerbocker past was, of course, itself factitious. Wharton recalled a complex pecking order in which New Yorkers of middle-class ancestry were distinguished from those with authentically aristocratic genealogies (*Backward Glance* 10).

11. In an 1896 letter to the *Newport Daily News*, Wharton chided "puerile" disciples of the Colonial Revival for their pretentiously "original" mansions

(*Uncollected* 56). "'Colonial' architecture," she insisted, was "simply a modest copy of Georgian models'" (*Decoration of Houses* 81–2). Displacing American originality by displacing American origins, Wharton urged a return to the nation's European roots.

12. *Decoration of Houses* 187. Wharton returned to this connection again in 1908, blaming the "chaos of ornament" marring a French church on the ethnically "strange fellowship" of Flemish, Lombard, German and Spanish artisans who had contributed to its "deluge of detail." Such "profusion – and confusion" of nationalities flouted Wharton's racialized aesthetic of "artistic unity" (*Motor-Flight* 151–2).

13. *Decoration of Houses* 186. In this sense, the stifling home of Lily's aunt, Mrs. Peniston, underscores patrician decline. Aunt Julia's unseemly replica of the Louvre's "Dying Gladiator" (*House* 98), her "ormulu clock" (made of a copper alloy imitating gold), and her derivative "steel engravings of an anecdotic character" all contradict the precepts inculcated in *The Decoration of Houses* (110).

14. While Wharton's critique of sham advances what I am suggesting is a conservative agenda, her conclusions were by no means inevitable. Gustav Stickley, influential proponent of the Arts and Crafts style, advocated a strikingly similar aesthetic. According to Stickley, however, "closer contact with real things, with real work, with real life" would reconnect Americans to "the common needs of the common people" (qtd. in Orvell 161–2).

15. Wharton embraced twentieth-century technology only in so far as it enhanced personal privacy (see chapter 3). Her beloved "motor-car," for instance, liberated her "from all the compulsions and contacts of the railway" (*Motor-Flight* 1).

16. *Motor-Flight* 154. The association between "personality" and racial singularity is evident in Wharton's 1908 description of French visitors to a Paris *salon*: "the angles of difference have been so rubbed down that personalities are as hard to differentiate as in a group of Orientals" (*Motor-Flight* 188). While "personality" was not the exclusive domain of the well born, its "slow but continuous growth" did require "space" – a "larger . . . symphonic plan" generally contingent upon affluence (*Writing of Fiction* 48). Indeed if "type" found refuge in the "temporary shelter" of the short story, "personality" thrived in the "slowly built-up monument" of the novel (*Writing of Fiction* 75, 50).

17. William E. Moddelmog argues that Wharton rejected a property-owning model of personality in favor of the "boundlessness" of depersonalization (353). I am suggesting, however, that because Wharton's model of selfhood was fundamentally racial – grounded, that is, in the invisible and the inaccessible – such unmarketable boundlessness is entirely compatible with the Whartonian personality.

18. Rosedale's threatening alliance with his employee, the char-woman Mrs. Haffen (who shares his propensity for blackmail), personifies the double

blow to the American patriciate – *nouveau riche* wealth fueled by intrusive working-class labor. As Hoeller has shown, Rosedale's ascent is less a comment on his own personal gumption than it is on elite complacency – a complacency that, in admitting the Jewish financier, guarantees Old New York's demise: "When Rosedale is increasingly incorporated into the upper class of New York, Wharton implies that we will distance ourselves from that class" (20).

19. Wharton regretted the democratization of museums in the age of mass-tourism. She sharply criticized the "museumised aspect" of Europe's ancient shrines, valuing only those sites that looked "like the house of a great collector who still lives among his treasures" (*Motor-Flight* 150, 154). Merging museum with ancestral home, Wharton reveals her paradoxical desire to preserve the privacy of patrician exclusivity while publicly exhibiting racial distinction.

    The Whartonian museum monastically conforms to Selden's "republic of the spirit," a place free from "everything – from money, from poverty, from ease and anxiety, from all the material accidents" (68). Lily's reply that Selden's republic is really "a close corporation" in fact echoes the well-publicized comments of Louis di Cesnola, the director of the Metropolitan Museum, who, in 1897, ejected a plumber in overalls from the gallery. The museum, Cesnola famously remarked, was "a closed corporation" entitled to regulate conduct within its walls (see Levine 185–6).

20. It is important to draw a clear distinction here between Lily's point of view and Wharton's own. While Lily's erratic behavior in Part II is symptomatic of her growing desperation (she consents to marry a Jew, struggles to trim hats, and becomes addicted to drugs), Wharton, by contrast, approached her work with a cool and definite purpose. As she reports in *A Backward Glance*, once she knew that the novel's heroine was Lily Bart, "the tale rushed on toward its climax" (207). "What that climax was to be I had known before I began. My last page is always latent in my first" (208). Thus although Lily is "no pure, dedicated spiritual pilgrim," in Carol Singley's wonderfully understated words, she *is* Wharton's sacrificial lamb, a complex martyr "destined to die for principles that her self-absorbed, ignorant 'well-wishers' fail to recognize or honor" (Singley, *Edith Wharton* 76, 81).

21. *Education* 387. As the traditional attribute of the Virgin in Christian iconography, the lily symbolizes whiteness, purity and immortality (see Whittlesey 217–18; J. Hall 192–3). Its conventional association with the Annunciation, moreover, speaks to what Wharton, in an 1891 sonnet, described as the Madonna's "strange presentiment" of "the Light's terrible eclipse." This "foreboding pain," paired with the Virgin's ultimate assurance that "He also rose again," mirrors the dynamic of sacrifice and salvation in *The House of Mirth* ("Botticelli's Madonna" 74).

22. *House* 35; Hanson 48. The word functions here as a curiously decadent palimpsest of aestheticized gospel. Bourget's oft-quoted definition of decadent style – the book is sacrificed to the page, the page to the sentence, and the

sentence to the "independence of the word" – thus gains numinous resonance in Wharton's novel (Calinescu 170). Lily's ecstatic renunciations at the end of her life, moreover, bear a striking resemblance to Wharton's ancient hermits in *Italian Backgrounds*: "from the strife of the circus factions and the incredible vices and treacheries of civilized life, the disenchanted Christian, aghast at the more than pagan corruption of a converted world, fled into the waste places to wear out his life in penance. The horrors he left behind surpassed anything the desert could show" (66–7). On monasticism and decadence, see Hanson 218–28.

3 "A CLOSE CORPORATION"

1. H. James, letter to Edith Wharton, 24 November 1907. While James ostensibly disliked the novel, he was jealous of its possible success. In "The Velvet Glove" (1909), a princess writes a novel entitled "The Top of the Tree" and requests a publicity "puff" from John Berridge, an established author. Berridge, however, thinks that the princess is seducing him, and only later finds out that he is humiliatingly wrong. For a full discussion of this connection, see Tintner and Blackall.
2. *Backward Glance* 198. Examples of Wharton's erotic plant imagery include "Beatrice Palmato" and *Summer* 34–5.
3. Wharton had recently done business with the Knickerbocker Trust. In a diary entry from February 1906, she reports selling her holdings in the Consolidated Exchange to the Trust for an undisclosed amount (Diary 1906).
4. For a detailed account of the Knickerbocker Trust Panic of 1907, see Sobel 297–321.
5. Wharton was not only one of the first American women to own and drive a "motor-car," but was also witness to the first airplane tests in France. She purchased a typewriter, moreover, soon after it had been marketed, and was delighted to see *The House of Mirth* adapted into a six-reel film (R. W. B. Lewis 6–7).
6. As Adams recalls in *The Education*: "He had entered a supersensual world, in which he could measure nothing except by chance collisions of movements imperceptible to his senses, perhaps even imperceptible to his instruments, but perceptible to each other, and so to some known ray at the end of the scale" (380, 381–2). While both Seltzer and Michaels (*The Gold Standard*) examine the issue of chance in *The House of Mirth*, I am interested in how Adams's "chance collisions" reveal what Alan Trachtenberg identifies as "a source of severe anxiety prevalent among middle- and upper-class Americans, that of impending chaos, the rule of accident, exigency, and rampant city mobs" (48). That such seemingly random forces "defied regulation" is precisely the troubling dynamic that preoccupies the discourse of technology and class in *The Fruit of the Tree*.
7. Joan Copjec explores this imbrication in her analysis of early twentieth-century psychiatry. Whereas in the nineteenth century the mind was considered a

sovereign served by an otherwise useless body, in the twentieth century it was newly reconceived by psychiatrists as a mechanized "instrument with a function," an active "worker" facilitating the Darwinian struggle for survival. According to Copjec, this blurred delineation between the mental and the mechanical signals an irremediable loss:

> The traumatic collision of the concepts of man and machine robbed man of a little bit of his existence, and technology, I would suggest, came to be symbolized as the embodiment of the very impossibility of man's complete identity. Technology incarnated the limit of man not merely because of its role in actual events, but – in a more primary way – because it interfered with man's comprehension of himself. (77)

8. *Fruit* 11. Interestingly enough, between the time that *The Fruit of the Tree* appeared serially in *Scribner's Magazine* and its eventual publication in book form in 1907, Wharton received a corrective letter from one Mr. C. Greene, a Rhode Island cotton mill worker. Greene pointed out that Wharton had mistakenly confused a "carder" with a "card" in the novel's opening sequence. According to Greene, "a 'carder' is a man not a machine. The machine itself is a card. Consequently 'bent perfunctorily above a carder' calls up a ridiculous picture. If one asked for the carder, he would mean the overseer of the carding department" (letter to Edith Wharton, February 11, 1907). In thematizing the confusion between man and machine, Wharton herself had inadvertently fallen into her own trap.
9. Shoshana Felman gives a similar reading of the "pocket" in her analysis of Balzac's "La Fille aux yeux d'or" (see Felman 24–5).
10. Mr. Palmato's name itself – "palm"-ato – suggests additional connections between the hand and the phallus.
11. "The House of the Dead Hand" 149. Barbara A. White reaches similar conclusions in her examination of the incestuous subtext of "The House of the Dead Hand" (see White 6–7).
12. In "Friends," a short story published in 1904, Wharton reveals her dismay at the dense overpopulation of working-class communities. In the industrial New England town of Sailport, "Nowhere is there the least peep of green, the smallest open space that spring may use as a sign-board; even in the outlying districts, where cottages and tenements are being 'run up' for the increasing population of labouring men and operatives, the patches of ground between the houses are not gardens, but waste spaces strewn with nameless refuse" (193–4). Like the "nameless refuse" that crowds out the natural "sign-board," machines and the mass-produced people who operate them threaten to compromise the writer's authentic project.
13. My reading departs from that of Katherine Joslin, who argues that *The Fruit of the Tree* privileges the "middle-class professional" over the "working-class laborer" and "the upper-class owner," neither of whom has "the expertise to craft social, economic, and political reform" ("Architectonic" 72). As I am suggesting, however, the seemingly middle-class reformers in the novel are, in fact, genteel elites whose motives are not altogether altruistic.

14. Qtd. in Rothman 103. Charlotte Perkins Gilman, the feminist activist, took a more cynical view of what she termed "that pretty fiction about 'the traces of a woman's hand'" reified in conservative thought. "We imagine that a woman – any woman – just because she is a woman, has an artistic touch, an æsthetic sense, by means of which she can cure ugliness as kings were supposed to cure scrofula, by the laying on of hands," Gilman sarcastically observed in 1903. "There are women in our farm-houses – women who painfully strive to produce beauty in many forms; crocheted, knitted, crazy-quilted, sewed together, stuck together, . . . made – of all awful things – of the hair of the dead! Here are traces of a woman's hand beyond dispute, but is it beauty?" (Gilman, *The Home* 53, 54).

15. *Fruit* 421. The title of Barbara Melosh's provocative study, *"The Physician's Hand": Work Culture and Conflict in American Nursing*, refers to three aspects of nursing. First, the "physician's hand" underscores not only the nurse's subordinate position in relation to the doctor, but also "the nurse's critical role in executing the physician's work." Second, the phrase aligns nursing with manual skills and "direct involvement with the sick." Finally, the title registers the struggle of American nurses to gain professional autonomy, independent of doctors. As the "physician's hand," the nurse is often treated as a mere biomechanical extension of the doctor's will (a prosthetic device of sorts). Wharton's Dr. Wyant thus compliments Justine "as the surgeon might commend a fine instrument fashioned for his use" (424). But as Melosh insists, the nurse is anything but a tool: instead, she or he is an active caretaker who physically tends to the patient's body. Nurses, in fact, are decisive agents who "have never been content to define their work solely in relation to doctors. Both in professional associations and on the job, nurses have sought to claim and defend their own sphere of legitimate authority. Leaders called it professional autonomy; nurses on the job might well have named it workers' control" (6–7).

16. The class-based ramifications of Wharton's idealized representation of hands becomes clear when compared to the more brutal descriptions of her naturalist peers. In *Sister Carrie* (1900), for example, Theodore Dreiser describes his heroine's excruciating discomfort as she finishes her first shift at a Chicago shoe-making factory: "Her hands began to ache at the wrists and then in the fingers, and toward the last she seemed one mass of dull complaining muscles, fixed in an eternal position and performing a single mechanical movement which became more and more distasteful until at last it was absolutely nauseating" (38–9). Similarly, Upton Sinclair emphasizes the expendability of hands (both corporeal and metonymic) in *The Jungle*. In one particularly gory description of the meat-packers' pickle rooms, he recounts how the hands of the beef-boners and trimmers "would have no nails – they had worn them off pulling hides; their knuckles were swollen so that their fingers spread out like a fan." Those who handle sheep pelts treated with acid, moreover, are forced to "pull out this wool with their bare hands, till the acid had eaten their fingers off" (87). Such accounts make Wharton's recital of Dillon's accident seem tepid indeed.

17. Bessy Amherst miscarries a son, thus eliminating the possibility that an alternative heir will disrupt the linearity of Westmore family succession.

18. A prescient Lily Bart, in *The House of Mirth*, recognizes that Selden's "republic of the spirit" is no republic at all. Instead, "It is a close corporation, and you create arbitrary objections in order to keep people out" (71). Corporate thinking, she realizes, rejects artificiality and "social shabbiness" in favor of an inheritance-based, authentic genealogical elite (70).

19. Defining a trust as "an artificial creature not wholly responsible to or controlled by any legislation, either by State or nation, and not subject to the jurisdiction of any one court," Theodore Roosevelt insisted in 1902 that such "artificial, and very powerful corporate beings" demanded oversight by a "governmental sovereign . . . the National Government" ("The Control of Corporations" 65–6). Roosevelt's language, pitting "artificial creatures" against "sovereigns," sets up the confrontation that Wharton takes up in *The Fruit of the Tree* between the prostheticized body and the integrated oligarchic body. Both Roosevelt and Wharton implicitly advocate corporate authority based on inborn "sovereignty" rather than man-made power.

20. Stephen 188. See also "Condemnation of Euthanasia" 510 and Herzog.

21. Wharton, *Backward Glance* 127. Wharton closely followed the aging scholar's work, and visited the Nortons' country home frequently during this period. In her memoirs, she called Norton "an awakener": "Every word he spoke, every question he asked, was like a signal pointing to the next height" (*Backward Glance* 154 and 155).

22. *Fruit* 418–19. As Mark Seltzer points out in his analysis of the "statistical persons" that populate the fiction of Stephen Crane, "One finds in . . . late nineteenth-century realism generally, something like a passion for cases, in several senses, and for case histories." Seltzer adds in an endnote that his formulation works "In several senses, because the word 'case' derives from and remains linked to 'casus' or fall; and the fallen man, the prostrate body, is the paradigmatic case of falling ill or out of luck" (Seltzer 106 and 207, n.27). It is worth noting, however, that elsewhere in his important book *Bodies and Machines*, Seltzer appears to contradict this position. Earlier in his analysis, he argues that the shift from realism to naturalism is marked by a shift "from histories of marriage and adultery to case histories of bodies, sexualities, and populations." The effort to distinguish realism from naturalism along these particular lines is thus rendered somewhat moot. See Seltzer 43.

23. *House* 319. For a fuller discussion of this subject, see chapter 1.

24. Wharton seems to draw a subtle class distinction between those who produce drugs and those who consume them. In *The Custom of the Country*, the déclassé Leota B. Spragg recounts how Undine's grandfather "opened a drug-store" after trying his hand first as an undertaker and then as a minister (*Custom* 48). Wharton connects the sale of drugs, once again, to familial rupture. As Leota recalls, her father later "got speculating in land out at Apex, and somehow everything went – though Mr Spragg did all he *could* –" (48). Beholden to his unscrupulous son-in-law, who swindles the older man out of some valuable

land, the former druggist fades ingloriously out of the picture. While the strategic consumption of drugs is frequently a mark of class privilege in much of Wharton's work, the sale or abuse of drugs is usually a sign of class inferiority. For a discussion of class and drug use among Victorian women, see Haller and Haller 271–303.

25. Wharton was compulsively attentive to the mechanics of publication. After reading the galleys of *The Fruit of the Tree*, she scribbled a postcard to William Crary Brownell at Scribner's objecting to the spacing of the ellipses. "I have returned proofs with an urgent marginal note & a diagram. *Please* reinforce by a few remarks, & show them *any* French novel!" (*Letters* 116). After *The Fruit of the Tree* was published, she grumbled that critics had faulted the novel's structure. "[T]hat rather discouraged me," she wrote to Robert Grant. "After all, one knows one's weak points so well, that it's rather bewildering to have the critics overlook them & invent others that (one is fairly sure) don't exist – or exist in a less measure" (*Letters* 124). Wharton's inability to control how her texts were read clearly irked her, as evidenced by the querulous peace she reaches in *A Backward Glance* (1934):

I made up my mind long ago that it is foolish and illogical to resent so puerile a form of criticism. If one has sought the publicity of print, and sold one's wares in the open market, one has sold to the purchasers the right to think what they choose about one's books; and the novelist's best safeguard is to put out of his mind the quality of the praise or blame bestowed on him by reviewers and readers, and to write only for that dispassionate and ironic critic who dwells within the breast. (212).

Notably, Wharton sees the dynamics of personal agency and the forces of a market economy as inextricably interwoven.

4 THE AGE OF EXPERIENCE

1. *Reef* 308. Both Wharton and Anna belittle the politicized figure of the New Woman. Sophy's declaration that "I'm all for self-development and the chance to live one's life. I'm awfully modern, you know" meets with genteel scorn: Anna later dismisses "The stuff that awful women rave about on platforms" (60, 280). For Wharton, the New Woman epitomized the emerging *parvenu* spirit of modern America. By pursuing a college education, a professional work identity and broader political rights, the New Woman had become a socially mobile representative of Progressive-era meritocracy (see Smith-Rosenberg 245–7). For a fuller discussion of Wharton's attitudes toward Progressive-era reform, see chapter 5.

2. See Epstein 123; Alexander 18; Peiss, and Lunbeck 535. To an anxious American public unsettled by rapid industrial and cultural change, the working woman's sexuality was fearfully manifest in the figure of the prostitute. As Ruth M. Alexander has pointed out, prostitution represented "in especially stark terms the tragic consequences of rampant commercialization, unchecked immigration, and unrestrained industrial exploitation" (37). The "white slavery" panic,

which hit its frantic peak around 1913, made it seem as though every white American girl was vulnerable to what one contemporary film luridly called "The Traffic in Souls." "Any girl, it seemed, who said hello to a stranger in a large city was likely to be pricked with a poisoned needle and spirited away" (May 343).

3. "Sex O'Clock" 113. In 1911, the Progressive-era activist Rheta Childe Dorr protested the practice of arresting so-called "wayward girls": "To dispose of an erring girl by ostracising her is exactly as dangerous as to dispose of typhoid-fever germs by throwing them into a public reservoir. The revenge the outcast girl reaps upon society is far more terrible than an epidemic of typhoid" (70). Wayward girls like Sophy Viner posed a viral threat to society as a whole.

4. See chapter 2.

5. *Reef* 17. As Amy Kaplan has pointed out, "the gaping mob in *The House of Mirth* threatens the power of the elite by entrapping them in its gaze, in their own dependence on publicity" (90). When Lily's father abruptly announces his financial ruin, Mrs. Hudson Bart immediately sends the butler away, who withdraws "with an air of silent disapproval" (32). More significantly, Mrs. Haffen, the charwoman at Selden's apartment-house, can bribe Lily with purloined love letters only because she is the *Benedict*'s eyes and ears. When Lily passes Mrs. Haffen on the stairwell, the charwoman "looked up curiously . . . and continued to stare as Miss Bart swept by . . . Lily felt herself flushing under the look. What did the creature suppose?" (13, 14). When the cleaning woman's undercover information eventually reaches Rosedale, the *Benedict*'s owner, we realize that espionage is common among workers and their parvenu employers. As the Jewish financier boasts, "Getting on to things is a mighty useful accomplishment in business, and I've simply extended it to my private affairs" (258). *The House of Mirth*'s vulnerable spectacle of class privilege is further destabilized in *The Reef*, where the elite find themselves aping working-class freedoms in morals and manners (see Lunbeck 537).

6. *Reef* 17. Such turnabouts register complex social changes. The "sensation of being seen" unsettles those accustomed to power, Sartre remarks in *Black Orpheus*, "For the white man has enjoyed for three thousand years the privilege of seeing without being seen" (qtd. in Doane 223).

7. *Reef* 35. On using the body as a disguise, see Doane 26.

8. *Reef* 252. Wharton frequently parodied the phallic assumptions that underwrote artistic production. In the 1908 short story "The Verdict," she evaluates the work of Jack Gisburn, a "fashionable" New York artist whose decision to paint a portrait of his wife produces a "picture [that] was one of Jack's 'strongest,' as his admirers would have put it – it represented, on his part, a swelling of muscles, a congesting of veins, a balancing, straddling and straining that reminded one of the circus-clown's efforts to lift a feather" (*The Hermit and the Wild Woman* 201).

9. As Richard A. Kaye has observed, Wharton depicts Sophy as "an androgynous *gamine*" (877). Her "boyish" appearance delights Darrow, to whom she is "less a sexually alluring female than an abstracted carnal temptation" (878). While

Sophy's androgyny may underscore the indeterminacy of Darrow's own sexual proclivities, it seems equally likely that her flapper-like boyishness serves to mark the gendered element of her overall cultural hybridity (see Kaye 876–7).

10. Wharton admired the ability of the poet Eugene Lee-Hamilton to write through what she called a "mysterious illness, presumably of nervous origin, which . . . kept him for over twenty years stretched on the low-wheeled couch – 'hybrid of rack and of Procrustes' bed'" (*Uncollected* 116). Prior to his death in 1907, Lee-Hamilton, the half-brother of Vernon Lee, found "increasing strength to bear his pain, and increasing consolation, in the very sensitiveness to imaginative reactions that had once been the cause of his intensest misery" (*Uncollected* 117).

11. Repplier 780. The debate over the social efficacy of pain reached its apex in the period between 1905 and 1912. Pain proponents argued that only suffering could grant real knowledge. In the 1907 poem "Pain," Margaret Steele Anderson rapturously wrote that "no man lives but quails before you – Pain! / And no man lives that learns to love your rod." Nevertheless, she concludes,

> You work a mystery. When you are done
> Lo, common living turns to heavenly bliss,
> Lo, the mere light is as the noonday sun!
>   (Anderson 117)

While critics countered that "it is better to teach humanity to know as much as it can happily and not to come at necessary truths through pain," it was William James who made the most lasting contribution when he identified the class assumptions that underwrote the strenuous life ("Suffering versus Training" 6). Those who valorized pain, he argued in his 1911 essay "The Moral Equivalent of War," were often those who were least likely to suffer it as a matter of course. "But that so many men, by mere accidents of birth and opportunity, should have a life of *nothing else* but toil and pain and hardness and inferiority imposed upon them . . . *this* is capable of arousing indignation in reflective minds" (1291). Surely, he argued, there must be a way to "preserve in the midst of a pacific civilization the manly virtues" without sacrificing morality (1291).

12. Throughout her career, Wharton insisted that writing could manage the conflicts "between the social order and individual appetites" (*Writing of Fiction* 14). Disinterestedness was the key. In 1925, she remarked that the "creative imagination" could achieve "an all-around view . . . only by mounting to a height; and that height, in art, is proportioned to the artist's power of detaching one part of his imagination from the particular problem in which the rest is steeped" (*Writing of Fiction* 15–16).

13. Santayana, "Genteel" 359. Pragmatism's "hard teachings" clearly appealed to the neurasthenic sensibility, whose "tender-minded" rationalism could be cured by the "tough-minded" elixir of experience (see W. James *Pragmatism* 13; see also Lutz 87). Americans suffered from "over-tension and jerkiness and breathlessness and intensity and agony of expression" because they devoted themselves to

high-minded, abstract "principles," William James argued in 1899 ("Gospel" 503). For overwrought New Englanders, James had this advice: "*Unclamp . . . your intellectual and practical machinery and let it run free*" ("Gospel" 505). "[S]ociety is refreshing . . . wherever people forget their scruples and take the brakes off their hearts and let their tongues wag as automatically and irresponsibly as they will" ("Gospel" 506).

14. Santayana, "Genteel" 380. Interestingly, Santayana's retreat to the mind had personal implications for Morton Fullerton, the philosopher's Class of 1886 Harvard College classmate. In her unconventional biography of Fullerton, Marion Mainwaring notes that Fullerton is notably absent from Santayana's later autobiographical accounts, this despite the fact that Santayana had modeled his womanizing Mario after Fullerton in *The Last Puritan* (1936). In avoiding even the most oblique reference to Fullerton in his later memoirs, however, Santayana, by Mainwaring's lights, betrayed the depths of his own animus. Either Fullerton had committed some "unstated offence" against his classmate, or the former bisexual lothario reminded his gay friend too much of "a long-past, less guarded self" better left forgotten (Mainwaring 268). In either case, Santayana's act of historical erasure served as a "snub absolute," and put an end to the two men's friendship (267).

15. Luckily, France had anticipated these possibilities. Unlike either the United States or Morocco, the French sanctioned extra-marital sexuality, thereby forging a sensible détente between the body's individual needs and the state's collective duties. "[T]hey allow it, frankly and amply, the part it furtively and shabbily, but no less ubiquitously, plays in Puritan societies" (*French Ways* 132).

16. *Reef* 304. Anna refers to "On Mercy," an essay written in 55 CE by the Stoic philosopher Seneca for the then 18-year-old emperor Nero. In urging the young monarch to exercise "wise moderation" when dispensing punishment, Seneca imagined the emperor as the restraining ego to the popular id (365). Just as "the whole body is the servant of the mind," he argued, so the "vast throng, encircling the life of one man, is ruled by his spirit, guided by his reason, and would crush and cripple itself with its own power if it were not upheld by wisdom" (367–9). Spectacles of retribution "show a state in how great a majority evil men are," just as injudicious punishment shows children "the way to the deed" (421). Seneca thus rejects the "proposal . . . once made to the senate to distinguish slaves from free men by their dress" (421). "[I]t . . . became apparent how great would be the impending danger if our slaves should begin to count our number . . . Numerous executions are not less discreditable to a prince than are numerous funerals to a physician" (421, 423).

17. Lears, *No Place of Grace* 118, 119. As Frank Lentricchia notes, the patrician fascination with the arduous regimes of the working class was ironic: "[t]o get in touch with their bodies was not exactly the desire of the immigrants who . . . became the backbone of our working class – [and who,] among other things . . . dug the subway tunnels of New York" (Lentricchia 794–5).

18. *Reef* 308. Wharton's words mirror those of Frederick Jackson Turner, another turn-of-the-century intellectual who celebrated the common man because the latter "had little patience with finely drawn distinctions or scruples of method" (Turner 292).

19. *Reef* 294. On Henry Osborne Taylor, see Wharton, *Letters* 257.

20. In a 1918 letter to an aspiring poet-soldier, Wharton insisted that it was not enough "to feel . . . ; poetry is an art as exact & arduous as playing the violin, or sculpture or painting . . . It takes a great deal of the deepest kind of culture to write one little poem" (*Letters* 411). Literary production demanded painful endeavor.

21. *Reef* 351. Despite her fleshiness, Laura is plainly artificial: the "immense powder-puff" on her bed reveals her dependence on the same cosmetics that Anna found "distinctly disagreeable" on Sophy (350; see 225). In *The Reef,* cosmetics pose a dangerous threat to aristocratic authenticity. Lady Ulrica, Darrow's old amour, is reportedly "false from head to foot." When "touch[ing] up" after tennis, the pseudo-aristocrat "took apart like a puzzle." As Sophy scandalously remarks, it was impossible to believe that Lady Ulrica was sleeping with Darrow "because I know she'd never dare un – [undress]" (18).

22. *Reef* 141. By situating *The Reef* in the hallowed corridors of a French manor, Wharton can exploit the incongruity generated by such a juxtaposition. Givré's "quiet rooms, so full of a fastidious taste" only emphasize the unruliness of their American inhabitants. As Owen tells Anna, he wants "to make it grin from wing to wing. I've a mad desire to say outrageous things to it – haven't you? After all, in old times there must have been living people here!'" (101). Fiercely resisting the possibility of being made "an adjunct of Givré," Owen declares that he "want[s] to get out of it, into a life that's big and ugly and struggling" (139–40). As I will suggest in chapter 5, Wharton takes up the conflict between the "old home" and the individual appetites of its inhabitants in *Summer.*

5 CHARITY BEGINS AT HOME

1. A generation of Wharton critics have, quite intuitively, read *Summer*'s incest plot as a sinister patriarchal trap of *Ethan Frome*ian doom. Most famously, Elizabeth Ammons concluded that "the final union" between Charity and lawyer Royall is "not merely depressing: it is sick." The 1917 novel, Ammons argues, is "Wharton's bluntest criticism of the patriarchal sexual economy" (*Edith Wharton's Argument* 133). Sandra Gilbert and Kathleen Pfeiffer agree. For Gilbert, Charity's marriage serves as a prime example of patriarchy's insidious ability to stifle a daughter's "natural" desires for lover/brother, mother and self by eroticizing the father (371). *Summer,* Pfeiffer maintains, "reverberates with strong feminist anger." Charity's growing intimacy with Royall marks the heroine's "evolving failure" and "her willing abdication of independence and autonomy" (152, 147). As Gloria Ehrlich concludes, the novel's "joyless union" between father and daughter marks Charity's "final defeat": trapped

in an "oedipal fantasy" in which her father is her only option, the Mountain girl surrenders to the "grim fatality" of her incestuous doom (126, 131). Despite the persuasiveness of these discerning readings, their reassuring implications threaten to obscure what I see as the radical conservatism of Wharton's vision. As Cynthia Griffin Wolff observed in 1977, "Why must society be so repressive? Because at the very core of social organization, within the innermost circle of the family itself, there lurks such attractive temptation" (308).

2. *Fighting France* 58. With the notable exceptions of Judith Sensibar and Alan Price, many critics have been misled, I think, by Wharton's propagandist tone in *Fighting France*, and her pro-militarist stance in both *The Marne* (1918) and *A Son at the Front* (1923). Jean Bethke Elshtain, for example, insists that Wharton had little conception of "war's realities." "Men 'fall' – they are not killed . . . It is all very pleasant, antiseptic; wounds are clean; the end is swift and merciful" (217). David Lundberg likewise faults Wharton and other women writers for supporting a war in which they did not directly participate. Wharton, he argues, hides "the true nature of fighting in France beneath a haze of romantic prose" (380). While women's exclusion from combat is true enough, such analyses rely on a far too limited conception of "war" – one that reifies the opposition between home front and battlefield. As Helen M. Cooper, Adrienne Auslander Munich and Susan Merrill Squier remind us,

[This] dualistic structure is emphatically at variance with facts of war in the modern era that was inaugurated by women's incursion with Florence Nightingale into battlefield nursing. The increasing toll of civilian casualties during the two world wars destroys the myth that in war men fight to protect their women, who remain secure at home caring for their children. Historically, women's new roles as war workers, ambulance drivers, soldiers, and terrorists, as well as victims of total war, put to rest the notion of inherently peaceable women, inherently warlike men. (16)

Wharton certainly would have agreed: the Great War, she felt, had fundamentally dismantled such binary oppositions, wreaking havoc in both the domestic and military arenas.

Recent feminist reassessments of women's wartime roles underscore Wharton's point. Margaret R. Higonnet, for instance, contends that women writers have generally responded differently to war. Unlike men, they tend to see the family as an integral part of military conflict: "From the male author's perspective, the family seems insulated from conflict; from that of the female author, political discourse and familial order lie on a continuum. Significantly, men rather than women construe the family as a depoliticized idyllic terrain" (93).

3. In *The Custom of the Country* (1913), Undine de Chelles' crude publicity offends her ex-husband's genteel reserve in much the same way that the roofless house insulted Wharton's sense of privacy. Ralph Marvell learns of his wife's remarriage only by reading the Sunday papers: "NEW YORK BEAUTY WEDS FRENCH NOBLEMAN" (*Custom* 243). Below the "hated headline," he finds the story "in all its long-drawn horror – an 'interview' – an 'interview' of Undine's about

her coming marriage! . . . Her confidences filled the greater part of a column" (243). Wharton deplored such violations of privacy. After the death of her young friend Ronald Simmons in 1918, she told Sara Norton that she knew "of one of our dear young war-friends, a young officer who died suddenly of Spanish grippe at Marseilles, & whose poor mother in America learned of his death only through the newspapers!" (letter, Oct. 5, [19]18).

4. See chapter 4.

5. *Backward Glance* 13, 14. Wharton's identification with Stevens is also clear in her unfinished manuscript, "The Happy Isles." As the aging Revolutionary general Mark Inwood, Stevens is "a man of the new age in spite of his conservative dress. A man who had passed through two Revolutions, had seen everything that his youth believed in and thought immutable shattered like glass and tossed to the winds like rubbish" (1–2).

6. See Hobsbawm. From its vaulted gallery and oak-paneled library, to its Louis XVI-style chairs, the Mount fully participated in the filiopietistic logic of the Colonial Revival (see Benstock 130–1). Its deliberately derivative architecture was, to borrow the words of Harvey Green, the "fabrication of the urban mind generations away from the rural reality" (Green 16). The sense of historical rupture produced by the era's spinning dynamos, soaring skyscrapers and teeming tenements had forced panicked conservatives to seek refuge in the architecture of their colonial past. In an country where "the latest new grain-elevator or office building is the only monument that receives homage from the surrounding architecture," as Wharton derisively put it, the Colonial Revival's imitative aesthetics seamlessly gave way to the essentialist demands of "colonial survival" (*Motor-Flight* 32; Betsky 266; see also Green).

   In this regard, the Mount dramatically materialized the hierarchical underpinnings of turn-of-the-century "culture." "[T]rue culture" in this period was "culture free of intrusion, free of dilution, free of the insistent demands of the people and the marketplace, culture that would ennoble, elevate, purify; culture that would provide a refuge from the turmoil, the feelings of alienation, the sense of impotence that were becoming all too common" (Levine 206). Like Lawrence Selden's "republic of the spirit" in *The House of Mirth* (1905), the Mount was a place apart – a place rich in "country cares and joys . . . the companionship of a few dear friends, and the freedom from trivial obligations" (*Backward Glance* 125).

7. Qtd. in Levine 202. Olmstead's desire for "the greatest possible contrast with the streets and the shops and the rooms of the town which will be consistent with convenience and the preservation of good order and neatness" matched Wharton's own view of the ideal suburban escape (qtd. in Levine 202). Writing in 1905 from Biltmore House, George Vanderbilt's expansive North Carolina estate, Wharton praised Olmstead's "divine landscape," which stood in marked contrast to "the horrors of the thrice-loathsome New York" (*Letters* 100). "Alas," she wrote Sara Norton, "that it is so far from everything, & that beyond the park, as James said, there is only 'a vast niggery wilderness'" (*Letters* 101). Both Biltmore House and the Mount expressed a central patrician fantasy: elite

citadels, they were designed to protect their inhabitants from the racial and class indeterminacies proliferating just beyond "the park."

8. Baltzell 118; Lindgren 7. In reality, seventeenth-century New England was home to a diverse population of Native Americans, English settlers, Africans and others, all of whom lived in close contact. The historical record notwithstanding, the "preserved past" of the late nineteenth century envisioned a land solely occupied by the "homogenized Yankee" (Lindgren 12).

9. Wendell, "Democracy" 166. In a 1913 letter from his Portsmouth, New Hampshire summer residence, Wendell told Wharton about his own "pleasant brick old home which has been in the family for a hundred years or so. The things in it – furniture, china, glass, what-not – have never been dispersed, and there are countless unimportant old papers, interesting to me because by and by they revive what little past we know in America, as little else can. So I plunge back into olden times." Wendell had evidently found a correspondent sympathetic to "this old New England." As he remarks elsewhere in the same letter, "I have always thought of you as among the few friends to whom one might turn newly should the time ever come when friendship calls for test" (letter, June 14, 1913).

10. Rollins, "New" 535. Rollins's campaign had its detractors. In 1928, Henry Bailey Stevens challenged the widespread shibboleth that summer tourists were to be "the very saviors of New England" (108). It was dangerous to think that "it is not cows we should milk but city people," he argued. "[O]ur urban friends, in relation to the soil itself, are largely parasitic," and "feeding upon their unproductiveness" would only encourage native apathy and dependence (108).

11. Rollins, "Renaissance" 70. Unbeknownst to the region's future visitors, Rollins was also fighting a rearguard campaign against his farmers' complacency. "Make your place attractive," he urged New Hampshire's agriculturalists; "pull down old, rattletrap buildings; paint the barn; straighten the fence" ("New" 539).

12. Morgan 582. Domestic and robust, these healthy country women were seen as a winsome antidote to Anglo-Saxon racial decline (see H. Green 21 and Gordon 137–42). As Harvey Green observes, the image of New England women as "nurturers of the children of the republic and keepers of the home," had a key role within Colonial Revival logic (21). The wholesome country maiden figured prominently in Old Home Week pageantry. As promoter Ralph Davol asked incredulously in 1914, "Should the pageant, as an expression of community ideals, exalt the denatured feminist who sniffs at responsibilities of home as a light and airy fiction, or should the pageant throw the weight of its influence to uphold the sweetness, charm, and sanctity of the home, on which America was founded and has been preserved?" (qtd. in Marling 200). In *Summer*, Charity's virginal appearance at Old Home Week – "third in the white muslin file" – forms a visual counterweight to the period's preoccupation with the "Anglo-Saxon woman's physiological 'decline'" (*Summer* 123; Green 21). Indeed, despite the minister's invocation of "the piety and purity of this group of innocent girls," Charity is, in fact, pregnant and eventually

faints (129). Manifestly fertile, she personifies both the sweet seductions and the reproductive possibilities of a revived New England.

13. The preferred comparison of the period was to Johnson's "Happy Valley" (Buell 311). Wharton herself borrowed the metaphor in 1901. After visiting Sara Norton and her father at their Massachusetts summer home, she regretted how "flat & commonplace" everything else looked by comparison. "The happy valley seems so far off already! Was it only yesterday we were picking our way through the blueberries & pignola and moonwort to the top of High Pastures?" (letter to Sara Norton, July 15 [1901]).

14. *Backward Glance* 294. Recent examples include Campbell, Marchand and Waid. For an opposing analysis of Wharton's recuperation of the sentimental, see Hoeller, *Edith Wharton's Dialogue*.

15. See D. Campbell 271.

16. *Summer* 55. Wharton valued these colonial details. In "Mother Earth," an unfinished story from the period, she lovingly describes the "family relics" found in a traditional New England home: "the crayon portraits, the silhouettes, the sallow samplers in little black frames, the rosewood what-nots garnished with shells & tea-cups, & the fire-screen worked by a great-aunt who had been a friend of Hawthorne," all of these were "records of what Mr. Edes sometimes called 'an historic past'" ("Mother Earth").

17. Like Alida, who is determined to purge her room of cheap decorations, Country Life reformers urged rural citizens to embrace "the stately beauty of the antique New England fashions, fashions little valued to-day in the country, and destined, unless redeemed by distinct effort, to pass away." "[H]ouses . . . adorned mainly with bad lithographs and crude advertisements," Rollin Lynde Hartt noted, would hardly attract tourists. New Englanders should instead follow the tasteful examples of their city-dwelling friends, who studiously shunned the "hideously ugly." Without proper guidance, rural inhabitants would transform their "grand old homesteads . . . into frightful Queen Anne abominations," trading their "quaint antique furniture" for "modern jig-saw monstrosities" (580).

18. Wharton admired Bernard Berenson's "great working library" at the Villa I Tatti in Settignano, Italy. Berenson's collection was "not a dusty mausoleum of dead authors but a glorious assemblage of eternally living ones." Like a garden, the library had been "continually weeded out and renewed," making it a "book-worm's heaven" (*Backward Glance* 327).

19. *Summer* 7. For Wharton, this was a potent combination. She recalled "a secret ecstasy of communion" during her "enraptured sessions" within her father's cozy library (*Backward Glance* 69–70). Speculating that her mother's "matter-of-factness must have shrivelled up any . . . buds of fancy" in George Frederic Jones, whose "stifled cravings" for poetry and art made him a frustrated and "lonely [man . . .] haunted by something always unexpressed and unattained," Wharton sought out the "secret wood" of her father's library as a child (*Backward* 39, 70). Luxuriating on the Turkish rug, she would experience near-amatory rapture as she read her father's books (70). Years later, after she had acquired "a little library of [her] own," Wharton understood Jones's isolation

all the more. Her own library, she remarked, similarly filled an affective void: as "the realms of gold swung wide . . . from that day to this I don't believe I was ever again . . . wholly lonely or unhappy" (*Backward Glance* 70, 71).

20. Currier 389. Harney's tour of old homes resembles the famous New England pilgrimage of architects McKim, Mead and White in 1877. Their journey, which "has assumed the status of the quest for the neocolonial grail" in Karal Ann Marling's colorful phrase, was at the time as much a flight from "the irregular, the untidy, and the grotesquely picturesque" as it was a search for architectural inspiration. The trip left the trio with a newfound appreciation for "a kind of classicism, a lost purity of shape, a hierarchical orderliness of form and design attached to colonial models" (Marling 88–9). The Mount's second architect, Francis L. V. Hoppin, had worked for McKim, Mead and White and shared Wharton's conviction that architecture should, in Judith Fryer's words, express "a sense of *order*" and "long-standing social traditions" (73).

21. *Summer* 113. A 1910 sonnet included in Wharton's secret love diary to Morton Fullerton describes the gothic, feminized allure of the decaying New England homestead:

> My soul is like a house that dwellers nigh
> Can see no light in. "Ah, poor house," they say,
> "Long since its owners died or went their way.
> Thick ivy-loops the rust door-latch tie,
> The chimney rises cold against the sky,
> And flowers turned weed down the bare paths decay . . ."
> Yet one stray passer, at the shut of day,
> Sees a light tremble in a casement high.
>
> Even so, my soul will set a light for you,
> A light invisible to all beside,
> As though a lover's ghost should yearn & glide
> From pane to pane, to let the flame shine through.
> Yet enter not, lest as it flit ahead,
> You see the hand that carries it is dead.
> ("The Life Apart")

Here, the feminized New England dwelling incarnates unrealized but ardent sexual potential. A haunted patrician birthplace, it awaits erotic renewal.

22. Gloria Ehrlich speculates that Royall himself is Charity's biological father and that "[b]y introducing this ambiguity," Wharton "fudges the incest issue, allowing readers to entertain the more piquant possibility of real incest while neutralizing it through the technicality of adoption." Either way, Ehrlich concedes, "the story is incestuous" (130).

23. Wharton had long been fascinated with Beatrice Cenci. A miniature of the Cenci appears in Lily Bart's room in Mrs. Peniston's house, and a full portrait overhangs Kate Clephane's guilty bed in *The Mother's Recompense* (1925).

24. Some would argue it was personal as well. Barbara A. White has gone so far as to suggest that Wharton was herself the victim of childhood incest. While I share Ehrlich's mistrust of the speculative nature of psychobiography, I am equally

troubled by the political implications of this move toward the biographical (see Ehrlich 182, n.30). Such approaches risk essentializing Wharton's deployment of incest by implying that, as a woman writer, she must have experienced trauma in order to write about it. While critics rarely, if ever, rely on Faulkner's childhood experiences to explain *The Sound and the Fury* or *Absalom, Absalom!*, the biographical approach in Wharton criticism is frequent. I think that it is important, however, that we see incest first and foremost as a deliberate *political* strategy in Wharton's writings, one that plays a pivotal role in her broader conservative critique.

25. *Summer* 16, 76, 124. Wharton's coy suggestion that "old man Royall" is the center of the story – "Of course, *he's* the book!" – has long puzzled critics (Wharton, *Letters* 398; see R. W. B. Lewis 397 and Benstock 328). At once father and husband, honored citizen and shameful debauchee, political patriot and incestuous peril, Royall is the site simultaneously of meaningful ancestry and of regal entitlement. He is named after Royall Tyler, the husband of Wharton's energetic wartime co-worker, Elisina, and an accomplished art historian of New England blue-blood descent. The man Bernard Berenson considered "the most attractive and finished and cultivated person of his age," Tyler could trace his genealogy to the noted eighteenth-century American playwright for whom he was named (qtd. in R. W. B. Lewis 372). In this sense, he was as "royal" as Americans come. The simultaneous embodiment of literary accomplishment, elite taste and genealogical distinction, Tyler underscores lawyer Royall's conservative role in *Summer's* drama of racial recuperation.

26. *Summer* 126. Royall shares the "long orator's jaw" of his own hero, Daniel Webster (21). Like the Old Home Week speaker, Webster had famously hailed New Englanders in 1843 with words calculated to unite all assembled in a common clan: "Welcome kindred names, with kindred blood!" Webster greeted celebrants at the completion of the Bunker Hill Monument. "Wherever else you may be strangers, here you are all at home . . . You come hither with a glorious ancestry of liberty" (Webster 140).

27. *French Ways* 102. Wharton's objection to women's higher education emanated from this critique. Women's colleges, she charged, had spawned a "'monstrous regiment' of . . . emancipated young women taught by their elders to despise the kitchen and the linen room, and to substitute the acquiring of University degrees for the more complex art of civilized living" (*Backward Glance* 60). Such statements, of course, must be taken with considerable irony. Wharton's nostalgia for "that ancient curriculum of house-keeping" was not a longing for the hands-on labor of actual housework, but instead a hunger for the racialized hierarchy that structured the patrician home of her youth (60). In *A Backward Glance*, she romantically recalls "our two famous negro cooks, Mary Johnson and Susan Minneman" who presided over her mother's kitchen and created "succulent repasts" with their "indefatigable blue-nailed hands" (*Backward Glance* 58–9). Secure in the knowledge that "the Dark Ladies" were laboring behind the scenes to create "my mother's big dinners," both the *gourmet* and the political traditionalist could "lean back in his chair and murmur 'Fate

cannot harm me'" (60, 59). In terms at once culinary and racial, Wharton nostalgically recalls such "long-lost day[s], when cream was cream and butter butter and coffee coffee" (59).

28. *Motor-Flight* 29. Mary V. Marchand discerningly identifies Wharton's "tendency to stigmatize low- and middlebrow tastes as feminine" by focusing on Wharton's class position. Like many other cultural elites, Wharton conflated "the political demands of [Progressive-era] activists with the undisciplined feminine tastes linked to the spread of middle- and lowbrow culture" (371, 374).

29. See MacMaster 192. Leslie J. Reagan points out that most Americans associated abortion, midwifery and prostitution with one another, because all were seen as promoting female sexual deviance (Reagan 99–100). Alarm at "the soaring incidence" of abortions in the United States among "married, native-born, Protestant women, frequently of middle- or upper-class status" only reinforced the widespread perception that abortion was a gendered and racial weapon in a larger demographic war (Mohr 86; see also Walkowitz 387; Petchesky 82). "Both contraception and abortion were associated by a male, upper-middle-class, WASP medical profession with obscenity, lewdness, sex, and worst of all, rebellious women," Rosalind Pollack Petchesky agrees (82). "Regular physicians" looked askance at "female doctors," midwives and abortionists, who were seen as serving the reproductive needs of immigrants and the poor (82). Wharton thus links Dr. Merkle to racial difference, class indeterminacy, the black-market economy and feminine autonomy. The abortionist's scurrilous efforts to blackmail Charity at the end of the novel reinforce her alienation from the more straightforward *quid pro quo* economy associated with the novel's men. Inflating the cost of Charity's visit by a factor of eight, Merkle represents the deviance, excess and indeterminacy of female enterprise.

30. Bauer 42–3. Although I am primarily concerned here with the European context, it is important to emphasize abortion's synchretic resonance in the novel. As Wharton no doubt knew, by the 1870s, a significant proportion of the New York abortionists who had been arrested were Germans – principally German Jews (Mohr 92). In 1869, George Ellington alleged that the majority of the city's "female abortionists" were "of foreign birth or extraction," many formerly "first-class nurses – in Germany, especially" (qtd. in Mohr 92–3).

31. By the end of World War I, these apprehensions had reached fever pitch. In 1920, France passed one of Europe's most draconian anti-contraception and abortion laws.

32. Wharton wearily apologized to her publisher, Charles Scribner, for her inability to complete the *kunstleroman* "Literature" which she had begun before the war: "In the first relief from war anxieties I thought it might be possible to shake off the question which is tormenting all novelists at present: 'Did the adventures related in this book happen before the war or did it happen since?' with the resulting difficulty that, if it happened before the war, I seem to have forgotten how people felt and what their point of view was" (*Letters* 425). The war had left her dry. "I can't talk or think of anything else," she told Robert Grant

in 1914. "Who *can*, who thinks at all?" (letter, Aug. 13, 1914). It was almost as if the war had itself aborted her own creative work: "I had a really big novel in me (excuse the gynecological metaphor) a year ago," she told Berenson in 1915, "but things have killed it – one thing after another" (letter, Feb. 10, 1915). When she *was* able to resume work, the results were painfully revitalizing. As Elisina Tyler reported in an October 1916 letter to her husband, Wharton had "all the inconveniences of spiritual childbirth on her" as she finished *Summer*. "They are very like the physical. She reminds me of tales about women who catch hold of furniture to assist them in the final throes" (Tyler).

33. When the *New York Evening Post* failed to extol the many "good works" of Frederic Bronson in its April 1900 obituary, Wharton fired off a letter to the editor to set the record straight. A treasurer for the New York Life Insurance company, Bronson had served the city well. His numerous philanthropic contributions bore witness to "the intelligent use of leisure" (*Uncollected* 187). For Wharton, class hierarchy had a benevolent trickle-down effect: with time and resources at their disposal, members of the leisured class could spread a wealth of good works to society's less fortunate.

34. S. Lewis 140. According to Amy Dru Stanley, by the late nineteenth century, many philanthropists had abandoned the "antiquated world of paternal relations that were based on protection and dependence," and adopted instead a more urban "relation of contract" (1265, 1292). Wharton, among others, regretted this transformation, and sought to restore a genteel model of personal benevolence.

35. Again, the hillbilly community on the Mountain plays a cautionary role. Like the refugees displaced by war and the soldiers lost in the trenches, Wharton's mountaineers are a potentially volatile population. "Here were a houseful of women and children, yesterday engaged in a useful task and now aimlessly astray over the earth," she observed in *Fighting France* (157). Indeed, both No Man's Land and the Mountain weirdly fulfill Jacob Riis's ominous 1903 prediction: "Just remember that it is one of two things, a gun on the shoulder or stripes on the back, where the home interposes no barrier" (137–8). "Wipe out the home and the whole structure totters and falls" (13).

36. In this sense, Harney serves as Wharton's surrogate in the novel. Like the proprietor of the Mount, he is a cosmopolitan tourist who is in New England to "[hunt] up old houses" (10). He shares Wharton's distaste for "the dapper weather-tight castles . . . on which the arch-restorer has worked his will, reducing them to mere museum specimens, archeological toys, from which all the growths of time have been ruthlessly stripped!" and similarly marvels at "How much more eloquently [the] tottering stones tell their story" (*Motor-Flight* 26). Harney frequently pauses "enchanted before certain neglected and paintless houses, while others, refurbished and 'improved' by the local builder, did not arrest a glance" (*Summer* 10, 48–9). As Miss Hatchard proudly observes, Lucius "has such a feeling for the past that he has roused us all to a sense of our privileges" (111).

37. Qtd. in Becker 59. For a rich discussion of the friendly visitor, see Boyer 155–61.

38. *Summer* 23, 21. Were Charity to reject Harney's and Royall's combined beneficence, she might easily become a "charity girl" – a young woman during the
First World War who would go out with a man "in return for dinners, auto-
mobile rides or any present he may give her . . . She is usually promiscuous
and, therefore, usually diseased" (Additon 155). As William I. Thomas noted
in his 1923 study *The Unadjusted Girl: With Cases and Standpoint for Behavior
Analysis*, "Girls . . . who have 'fellows' tend to justify sexual intimacy . . . if the
man says he will marry if there are 'consequences,' if the relation is with only
one man, and not for money. These are called 'charity girls' by the professional
prostitutes." The slope, however, was a slippery one. "When the girl has had
some experience in sexual life she will multiply and commercialize her casual
relationships" (119).

6 CODA

1. Editorial, *New York Times*, May 14, 1881. As if to guarantee their singularity,
Cesnola reacted to the controversy by forbidding visitors from sketching or
copying the disputed statues. Wyatt Eaton, a teacher at Cooper Union and later
the founder of the American Society of Artists, complained that he had been
"ejected from the Metropolitan Museum of Art with unwarrantable rudeness"
after making a rough drawing (McFadden 195). Cesnola evidently displaced his
anxiety over the artifacts' authenticity on to those who attempted to copy the
copies.
2. To this recognition, Wharton's later novellas make grudging concessions. "False
Dawn," subtitled "*The Forties*," is the first of her four-part *Old New York*
cycle (1924) and articulates this understanding most clearly. By lampooning
Halston Raycie, a forerunner to Faulkner's Thomas Sutpen, Wharton brings
her critical eye to bear on the conservative convictions that had animated
the first half of her career. "The dream, the ambition, the passion of Mr.
Raycie's life, was . . . to found a Family," the narrator tells us. "He believed in
primogeniture, in heirlooms, in entailed estates, in all the ritual of the English
'landed' tradition" (*Old New York* 23). When Halston's heir, Lewis Raycie,
decides to marry the "small and black and skinny" Beatrice Kent, however, racial
heterogeneity disrupts the patriarch's exalted scheme of dynastic succession
(7). The narrative goes so far as to equate Lewis's determination to marry
the half-Italian Treeshy with his equally revolutionary decision to invest in a
collection of unknown Pre-Raphaelite paintings on the advice of an Englishman
he has befriended in Europe, one equally unknown John Ruskin. Both gestures
underscore the new world that Lewis embodies. Determined to dethrone "the
old Powers and Principalities, and [set] up these new names in their place," Lewis
becomes a representative of new blood – both genealogically and aesthetically
(49).
3. While it is important to remember, in Lutz Koepnick's words, that "neither
pre- nor postfascist societies entail structures of experience identical with those
that enabled fascist aestheticization to assume its ultimately catastrophic role"

(13), it is equally crucial that we acknowledge, as Molly Abel Travis has, that "fascism was not the alien or pathological Other; rather, fascism inhabited the home haunts" (177). As Umberto Eco reminds us, sometimes fascism can wear "plainclothes" (15). Erin G. Carlston, for example, has pointed out the "conjunctions between the Decadence (and aestheticism more generally), a particular strain of romantic Catholicism, and fascism . . . from the mid-nineteenth-century through the 1930s" (43), while Koepnick has observed fascism's ability to "recycle decadent notions of artistic practice so as to refashion politics as a space of authenticity and existential self-assertion" (3). Clearly, Hal Foster is correct in conceding that "any mention of fascism" creates the "nasty *frisson*" that only "the great antitype of twentieth-century modernism" can provoke (65). Nonetheless, I think it important to acknowledge that, for Wharton and others who dabbled in the genteel anti-Semitism of the day, fascism must have seemed what Susan Buck-Morss calls the "reflecting mirror [in which] we recognize ourselves" (41).

4. Wharton self-consciously appeals to her conceptions about race and aesthetics to anesthetize herself against the "bestial horror" of this "repulsive scene" (*In Morocco* 54). By imaging herself to be a spectator at a ballet, she endows the ritual with "a blessed air of unreality . . . In that unreal golden light the scene became merely symbolical: it was like one of those strange animal masks which the Middle Ages brought down from antiquity by way of the satyr-plays of Greece" (54–5). Assumptions about race and class likewise augment this inoculating effect. Wharton writes with evident relief that "Gradually . . . it became evident that many of the dancers simply rocked and howled without hacking themselves, and that most of the bleeding skulls and breasts belonged to Negroes" (56). Future research into this complex text may wish to consider how Wharton's anti-modern assumptions permit her to assume what T. J. Jackson Lears calls a "negative identity – a means of shoring up selfhood by disowning impulses" that one distrusts in oneself (*No Place of Grace* 108). In this case, classicism and racism simultaneously mirror and deflect the "cataleptic anæsthesia" of the dancing participants.

Bibliography

Adams, Brooks. *The Law of Civilization and Decay: An Essay on History*. New York: Macmillan, 1897.

Adams, Henry. *The Degradation of Democratic Dogma*. New York: Macmillan, 1919.

    The Education of Henry Adams. 1918. New York: Houghton Mifflin, 1973.

    The Letters of Henry Adams. Vol. 6. Eds. J. C. Levenson, Ernest Samuels, Charles Vandersee and Viola Hopkins Winner. Cambridge, MA: Harvard University Press, 1988. 6 vols.

Addams, Jane. *Twenty Years at Hull-House*. 1910. New York: Signet Classic, 1961.

Alexander, Ruth M. *The "Girl Problem": Female Sexual Delinquency in New York, 1900–1930*. Ithaca: Cornell University Press, 1995.

The American Heritage Dictionary of the English Language. Ed. William Morris. Boston: Houghton Mifflin, 1976.

Ammons, Elizabeth. "Edith Wharton and Race." *The Cambridge Companion to Edith Wharton*. Ed. Millicent Bell. Cambridge: Cambridge University Press, 1995. 68–86.

    Edith Wharton's Argument with America. Athens: University of Georgia Press, 1980.

Amory, Cleveland. *The Last Resorts*. New York: Grosset and Dunlap, 1952.

Anderson, Harriet. "Woman." *Atlantic Monthly* 110 (1912): 177–83.

Anderson, Margaret Steele. "Pain." *Century* (May 1907): 117.

Anderson, Thomas F. "Old Home Week in New England." *New England Magazine* (Aug. 1906): 673–85.

"Another Title for Di Cesnola." *New York Times* Dec. 22, 1883: 8.

Appleton, William Sumner. "Destruction and Preservation of Old Buildings in New England." *Art and Archeology* 8 (1919): 131–83.

Arnesen, Eric. "Whiteness and the Historians' Imagination." *International Labor and Working-Class History* 60 (2001): 3–32.

Auchard, John. *Silence in Henry James: The Heritage of Symbolism and Decadence*. University Park, PA: Pennsylvania State University Press, 1986.

Baltzell, E. Digby. *The Protestant Establishment: Aristocracy and Caste in America*. New York: Random House, 1964.

Barker-Benfield, G. J. *Horrors of the Half-Known Life: Male Attitudes Toward Women and Sexuality in Nineteenth-Century America*. 1976. New York: Routledge, 2000.

Baron, Dennis. *The English-Only Question: An Official Language for Americans?* New Haven: Yale University Press, 1990.

Barron, Hal S. *Those Who Stayed Behind: Rural Societies in Nineteenth-Century New England.* Cambridge: Cambridge University Press, 1984.

Bauer, Dale M. *Edith Wharton's Brave New Politics.* Madison: University of Wisconsin Press, 1994.

Beard, George M. *American Nervousness: Its Causes and Consequences.* New York: Putnam's, 1881.

Beard, Miriam. "Anti-Semitism – Product of Economic Myths." *Jews in a Gentile World.* Eds. Isacque Graeber and Steuart Britt. New York: Macmillan, 1942. 362–401.

Becker, Dorothy G. "Exit Lady Bountiful: The Volunteer and the Professional Social Worker." *Social Service Review* 38 (1964): 57–72.

Bederman, Gail. *Manliness and Civilization: A Cultural History of Gender and Race in the United States, 1880–1917.* Chicago: University of Chicago Press, 1995.

Bendixen, Alfred, ed. "Lewises Discuss the Letters: R. W. B. Lewis and Nancy Lewis on *The Letters of Edith Wharton*; Highlights from a Question and Answer Session." *Edith Wharton Newsletter* 6.1 (1989): 1, 4–5.

Benjamin, Walter. *Illuminations.* Ed. Hannah Arendt. Trans. Harry Zohn. 1936. New York: Schocken, 1968.

Benstock, Shari. *No Gifts from Chance: A Biography of Edith Wharton.* New York: Scribner's, 1994.

Bentley, Nancy. *The Ethnography of Manners: Hawthorne, James, Wharton.* Cambridge: Cambridge University Press, 1995.

Berenson, Bernard. *Aesthetics and History.* Garden City, NY: Doubleday, 1953.

Bergland, Renée L. *The National Uncanny: Indian Ghosts and American Subjects.* Hanover, NH: University Press of New England, 2000.

Berlant, Lauren. "Fantasies of Utopia in *The Blithedale Romance.*" *American Literary History* 1 (1989): 30–62.

Betsky, Celia. "Inside the Past: The Interior and the Colonial Revival in American Art and Literature, 1860–1914." *The Colonial Revival in America.* Ed. Alan Axelrod. New York: Norton, 1985. 241–77.

Biel, Steven. *Down with the Old Canoe: A Cultural History of the Titanic Disaster.* New York: Norton, 1997.

The Black Book of the War: German Atrocities in France and Belgium. London: The Daily Chronicle, 1915.

Blackall, Jean Frantz. "Henry and Edith: 'The Velvet Glove' as an 'In' Joke." *Henry James Review* 7.1 (1985): 21–5.

Blum, John Morton. *The Republican Roosevelt.* 1954. Cambridge, MA: Harvard University Press, 1981.

Boone, Joseph Allen. *Tradition Counter Tradition: Love and the Form of Fiction.* Chicago: University of Chicago Press, 1987.

Bowers, William L. *The Country Life Movement in America, 1900–1920.* Port Washington, NY: Kennikat, 1974.

Boyer, Paul. *Urban Masses and Moral Order in America, 1820–1920.* Cambridge, MA: Harvard University Press, 1978.

Brooks, Van Wyck. *New England: Indian Summer 1865–1915.* New York: E. P. Dutton, 1940.

Brown, Bill. "Science Fiction, the World's Fair, and the Prosthetics of Empire, 1910–1915." *Cultures of United States Imperialism.* Eds. Amy Kaplan and Donald E. Pease. Durham: Duke University Press, 1993. 129–63.

Brown, Dona L. "The Tourist's New England: Creating an Industry, 1820–1900." Diss. University of Massachusetts, 1989.

Brown, James A. "Mound Builders." *Encyclopedia of North American Indians.* Ed. Frederick E. Hoxie. Boston: Houghton Mifflin, 1996. 398–401.

Buck-Morss, Susan. "Aesthetics and Anaesthetics: Walter Benjamin's Artwork Essay Reconsidered." *October* 62.4 (1992): 3–41.

Buell, Lawrence. *New England Literary Culture: From Revolution through Renaissance.* Cambridge: Cambridge University Press, 1986.

Buffet, E. P. "Euthanasia: The Pleasures of Dying." *New Englander and Yale Review* 55 (1891): 231–42.

Burnham, John C. *Paths into American Culture: Psychology, Medicine, and Morals.* Philadelphia: Temple University Press, 1988.

Burrows, Edwin G. and Mike Wallace. *Gotham: A History of New York City to 1898.* New York: Oxford University Press, 1999.

Calinescu, Matei. *Five Faces of Modernity: Modernism, Avante-Garde, Decadence, Kitsch, Postmodernism.* Durham: Duke University Press, 1987.

Campbell, Donna M. "Rewriting the 'Rose and Lavender Pages': *Ethan Frome* and Women's Local Color Fiction." *Speaking the Other Self: American Women Writers.* Ed. Jeanne Campbell Reesman. Athens: University of Georgia Press, 1997. 263–77.

Campbell, George A. "The Fatal Delusion." *Christian Century* May 9, 1912: 3.

Canby, Henry Seidel. "Edith Wharton." *Saturday Review of Literature* Aug. 21, 1937: 6–7.

Carlin, Deborah. "To Form a More Perfect Union: Gender, Tradition, and the Text in Wharton's *The Fruit of the Tree.*" *Edith Wharton: New Critical Essays.* Eds. Alfred Bendixen and Annette Zilversmit. New York: Garland, 1992. 57–77.

Carlston, Erin G. *Thinking Fascism: Sapphic Modernism and Fascist Modernity.* Stanford: Stanford University Press, 1998.

Carver, Thomas N. "Economic Significance of Changes in Country Population." *Annals of the American Academy of Political and Social Science* 40.12 (1912): 21–5.

Castiglia, Chris. "The Genealogy of a Democratic Crush." *Materializing Democracy: Toward a Revitalized Cultural Politics.* Eds. Russ Castronovo and Dana D. Nelson. Durham: Duke University Press, 2002. 195–217.

Cesnola, General Louis Palma di. *Cyprus: Its Ancient Cities, Tombs, and Temples.* 1877. New York: Harper & Brothers, 1878.

"The Cesnola Investigation." *New York Times* Dec. 19, 1880: 6.

Chandler, Alfred D., Jr. *The Visible Hand: The Managerial Revolution in American Business*. Cambridge, MA: Harvard University Press, 1977.

Chandler, Joseph Everett. *The Colonial House*. New York: Robert A. McBride, 1924.

"The Charges against Cesnola." *New York Post* Aug. 6, 1880: 4.

"Columbia's President Angry." *New York Times* Dec. 7, 1883: 3.

"Condemnation of Euthanasia." Editorial. *Journal of the American Medical Association* 25 (1899): 674.

Conn, Steven. *Museums and American Intellectual Life, 1876–1926*. Chicago: University of Chicago Press, 1998.

Cooper, Helen M., Adrienne Auslander Munich and Susan Merrill Squier. "Arms and the Woman: The Con[tra]ception of the War Text." *Arms and the Woman*. Eds. Helen M. Cooper, Adrienne Auslander Munich, and Susan Merrill Squier. Chapel Hill: University of North Carolina Press, 1989. 9–24.

Copjec, Joan. "The Sartorial Superego." *October* 50.4 (1989): 57–95.

Corbey, Raymond. "Ethnographic showcases, 1870–1939." *Cultural Anthropology* 8 (1993): 338–69.

Cowling, Mary. *The Artist as Anthropologist: The Representation of Type and Character in Victorian Art*. Cambridge: Cambridge University Press, 1989.

Crozier, Alfred O. "The Recent Panic and the Present Deadly Peril to American Prosperity." *Arena* 39 (1908): 272–5.

Crunden, Robert M. *Ministers of Reform: The Progressives' Achievement in American Civilization, 1889–1920*. New York: Basic Books, 1982.

Culver, Stuart. "What Manikins Want: *The Wonderful Wizard of Oz* and *The Art of Decorating Dry Goods Windows*." *Representations* 21 (1988): 97–116.

Currier, Amos N. "The Decline of Rural New England." *Popular Science Monthly* 38 (1891): 383–90.

Daniels, Harvey A. *Famous Last Words: The American Language Crisis Reconsidered*. Carbondale, IL: Southern Illinois University Press, 1983.

Deloria, Philip J. *Playing Indian*. New Haven: Yale University Press, 1998.

Denison, John H. "The Survival of the American Type." *Atlantic Monthly* 75 (1895): 16–28.

"Di Cesnola's Statuettes." *New York Times* Jan. 6, 1881: 2.

Dickinson, G. Lowes. "Euthanasia: From the Note-Book of an Alpinist." *Littell's Living Age* Feb. 17, 1906: 445–7.

Dilworth, Leah. *Imagining Indians in the Southwest: Persistent Visions of a Primitive Past*. Washington, DC: Smithsonian Institution Press, 1996.

Dimock, Wai-Chee. "Debasing Exchange: Edith Wharton's *The House of Mirth*." *The House of Mirth*. Ed. Shari Benstock. Boston: Bedford, 1994. 375–90.

Doane, Mary Ann. *Femmes Fatales: Feminism, Film Theory, Psychoanalysis*. New York: Routledge, 1991.

Dorr, Rheta Childe. "Reclaiming the Wayward Girl." *Hampton's Magazine* 26 (1911): 67–78.

"Dr. Norton on Euthanasia." Editorial. *New York Times* Jan. 6, 1906: 8.

Dreiser, Theodore. *Sister Carrie*. 1900. Philadelphia: University of Pennsylvania Press, 1981.

"The Drift of the Testimony." *New York Times* April 20, 1912: 14.

DuBois, W. E. B. *The Souls of Black Folk*. 1903. New York: Bedford, 1997.

Duncan, Hugh Dalziel. *Culture and Democracy: The Struggle for Form in Society and Architecture in Chicago and the Middle West during the Life and Times of Louis H. Sullivan*. Totowa, NJ: Bedminster Press, 1965.

Eco, Umberto. "Ur-Fascism." *New York Review of Books* June 22, 1995: 12–15.

Editorial. *New York Times* May 14, 1881: 4.

Ehrlich, Gloria. *The Sexual Education of Edith Wharton*. Berkeley: University of California Press, 1992.

Eliot, T. S. Review of *Summer*, by Edith Wharton. *The Egoist: An Individualist Review* (Jan. 1918): 10.

Ellis, Havelock. Introduction. J. K. Huysmans, *Against the Grain (A Rebours)*. New York: Illustrated Editions, 1931.

Elshtain, Jean Bethke. *Women and War*. New York: Basic Books, 1987.

Epstein, Barbara. "Family, Sexual Morality, and Popular Movements in Turn-of-the-Century America." *Powers of Desire: The Politics of Sexuality*. Eds. Ann Snitow, Christine Stansell and Sharon Thompson. New York: Monthly Review Press, 1983. 117–30.

Estabrook, Arthur H. and Charles B. Davenport. *The Nam Family: A Study in Cacogenics*. Long Island, NY: Cold Spring Harbor, 1912.

"Euphoria vs. Euthanasia." Editorial. *Journal of the American Medical Association* 25 (1899): 674.

"Euthanasia." *Littell's Living Age* Mar. 8, 1902: 635–7.

"Euthanasia." *Oxford English Dictionary*. 2nd edn. 1989.

"Euthanasia and Civilization." Editorial. *New York Times* Feb. 3, 1906: 8.

"'Euthanasia' Bobs Up Again." Editorial. *New York Times* Jan. 25, 1906: 8.

"Euthanasia from the Physician's View-Point." *Review of Reviews* 33 (1906): 628–9.

Farb, Peter. *Word Play: What Happens When People Talk*. New York: Knopf, 1974.

Felman, Shoshana. "Rereading Femininity." *Yale French Studies* 62 (1981): 19–44.

Feuardent, Gaston L. Letter to the Editor. *The Art Amateur* 3.4 (1880): 68.

   "Tampering with Antiquities." *The Art Amateur* 3.3 (1880): 48–50.

"The Feuardent–Cesnola Controversy." *The Art Amateur* 3.5 (1880): 90.

Fields, Barbara. "Whiteness, Racism, and Identity." *International Labor and Working-Class History* 60 (2001): 48–56.

"Find a Rare Aborigine." *New York Times* Sept. 7, 1911: 3.

Fletcher, Henry U. "The Doom of the Small Town." *The Forum* 19 (1895): 214–23.

Fogelson, Raymond D. "The Red Man in the White City." *Columbia Consequences*. Vol. 3. Ed. David Hurst-Thomas. Washington: Smithsonian Institution Press, 1991. 3 vols. 73–90.

Foner, Eric. *Free Soil, Free Labor, Free Men: The Ideology of the Republican Party before the Civil War*. New York: Oxford University Press, 1970.

"Response to Eric Arnesen." *International Labor and Working-Class History* 60 (2001): 57–60.

The Story of American Freedom. New York: Norton, 1998.

Foreman, P. Gabrielle. "Who's Your Mama? 'White' Mulatta Genealogies, Early Photography, and Anti-Passing Narratives of Slavery and Freedom." *American Literary History* 14 (2002): 505–39.

Foster, Hal. "Armor Fou." *October* 56.2 (1991): 65–97.

Foucault, Michel. *Language, Counter-Memory, Practice*. Eds. Donald F. Bouchard and Sherry Simon. Ithaca: Cornell University Press, 1977.

Frankenberg, Ruth. *White Women, Race Matters: The Social Construction of Whiteness*. Minneapolis: University of Minnesota Press, 1993.

French, W. E. P. Letter. *New York Times* March 12, 1906: 8.

Fried, Michael. *Realism, Writing, Disfiguration: On Thomas Eakins and Stephen Crane*. Chicago: University of Chicago Press, 1987.

Frost, Robert. "The Generations of Men." *Collected Poems, Prose, & Plays*. New York: Library of America, 1995. 74–81.

Fryer, Judith. *Felicitous Space: The Imaginative Structures of Edith Wharton and Willa Cather*. Chapel Hill: University of North Carolina Press, 1986.

Gallagher, Catherine and Stephen Greenblatt. *Practicing New Historicism*. Chicago: University of Chicago Press, 2000.

Galton, Francis. "Photographic Composites" *The Photographic News* 17 (1885): 243–5.

Gates, Henry Louis, Jr. "The Trope of a New Negro and the Reconstruction of the Image of the Black." *Representations* 24 (1988): 129–55.

Gibbs, S. E. Letter. *New York Times* Feb. 2, 1906: 10.

Gilbert, Sandra M. "Life's Empty Pack: Notes toward Literary Daughteronomy." *Critical Inquiry* 11 (1985): 355–84.

Gilbert, Sandra M. and Susan Gubar. *No Man's Land: The Place of the Woman Writer in the Twentieth Century*. New Haven: Yale University Press, 1989.

Giles, William A. "Is New England Decadent?" *The World To-day* 9 (1905): 991–5.

Gilman, Charlotte Perkins. *The Home: Its Work and Influence*. 1903. Urbana: University of Illinois Press, 1972.

Women and Economics. 1898. New York: Harper & Row, 1966.

Glassberg, David. *American Historical Pageantry*. Chapel Hill: University of North Carolina Press, 1990.

"History and the Public: Legacies of the Progressive Era." *Journal of American History* 73 (1987): 979–80.

Gleason, Herbert Wendell. "The Old Farm Revisited." *New England Magazine* 22 (1900): 668–80.

Godkin, Edwin L. "Chromo-civilization." *The Nation* 19 (1874): 201–2.

"The Feuardent–Cesnola Trial." *The Nation* 38 (1884): 113–14.

Goodman, Susan. *Edith Wharton's Inner Circle*. Austin: University of Texas Press, 1994.

Gordon, Linda. *Woman's Body, Woman's Right: A Social History of Birth Control in America*. New York: Penguin, 1977.

"The Gospel of Pain." *Harper's Weekly* July 8, 1911: 6.

Gossett, Thomas F. *Race: The History of an Idea in America*. Dallas: Southern Methodist University Press, 1964.

Green, Harvey. "Popular Science and Political Thought Converge: Colonial Survival Becomes Colonial Revival, 1830–1910." *Journal of American Culture* 6 (1983): 3–24.

Green, Jesse, ed. *Cushing at Zuni: The Correspondence and Journals of Frank Hamilton Cushing, 1879–1884*. Albuquerque: University of New Mexico Press, 1990.

Green, Rayna. "The Tribe Called Wannabee: Playing Indian in America and Europe." *Folklore* 99 (1988): 30–55.

Greenblatt, Stephen. "Resonance and Wonder." *Exhibiting Cultures: The Poetics and Politics of Museum Display*. Eds. Ivan Karp and Steven D. Lavine. Washington: Smithsonian Institution Press, 1991. 42–56.

Greene, C. Letter to Edith Wharton. February 11, 1907. Scribner's Collection. Firestone Library, Princeton University, Princeton.

Haber, Samuel. *The Quest for Authority and Honor in the American Professions, 1750–1900*. Chicago: University of Chicago Press, 1991.

Hale, Nathan G. *Freud and the Americans: The Beginnings of Psychoanalysis in the United States, 1876–1917*. New York: Oxford University Press, 1971.

Hall, Gertrude. "One of the Unconquerable Army." *The Book Buyer* 24 (1902): 196–8.

Hall, James. *Dictionary of Subjects and Symbols in Art*. Boulder, CO: Westview, 1974.

Haller, John S. and Robin M. Haller. *The Physician and Sexuality in Victorian America*. Carbondale: Southern Illinois University Press, 1974.

Hanson, Ellis. *Decadence and Catholicism*. Cambridge, MA: Harvard University Press, 1997.

Haraway, Donna. "Teddy Bear Patriarchy: Taxidermy in the Garden of Eden, New York City, 1908–1936." *Cultures of United States Imperialism*. Eds. Amy Kaplan and Donald E. Pease. Durham: Duke University Press, 1993. 237–91.

Hartt, Mary Bronson. "The Skansen Idea." *The Century* 83 (1912): 916–20.

Hartt, Rollin Lynde. "The Regeneration of Rural New England." *The Outlook* 64 (1900): 571–83.

Hattam, Victoria C. "Whiteness: Theorizing Race, Eliding Ethnicity." *International Labor and Working-Class History* 60 (2001): 61–8.

Herman, Arthur. *The Idea of Decline in Western History*. New York: Free Press, 1997.

Herzog, Alfred W. "Euthanasia." *Medico-Legal Journal* 35.2 (1918): 21–2.

Hibbard, George A. *Lenox*. New York: Scribner's, 1894.

Higham, John. "The Reorientation of American Culture in the 1980s." *The Origins of Modern Consciousness*. Ed. John Weiss. Detroit: Wayne State University Press.

  Strangers in the Land: Patterns of American Nativism 1860–1925. 1955. New York: Atheneum, 1981.

Higonnet, Margaret R. "Civil Wars and Sexual Territories." *Arms and the Woman.* Eds. Helen M. Cooper, Adrienne Auslander Munich and Susan Merrill Squier. Chapel Hill: University of North Carolina Press, 1989. 80–96.

Hobsbawm, Eric. "Introductions: Invented Traditions." *The Invention of Tradition.* Eds. Eric Hobsbawm and Terence Ranger. Cambridge: Cambridge University Press, 1983. 1–14.

Hoeller, Hildegard. *Edith Wharton's Dialogue with Realism and Sentimental Fiction.* Gainesville: University Press of Florida, 2000.

"'The Impossible Rosedale': 'Race' and the Reading of Edith Wharton's *The House of Mirth.*" *Studies in American Jewish Literature* 13 (1994): 14–20.

Hofstadter, Richard. *The Age of Reform from Bryan to F. D. R.* New York: Vintage, 1955.

Hoopes, James. "The Culture of Progressivism: Croly, Lippman, Brooks, Bourne, and the Idea of American Artistic Decadence." *Clio* 7 (1977): 91–111.

Hornaday, William T. *Taxidermy and Zoological Collecting.* 7th edn. New York: Scribner's, 1900.

Howe, Irving, ed. *Edith Wharton: A Collection of Critical Essays.* Englewood Cliffs, NJ: Prentice-Hall, 1962.

Hugh Smith, John. [Reminiscence], ts. Edith Wharton Collection. Beinecke Library, Yale University, New Haven.

Hutchinson, Stuart. "Sex, Race, and Class in Edith Wharton." *Texas Studies in Literature and Language* 42 (2000): 431–44.

James, Henry. *The American Scene.* 1907. New York: Penguin, 1994.

Collected Travel Writings: Great Britain and America. New York: Library of America, 1993.

Hawthorne. 1879. Garden City, NY: Dolphin Books, n.d.

Letters. Vol. 4. Ed. Leon Edel. Cambridge, MA: Harvard University Press, 1984. 4 vols.

"Paste." 1899. *The Complete Tales of Henry James.* Ed. Leon Edel. Vol. 10. Philadelphia: J. B. Lippincott, 1964. 12 vols. 451–69.

James, William. "The Gospel of Relaxation." *Scribner's Magazine* 25 (1899): 499–507.

Letter to Edith Wharton. April 25, 1910. Edith Wharton Collection. Beinecke Library, Yale University, New Haven.

"The Moral Equivalent of War." *Writings, 1902–1910.* New York: Library of America, 1987. 1281–93.

Pragmatism and The Meaning of Truth. Intro. A. J. Ayer. Cambridge, MA: Harvard University Press, 1978.

The Varieties of Religious Experience. 1902. Cambridge, MA: Harvard University Press, 1985.

Jefferson, Thomas. *Writings.* New York: Library of America, 1984.

Jehlen, Myra. *American Incarnation: The Individual, the Nation, and the Continent.* Cambridge, MA: Harvard University Press, 1986.

Johnson, Clifton. "The Deserted Homes of New England." *The Cosmopolitan* 15 (1893): 215–22.

Johnson, Joseph French. "The Crisis and Panic of 1907." *Political Science Quarterly* 23 (1908): 454–67.

Jones, George Frederick. "Diary of George F. Jones 1847–1848." Edith Wharton Collection. Lilly Library, Indiana University, Bloomington.

Joslin, Katherine. "Architectonic or Episodic? Gender and *The Fruit of the Tree*." *A Forward Glance: New Essays on Edith Wharton*. Eds. Clare Colquitt, Susan Goodman and Candace Waid. Newark: University of Delaware Press, 1999. 62–75.

Edith Wharton. New York: St. Martin's, 1991.

Judd, Richard W. *Common Lands, Common People: The Origins of Conservation in Northern New England*. Cambridge, MA: Harvard University Press, 1997.

Julien, Eileen. "Visible Woman; or, a Semester among the Great Books." *Profession* (1999): 225–35.

Kammen, Michael. *Mystic Chords of Memory: The Transformation of Tradition in American Culture*. New York: Knopf, 1991.

Kaplan, Amy. *The Social Construction of American Realism*. Chicago: University of Chicago Press, 1988.

Kaye, Richard A. "Edith Wharton and the 'New Gomorrahs' of Paris: Homosexuality, Flirtation, and Incestuous Desire in *The Reef*." *Modern Fiction Studies* 43 (1997): 860–97.

Keller, Morton. *Affairs of State: Public Life in Late Nineteenth-Century America*. Cambridge, MA: Harvard University Press, 1977.

Kennedy, Roger G. *Hidden Cities: The Discovery and Loss of Ancient North American Civilization*. New York: Free Press, 1994.

"Kill to End Suffering." *Washington Post* Jan. 5, 1906: 1.

King, C. Richard. *Colonial Discourses, Collective Memories, and the Exhibition of Native American Cultures and Histories in the Contemporary United States*. New York: Garland, 1998.

Kirwin, Susie. Letter. *New York Herald* Aug. 19, 1894: sec. 4, 7.

Koepnick, Lutz. *Walter Benjamin and the Aesthetics of Power*. Lincoln: University of Nebraska Press, 1999.

Kroeber, A. L. "Ishi, the Last Aborigine." *World's Work* 24 (1912): 304–8.

Kuepper, Stephen Louis. "Euthanasia in America, 1890–1960: The Controversy, the Movement, and the Law." Diss. Rutgers Univesity, 1981. Ann Arbor: UMI, 1981. 8122092.

Kulik, Gary. "Designing the Past: History-Museum Exhibitions from Peale to the Present." *History Museums in the United States: A Critical Assessment*. Eds. Warren Leon and Roy Rosenzweig. Urbana: University of Illinois Press, 1989.

Larabee, Ann E. "The American Hero and His Mechanical Bride: Gender Myths of the *Titanic* Disaster." *American Studies* 31.1 (1990): 5–23.

"The Law of the Sea." *Independent* 72 (1912): 901.

Lears, T. J. Jackson. *Fables of Abundance: A Cultural History of Advertising in America*. New York: Basic Books, 1994.

No Place of Grace: Antimodernism and the Transformation of American Culture, 1880–1920. New York: Pantheon, 1981.

Lee, Joseph. "The Philanthropist's Place in a Democracy." *Family* 3.6 (1922): 139–43.

Lee, Vernon [Violet Paget]. *Euphorion: Being Studies of the Antique and the Mediaeval in the Renaissance*. Vol. 1. Boston: Roberts, 1884. 2 vols.

Lentricchia, Frank. "Philosophers of Modernism at Harvard, circa 1900." *The South Atlantic Quarterly* 89 (1990): 787–834.

Levin, Jonathan. *The Poetics of Transition: Emerson, Pragmatism, and American Literary Modernism*. Durham: Duke University Press, 1999.

Levine, Lawrence W. *Highbrow/Lowbrow: The Emergence of Cultural Hierarchy in America*. Cambridge, MA: Harvard University Press, 1988.

Lewis, R. W. B. *Edith Wharton: A Biography*. New York: Fromm International, 1985.

Lewis, Sinclair. *Main Street*. 1920. New York: Signet, 1980.

Lindgren, James M. *Preserving Historic New England: Preservation, Progressivism, and the Remaking of Memory*. New York: Oxford University Press, 1995.

Lippmann, Walter. *A Preface to Politics*. 1914. Ann Arbor: University of Michigan Press, 1965.

Lipsitz, George. *Time Passages: Collective Memory and American Popular Culture*. Minneapolis: University of Minnesota Press, 1990.

Lodge, Henry Cabot. *Early Memories*. New York: Scribner's, 1913.

Lott, Eric. *Love and Theft: Blackface Minstrelsy and the American Working Class*. New York: Oxford University Press, 1993.

Lovett, Robert Morss. *Edith Wharton*. New York: Robert M. McBridge, 1925.

Lowenthal, David. *The Past is a Foreign Country*. New York: Cambridge University Press, 1985.

Lunbeck, Elizabeth. "'A New Generation of Women': Progressive Psychiatrists and the Hypersexual Female." *Feminist Studies* 13 (1987): 513–43.

Lundberg, David. "The American Literature of War: The Civil War, World War I, and World War II," *American Quarterly* 36 (1984): 373–88.

Lutz, Tom. *American Nervousness, 1903: An Anecdotal History*. Ithaca: Cornell University Press, 1991.

MacCannell, Dean. *The Tourist: A New Theory of the Leisure Class*. New York: Schocken, 1976.

McCullough, Jack. *Living Pictures on the New York Stage*. Ann Arbor: UMI Research Press, 1983.

McFadden, Elizabeth. *The Glitter and the Gold: A Spirited Account of the Metropolitan Museum of Art's First Director, the Audacious and High-Handed Luigi Palma di Cesnola*. New York: Dial Press, 1971.

McLaren, Angus. *Sexuality and Social Order: The Debate over the Fertility of Women and Workers in France, 1770–1920*. New York: Holmes & Meier, 1983.

MacMaster, Anne. "Wharton, Race, and *The Age of Innocence*: Three Historical Contexts." *A Forward Glance: New Essays on Edith Wharton*. Eds. Clare

Colquitt, Susan Goodman and Candace Waid. Newark: University of Delaware Press, 1999. 188–205.

Mainwaring, Marion. *Mysteries of Paris: The Quest for Morton Fullerton.* Hanover, NH: University Press of New England, 2001.

Makowsky, Veronica and Lynn Z. Bloom. "Edith Wharton's Tentative Embrace of Charity: Class and Character in *Summer.*" *American Literary Realism* 32 (2000): 220–33.

Mallan, John P. "Roosevelt, Brooks Adams, and Lea: The Warrior Critique of the Business Civilization." *American Quarterly* 8 (1956): 216–30.

Mallary, Raymond DeWitt. *Lenox and the Berkshire Highlands.* New York: G. P. Putnam's Sons, 1902.

Marchand, Mary V. "Cross Talk: Edith Wharton and the New England Women Regionalists." *Women's Studies* 30 (2001): 369–95.

Marling, Karal Ann. *George Washington Slept Here: Colonial Revivals and American Culture, 1876–1986.* Cambridge, MA: Harvard University Press, 1988.

Martin, Ruth Moxcey. "Three Old New England Communities." *Scientific Proceedings of the Second International Congress of Eugenics, held at American Museum of Natural History, New York, September 22–28, 1921.* Vol 1. Baltimore: Williams & Williams, 1923. 2 vols. 278–84.

May, Henry F. *The End of American Innocence: A Study in the First Years of Our Own Time, 1912–1917.* New York: Knopf, 1969.

Mechling, Jay. "The Collecting Self and American Youth Movements." *Consuming Visions: Accumulation and Display of Goods in America 1880–1920.* Ed. Simon J. Bronner. New York: W. W. Norton, 1989. 255–85.

Melosh, Barbara. *"The Physician's Hand": Work Culture and Conflict in American Nursing.* Philadelphia: Temple University Press, 1982.

Meltzer, David J. "On 'Paradigms' and 'Paradigm Bias' in Controversies over Human Antiquity in America." *The First Americans: Search and Research.* Eds. Tom D. Dillehay and David J. Meltzer. Boca Raton, FL: CRC Press, 1991. 13–49.

Mencken, H. L. *The American Language: An Inquiry into the Development of English in the United States.* 1919. New York: Knopf, 1927.

Merwin, Henry Childs. "On Being Civilized Too Much." *Atlantic Monthly* 79 (1897): 838–46.

Meyerowitz, Joanne. *Women Adrift: Independent Wage Earners in Chicago, 1880–1930.* Chicago: University of Chicago Press, 1983.

Meyn, Susan Labry. "Who's Who: The 1896 Sicangu Sioux Visit to the Cincinnati Zoological Gardens." *Museum Anthropology* 16.2 (1992): 21–6.

Michaels, Walter Benn. *The Gold Standard and the Logic of Naturalism.* Berkeley: University of California Press, 1987.

  Our America: Nativism, Modernism, and Pluralism. Durham: Duke University Press, 1995.

  "The Souls of White Folk." *Literature and the Body: Essays on Population and Persons.* Ed. Elaine Scarry. Baltimore: Johns Hopkins University Press, 1988. 185–209.

Milton, John. *Paradise Lost and Other Poems*. New York: Mentor, 1981.

Mitchell, Lee Clark. *Witnesses to a Vanishing America: The Nineteenth-Century Response*. Princeton: Princeton University Press, 1981.

Mitchell, S. Weir. *Fat and Blood: An Essay on the Treatment of Certain Forms of Neurasthenia and Hysteria*. Philadelphia: J. B. Lippincott, 1884.

Moddelmog, William E. "Disowning 'Personality': Privacy and Subjectivity in *The House of Mirth*." *American Literature* 70 (1998): 337–63.

"Modern Science in its Relations to Pain." *Century* 36 (1888): 632–4.

Mohr, James C. *Abortion in America: The Origins and Evolution of National Policy, 1800–1900*. New York: Oxford University Press, 1978.

Morgan, Philip. "The Problems of Rural New England: A Remote Village." *Atlantic Monthly* 79 (1897): 577–87.

"Mr. Choate's Argument." *New-York Tribune* Jan. 30, 1884: 3.

Myers, John L. *Handbook of the Cesnola Collection of Antiquities from Cyprus*. New York: The Metropolitan Museum of Art, 1914.

Navarette, Susan J. *The Shape of Fear: Horror and the Fin de Siècle Culture of Decadence*. Lexington: University Press of Kentucky, 1998.

Nelson, Dana D. *National Manhood: Capitalist Citizenship and the Imagined Fraternity of White Men*. Durham: Duke University Press, 1998.

"Representative/Democracy: The Political Work of Countersymbolic Representation." *Materializing Democracy: Toward a Revitalized Cultural Politics*. Eds. Russ Castronovo and Dana D. Nelson. Durham: Duke University Press, 2002. 218–47.

Nelson, Dana D. and Russ Castronovo. "Introduction." *Materializing Democracy: Toward a Revitalized Cultural Politics*. Eds. Russ Castronovo and Dana D. Nelson. Durham: Duke University Press, 2002. 1–21.

Nemerov, Alex. "Doing the 'Old America': The Image of the American West, 1880–1920." *The West as America: Reinterpreting Images of the Frontier*. Ed. William H. Truettner. Washington, DC: Smithsonian Institution Press, 1991. 285–343.

New England Society of the City of New York. *Ninety-Eighth Anniversary Celebration of the New England Society in the City of New York*. New York: New England Society, 1903.

The New Oxford Annotated Bible with Apocrypha. Ed. Herbert G. May and Bruce M. Metzger. New York: Oxford University Press, 1977.

Norton, Charles Eliot. "The Intellectual Life of America." *New Princeton Review* Nov. 1888: 312–24.

Letters of Charles Eliot Norton. Eds. Sara Norton and M. A. DeWolfe Howe. Boston: Houghton Mifflin, 1913.

Nutting, Wallace. *Massachusetts Beautiful*. Framingham: Old America Company, 1923.

Nye, Robert. *Crime, Madness, and Politics in Modern France: The Medical Concept of National Decline*. Princeton: Princeton University Press, 1984.

Orvell, Miles. *The Real Thing: Imitation and Authenticity in American Culture, 1880–1940*. Chapel Hill: University of North Carolina Press, 1989.

Otis, Laura. *Organic Memory: History and the Body in the Late Nineteenth and Early Twentieth Centuries*. Lincoln: University of Nebraska Press, 1994.

Outlaw, Lucius. "Toward a Critical Theory of 'Race.'" *Anatomy of Racism*. Ed. David Theo Goldberg. Minneapolis: University of Minnesota Press, 1990. 58–82.

Paine, Robert Treat. *The Empire of Charity Established by the Revolution of This Century; Its New Allies, Broader Functions, and Stupendous Tasks*. Boston: G. H. Ellis, 1895.

Parrington, Vernon L. "Our Literary Aristocrat." *Edith Wharton: A Collection of Critical Essays*. Ed. Irving Howe. Englewood Cliffs, NJ: Prentice-Hall, 1962. 151–4.

Pascoe, Peggy. "Miscegenation Law, Court Cases, and Ideologies of 'Race' in Twentieth-Century America." *Journal of American History* 83.1 (1996): 44–69.

Peiss, Kathy. *Cheap Amusements: Working Women and Leisure in Turn-of-the-Century New York*. Philadelphia: Temple University Press, 1986.

Petchesky, Rosalind Pollack. *Abortion and Woman's Choice: The State, Sexuality, and Reproductive Freedom*. Rev. edn Boston: Northeastern University Press, 1990.

Pfeiffer, Kathleen. "*Summer* and Its Critics' Discomfort." *Women's Studies* 20 (1991): 141–52.

Phillips, Forbes. "Ancestral Memory: A Suggestion." *The Nineteenth Century* 59 (1906): 977–83.

Pittenger, Mark. "A World of Difference: Constructing the 'Underclass' in Progressive America." *American Quarterly* 49.1 (1997): 26–65.

Posnock, Ross. "The Influence of William James on American Culture." *The Cambridge Companion to William James*. Ed. Ruth Anna Putnam. Cambridge: Cambridge University Press, 1997. 322–42.

Pound, Ezra. Letter to Margaret Anderson. 6 August 1917. *Pound / The Little Review; The Letters of Ezra Pound to Margaret Anderson: The Little Review Correspondence*. Eds. Thomas L. Scott, Melvin J. Friedman and Jackson R. Bryher. New York: New Directions, 1988. 106.

Powers, Lyall H., ed. *Henry James and Edith Wharton; Letters: 1900–1915*. New York: Scribner's, 1990.

Price, Alan. *The End of the Age of Innocence: Edith Wharton and the First World War*. New York: St. Martin's, 1998.

Quint, David. *Origin and Originality in Renaissance Literature: Versions of the Source*. New Haven: Yale University Press, 1983.

A Race at Bay: New York Times Editorials on "The Indian Problem," 1860–1900. Ed. Robert G. Hays. Carbondale, IL: Southern Illinois University Press, 1997.

Ramsden, George. *Edith Wharton's Library*. Foreword by Hermione Lee. Settrington: Stone Trough Books, 1999.

Rath, Sura P. "Romanticizing the Tribe: Stereotypes in Literary Portraits of Tribal Cultures." *Diogenes* 148.1 (1989): 61–77.

Read, James Morgan. *Atrocity Propaganda, 1914–1919*. New Haven: Yale University Press, 1941.

Reagan, Leslie J. *When Abortion Was a Crime: Women, Medicine, and Law in the United States, 1867–1973*. Berkeley: University of California Press, 1997.

"Realities and Mockeries." Editorial. *Independent* April 25, 1912: 904–5.

Reid, Whitelaw. "Speech by the Honorable Whitelaw Reid." *Anniversary Celebration of the New England Society in the City of New York*. New York: Green, 1903. 41–52.

"Religious Views of the 'Titanic.'" *Literary Digest* May 4, 1912: 938–9.

Repplier, Agnes. "Ennui." *Review of Reviews* 71 (1893): 775–84.

Riis, Jacob. *The Perils and Preservation of the Home*. Philadelphia: George W. Jacobs, 1903.

Roediger, David R. *The Wages of Whiteness: Race and the Making of the American Working Class*. London: Verso, 1991.

Rohrbach, Augusta. *Truth Stranger than Fiction: Race, Realism, and the U.S. Literary Marketplace*. New York: Palgrave, 2002.

Rollins, Frank West. "New Hampshire's Opportunity." *New England Magazine* 16 (1897): 534–43.

"The Renaissance of New England." *Independent* 53 (1901): 69–71.

Romero, Lora. *Home Fronts: Domesticity and Its Critics in the Antebellum United States*. Durham: Duke University Press, 1997.

Roosevelt, Theodore. "Character and Success." *Outlook* Mar. 1900: 745.

"Citizenship in a Republic." *The Works of Theodore Roosevelt*. Ed. Hermann Hagedorn. Vol. 15. New York: Scribner's, 1925. 20 vols. 349–76.

"The Conservation of Wild Life." *The Works of Theodore Roosevelt*. Ed. Hermann Hagedorn. Vol. 12. New York: Scribner's, 1926. 20 vols. 423–31.

"The Control of Corporations." *The Works of Theodore Roosevelt*. Ed. Hermann Hagedorn. Vol. 16. New York: Scribner's, 1925. 20 vols. 61–8.

"A Letter from President Roosevelt on Race Suicide." *Review of Reviews* 85 (1907): 550–1.

"To Douglas Robinson." 16 November 1907. Letter 4501 of *The Letters of Theodore Roosevelt*. Ed. Elting E. Morison. Vol. 5. Cambridge, MA: Harvard University Press, 1952. 8 vols. 845–6.

"The Man Who Works with His Hands." *The Works of Theodore Roosevelt*. Ed. Hermann Hagedorn. Vol. 16. New York: Scribner's, 1925. 20 vols. 129–44.

The Strenuous Life: Essays and Addresses. New York: Century, 1902.

Rothman, Sheila M. *Woman's Proper Place: A History of Changing Ideals and Practices, 1870 to the Present*. New York: Basic Books, 1978.

Said, Edward W. *The World, the Text, and the Critic*. Cambridge, MA: Harvard University Press, 1983.

Santayana, George. "The Genteel Tradition in American Philosophy." *University of California Chronicle* Oct. 1911: 357–80.

The Winds of Doctrine: Studies in Contemporary Opinion. New York: Scribner's, 1913.

Saveth, Edward N. "Patrician Philanthropy in America: The Late Nineteenth and Early Twentieth Centuries." *Social Service Review* 54.1 (1980): 76–91.

Scheckel, Susan. *The Insistence of the Indian: Race and Nationalism in Nineteenth-Century American Culture*. Princeton: Princeton University Press, 1998.

Scribner, Charles. Letter to Edith Wharton. November 22, 1907. Scribner's Collection. Firestone Library, Princeton University, Princeton.

  Letter to Edith Wharton. [Undated.] Scribner's Collection. Firestone Library, Princeton University, Princeton.

Seaton, James. *Cultural Conservatism, Political Liberalism: From Criticism to Cultural Studies*. Ann Arbor: University of Michigan Press, 1996.

Sekula, Allan. "The Body and the Archive." *The Contest of Meaning: Critical Histories of Photography*. Ed. Richard Bolton. Cambridge, MA: MIT Press, 1992. 342–89.

Seltzer, Mark. *Bodies and Machines*. New York: Routledge, 1992.

Seneca, Lucius Annaeus. "On Mercy." *Moral Essays*. Trans. John W. Basore. Cambridge, MA: Harvard University Press, 1950. 357–429.

Sensibar, Judith L. "Edith Wharton as Propagandist and Novelist: Competing Visions of 'The Great War.'" *A Forward Glance: New Essays on Edith Wharton*. Eds. Clare Colquitt, Susan Goodman and Candace Waid. Newark: University of Delaware Press, 1999. 149–71.

Seton, Ernest Thompson. *The Book of Woodcraft and Indian Lore*. Garden City, NY: Doubleday, Page, 1915.

"Sex O'Clock in America." *Current Opinion* 55 (1913): 113–14.

"Shall We Legalize Homicide?" Editorial. *The Outlook* 82 (1906): 252–3.

Sheldon, Lurana W. Letter. *New York Times* Feb. 9, 1906: 8.

Showalter, Elaine. *Sister's Choice: Tradition and Change in American Women's Writing*. Oxford: Clarendon Press, 1991.

  "Spragg: The Art of the Deal." *The Cambridge Companion to Edith Wharton*. Ed. Millicent Bell. Cambridge: Cambridge University Press, 1995. 87–97.

Silverberg, Robert. *Mound Builders of Ancient America: The Archeology of a Myth*. Greenwich, CT: New York Graphic Society, 1968.

Sinclair, Upton. *The Jungle*. 1906. Memphis: Peachtree Publishers, 1988.

Singley, Carol J. *Edith Wharton: Matters of Mind and Spirit*. Cambridge: Cambridge University Press, 1995.

Skillern, Rhonda. "Becoming a 'Good Girl': Law, Language, and Ritual in Edith Wharton's *Summer*." *The Cambridge Companion to Edith Wharton*. Ed. Millicent Bell. Cambridge: Cambridge University Press, 1995. 117–36.

Slotkin, Richard. *The Fatal Environment: The Myth of the Frontier in the Age of Industrialization, 1800–1890*. New York: Atheneum, 1985.

Smith-Rosenberg, Carroll. *Disorderly Conduct: Visions of Gender in Victorian America*. New York: Knopf, 1985.

Sobel, Robert. *Panic on Wall Street: A History of America's Financial Disasters*. New York: Macmillan, 1968.

Sollors, Werner. *Beyond Ethnicity: Consent and Descent in American Culture.* New York: Oxford University Press, 1986.

Solomon, Barbara Miller. *Ancestors and Immigrants: A Changing New England Tradition.* Cambridge, MA: Harvard University Press, 1956.

"The Intellectual Background of the Immigration Restriction Movement in New England." *New England Quarterly* 25 (1952): 47–59.

Spencer, Herbert. *Facts and Comments.* New York: Appleton, 1902.

Stanley, Amy Dru. "Beggars Can't be Choosers: Compulsion and Contract in Postbellum America." *The Journal of American History* 78 (1992): 1265–93.

Stephen, Herbert. "Murder from the Best Motives." *Law Quarterly Review* 5 (1889): 188–9.

Stewart, Susan. *On Longing: Narratives of the Miniature, the Gigantic, the Souvenir, the Collection.* Durham: Duke University Press, 1993.

Straus, Isidor. "Causes of the Present Business Situation." *Annals of the American Academy of Political and Social Science* July 1908: 50–4.

Strong, Josiah. *Our Country: Its Possible Future and Its Present Crisis.* New York: Baker & Taylor, 1891.

The New Era. New York: Baker & Taylor, 1893.

"Suffering versus Training." *Harper's Weekly* 56 (1912): 6.

Sundquist, Eric J. *To Wake the Nations: Race in the Making of American Literature.* Cambridge, MA: Harvard University Press, 1993.

Susman, Warren I. "'Personality' and the Making of Twentieth-Century Culture." *New Directions in American Intellectual History.* Eds. John Higham and Paul K. Conkin. Baltimore: The Johns Hopkins University Press, 1979. 212–26.

Taylor, Henry Osborn. *The Mediaeval Mind: A History of the Development of Thought and Emotion in the Middle Ages.* Vol 1. 1911. Cambridge, MA: Harvard University Press, 1951. 2 vols.

Thomas, David Hurst. *Skull Wars: Kennewick Man, Archeology, and the Battle for Native American Identity.* New York: Basic Books, 2000.

Thomas, John M. *The Idealization of the Near: A Plea for the Small Towns of Vermont.* Middlebury, VT, 1913.

Thompson, Shirley E. "'*Ah Toucoutou, ye conin vous*': History and Memory in Creole New Orleans." *American Quarterly* 53 (2001): 232–66.

Tintner, Adeline R. "James's Mock Epic: 'The Velvet Glove,' Edith Wharton, and Other Late Tales." *Modern Fiction Studies* 17 (1971–72): 483–99.

"Titanic Verdict is Negligence." *New York Times* May 29, 1912: 3.

Tomlinson, Augustus. Letter. *New York Times* Feb. 5, 1906: 8.

Trachtenberg, Alan. *The Incorporation of America: Culture and Society in the Gilded Age.* New York: Hill and Wang, 1982.

Travis, Molly Abel. "Eternal Fascism and Its 'Home Haunts' in the Leavises' Attacks on Bloomsbury and Woolf." *Virginia Woolf and Fascism: Resisiting the Dictators' Seduction.* Ed. Merry M. Pawlowski. New York: Palgrave, 2001. 165–77.

Trigger, Bruce C. *A History of Archeological Thought*. Cambridge: Cambridge University Press, 1989.

Trombold, John. "The Uneven Development of Multiculturalism." *Profession* (1999): 236–47.

Trumpener, Katie and James M. Nyce. "The Recovered Fragments: Archeological and Anthropological Perspectives in Edith Wharton's *The Age of Innocence*." *Literary Anthropology: A New Interdisciplinary Approach to People, Signs and Literature*. Ed. Fernando Poyatos. Amsterdam: John Benjamins, 1988. 161–9.

Turner, Frederick J. "The Problem of the West." *Review of Reviews* 78 (1896): 289–97.

Tyler, Elisina. Letter to Royall Tyler. October 27, 1916. Ts. Edith Wharton Collection. Lilly Library, Indiana University, Bloomington.

van Rensselaer, M. G. "American Country Dwellings." *Century Illustrated Monthly Magazine* 10 (1886): 3–20.

Veblen, Thorstein. *The Theory of the Leisure Class*. 1899. Mineola, NY: Dover, 1994.

Waid, Candace. *Edith Wharton's Letters from the Underworld: Fictions of Women and Writing*. Chapel Hill: University of North Carolina Press, 1991.

Walkowitz, Judith. "Dangerous Sexualities." *A History of Women in the West: Emerging Feminism from Revolution to World War*. Eds. Genevieve Fraisse and Michelle Perrot. Cambridge, MA: Harvard University Press, 1993. 369–98.

Walton, William. "The Artist-Taxidermist and the Great African Hall of the American Museum of Natural History." *Scribner's Magazine* 56 (1914): 555–8.

Wayne, Frances. "Men of Brains and Millions Sacrificed for Lowly Women." *Denver Post* April 16, 1912: 18.

Webster, Daniel. *The Great Speeches and Orations of Daniel Webster*. Ed. Edwin P. Whipple. Boston: Little, Brown, 1891.

Wegener, Frederick. "Form, 'Selection,' and Ideology in Edith Wharton's Anti-modernist Aesthetic." *A Forward Glance: New Essays on Edith Wharton*. Eds. Clare Colquitt, Susan Goodman and Candace Waid. Newark: University of Delaware Press, 1999. 116–38.

"'Rabid Imperialist': Edith Wharton and the Obligations of Empire in Modern American Fiction." *American Literature* 72 (2000): 783–812.

Wendell, Barrett. *A Literary History of America*. New York: Scribner's, 1900.

"Democracy." *Literature, Society, and Politics: Selected Essays*. Ed. Robert T. Self. St. Paul, MN: John Colet Press, 1977. 161–89.

Letter to Edith Wharton. June 14, 1913. Edith Wharton Collection. Beinecke Library, Yale University, New Haven.

Stelligeri and Other Essays Concerning America. New York: Scribner's, 1893.

Westbrook, Perry D. *The New England Town in Fact and Fiction*. Madison, NJ: Fairleigh Dickinson University Press, 1982.

Wharton, Edith. *The Age of Innocence*. 1920. New York: Penguin, 1985.

A Backward Glance. 1934. London: Century, 1987.

"Beatrice Palmato." Lewis, *Edith Wharton* 544–8.

Ed. *The Book of the Homeless (Le Livre des Sans-Foyer)*. New York: Scribner's, 1916.

"Botticelli's Madonna in The Louvre." *Scribner's Magazine* Jan. 1891: 74.

"Bunner Sisters." *Madame de Treymes and Others: Four Short Novels by Edith Wharton*. Intro. Marilyn French. London: Virago, 1984. 225–314.

The Collected Short Stories of Edith Wharton. Vol 1. New York: Scribner's, 1968. 2 vols.

The Custom of the Country. 1913. New York: Penguin, 1987.

Diary, 1906, ms. Edith Wharton Collection. Beinecke Library, Yale University, New Haven.

"Disintegration," ts. and ms. Edith Wharton Collection. Beinecke Library, Yale University, New Haven.

"Documentation in Fiction," ms. Edith Wharton Collection. Beinecke Library, Yale University, New Haven.

Edith Wharton: The Uncollected Critical Writings. Ed. Frederick Wegener. Princeton: Princeton University Press, 1996.

Ethan Frome. 1911. New York: Macmillan, 1987.

"The Eyes." *"The Muse's Tragedy" and Other Stories*. Ed. Candace Waid. New York: Signet, 1990. 321–41.

Fighting France: From Dunkerque to Belfort. New York: Scribner's, 1915.

French Ways and Their Meaning. 1919. Lee, MA: Berkshire, 1997.

"Friends." *Fifty-Two Stories of Head, Heart, and Hand for Girls*. Ed. Alfred H. Miles. London: Hutchinson, 1905. 193–216.

The Fruit of the Tree. New York: Scribner's, 1907.

"The Fullness of Life." *The Muse's Tragedy and Other Stories*. Ed. Candace Waid. New York: Signet, 1990. 20–31.

The Greater Inclination. New York: Scribner's, 1899.

"The Happy Isles," ts. Edith Wharton Collection. Beinecke Library, Yale University, New Haven.

The Hermit and the Wild Woman. London: Macmillan, 1908.

The House of Mirth. 1905. New York: Penguin, 1985.

"The House of the Dead Hand." *Atlantic Monthly* 94 (1904): 145–60.

In Morocco. 1920. London: Century Hutchinson, 1984.

"The Intruders," ms. Edith Wharton Collection. Beinecke Library, Yale University, New Haven.

Italian Backgrounds. 1905. Hopewell, NJ: Ecco, 1998.

Italian Villas and Their Gardens. 1904. New York: Da Capo, 1976.

Letter to Bernard Berenson. May 19, 1911. Villa I Tatti. Florence.

Letter to Bernard Berenson. Dec. 16, 1911. Villa I Tatti. Florence.

Letter to Bernard Berenson. Jan. 27, [1915]. Villa I Tatti. Florence.

Letter to Bernard Berenson. May 4, 1915. Villa I Tatti. Florence.

Letter to Bernard Berenson. Feb. 10, 1915. Villa I Tatti. Florence.

Letter to Robert Bridges. May 27, [19]15. Scribner's Collection. Firestone Library, Princeton University, Princeton.

Letter to Edward Burlingame. March 12, 1906. Scribner's Collection. Firestone Library, Princeton University, Princeton.

Letter to Edward Burlingame. July 30, 1906. Scribner's Collection. Firestone Library, Princeton University, Princeton.

Letter to Edward Burlingame. March 30, 1907. Scribner's Collection. Firestone Library, Princeton University, Princeton.

Letter to Robert Grant. Aug. 31 [1914]. Edith Wharton Collection. Beinecke Library, Yale University, New Haven.

Letter to Robert Grant. Feb. 13, [19]15. Edith Wharton Collection. Beinecke Library, Yale University, New Haven.

Letter to Sara Norton. June 3, 1901. Edith Wharton Collection. Beinecke Library, Yale University, New Haven.

Letter to Sara Norton. July 15, 1901. Edith Wharton Collection. Beinecke Library, Yale University, New Haven.

Letter to Sara Norton. Nov. 22 [1901]. Edith Wharton Collection. Beinecke Library, Yale University, New Haven.

Letter to Sara Norton. Dec. 29, [1901]. Edith Wharton Collection. Beinecke Library, Yale University, New Haven.

Letter to Sara Norton. Sept. 1, [1902]. Edith Wharton Collection. Beinecke Library, Yale University, New Haven.

Letter to Sara Norton. July 25, 1905. Edith Wharton Collection. Beinecke Library, Yale University, New Haven.

Letter to Sara Norton. Sept. 15, 1905. Edith Wharton Collection. Beinecke Library, Yale University, New Haven.

Letter to Sara Norton. Oct. 26, [1907]. Edith Wharton Collection. Beinecke Library, Yale University, New Haven.

Letter to Sara Norton. Oct. 5, 1908. Edith Wharton Collection. Beinecke Library, Yale University, New Haven.

Letter to Sara Norton. Oct. 19, 1908. Edith Wharton Collection. Beinecke Library, Yale University, New Haven.

Letter to Sara Norton. Oct. 21, 1908. Edith Wharton Collection. Beinecke Library, Yale University, New Haven.

Letter to Sara Norton. Oct. 5, [19]18. Edith Wharton Collection. Beinecke Library, Yale University, New Haven.

Letter to Sara Norton. Oct. 15, [19]18. Edith Wharton Collection. Beinecke Library, Yale University, New Haven.

Letter to Charles Scribner. November 22, 1905. Scribner's Collection. Firestone Library, Princeton University Princeton.

Letter to Charles Scribner. December 18, 1907. Scribner's Collection. Firestone Library, Princeton University Princeton.

Letter to Charles Scribner. Aug. 16, 1916. Scribner's Collection. Firestone Library, Princeton University Princeton.

Letter to John Hugh Smith. March 9, 1910. Edith Wharton Collection. Beinecke Library, Yale University, New Haven.

Letter to Elisina Tyler. Oct. 11 [1914]. Edith Wharton Collection. Lilly Library, Indiana University Bloomington.

Letter to Elisina Tyler. July 29, 1936. Edith Wharton Collection. Lilly Library, Indiana University Bloomington.

The Letters of Edith Wharton. Eds. R. W. B. Lewis and Nancy Lewis. New York: Collier Books, 1988.

"'The Life Apart' (L'ame close)." Unpublished diary, ms. Edith Wharton Collection. Lilly Library, Indiana University Bloomington.

"Mother Earth." Holograph ms. Edith Wharton Collection. Beinecke Library, Yale University New Haven.

The Mother's Recompense. New York: D. Appleton, 1925.

A Motor-Flight through France. 1908. DeKalb: Northern Illinois University Press, 1991.

"My ruling passions." Holograph fragment, ms. Edith Wharton Collection. Lilly Library, Indiana University Bloomington.

"New England." Holograph and ts. Edith Wharton Collection. Beinecke Library, Yale University New Haven.

Old New York. 1924. London: Virago, 1985.

"A Patient Soul." Notebook 2. Edith Wharton Collection. Lilly Library, Indiana University Bloomington.

The Reef. 1912. New York: Penguin, 1994.

Sanctuary. 1903. *Madame de Treymes and Others: Four Short Novels.* London: Virago, 1984. 85–162.

"A Study by Mrs. Wharton of a Woman in Love." *New-York Tribune* Nov. 23, 1912.

"Subjects and Notes 1918–1923." Notebook, ms. Edith Wharton Collection. Beinecke Library, Yale University New Haven.

Summer. 1917. New York: Penguin, 1993.

"Terminus." *Edith Wharton: A Biography.* By R. W. B. Lewis. New York: Fromm International, 1985. 259–60.

Twilight Sleep. New York: Appleton, 1927.

The Valley of Decision. 2 vols. New York: Scribner's, 1902.

The Writing of Fiction. 1925. New York: Scribner's, 1997.

Wharton, Edith, and Ogden Codman, Jr. *The Decoration of Houses.* 1897. New York: Classical America, 1997.

White, Barbara A. "Neglected Areas: Wharton's Short Stories and Incest, Part I." *Edith Wharton Review* 7.1 (1991): 3–12.

"Neglected Areas: Wharton's Short Stories and Incest, Part II." *Edith Wharton Review* 7.2 (1991): 3–10, 32.

White, Shane. *Somewhat More Independent: The End of Slavery in New York City, 1770–1810.* Athens: University of Georgia Press, 1991.

Whittlesey, E. S. *Symbols and Legends in Western Art.* New York: Scribner's, 1972.

Wiebe, Robert H. *The Search for Order, 1877–1920.* New York: Hill and Wang, 1967.

Williams, Sherwood. "The Rise of a New Degeneration: Decadence and Atavism in *Vandover and the Brute*." *ELH* 57 (1990): 709–36.

Williams, Stephen. *Fantastic Archeology: The Wild Side of North American Prehistory*. Philadelphia: University of Pennsylvania Press, 1991.

Williamson, Joel. *New People: Miscegenation and Mulattoes in the United States*. New York: Free Press, 1980.

Wolfe, Cary. "Ezra Pound and the Politics of Patronage." *American Literature* 63 (1991): 26–42.

Wolff, Cynthia Griffin. *A Feast of Words: The Triumph of Edith Wharton*. Oxford: Oxford University Press, 1977.

"Women in Silk and Rags Together Await News – Patricians Weep in Peasants' Arms." *Denver Post* 17 April 1912: 4.

Wood, Joseph S. "'Build, Therefore, Your Own World': The New England Village as Settlement Ideal." *Annals of the Association of American Geographers* 81.1 (1991): 32–50.

Woodberry, George Edward. *The Torch: Eight Lectures on Race Power in Literature Delivered before the Lowell Institute*. 1905. Freeport, ME: Books for Libraries, 1969.

Index

abortion, 145–7, 189
Adams, Brooks, 54
Adams, Henry
    on American society as trying to realize itself, 162
    on "chance collisions of movements," 10, 174
    on democracy and anarchy, 10
    on entropy and social decline, 54
    Lily Bart compared to the Virgin in work of, 58
    on modern inventions, 64
    and myth of Nordic economic innocence, 94
    on "race suicide," 3
    on specialization and degradation, 44
    the *Titanic* disaster, 83
Addams, Jane, 151
aestheticism, 44, 163, 192
African Americans
    American ambivalence about, 8
    blackness, 9, 40
    mulatto servants in Wharton's fiction, 145
    national hysteria about race, 9
    and New England villages, 122, 135
    the New Negro, 170
    one-drop rule, 41
    photographs of light-skinned, 9
    self-definition and race for, 41
    slavery in New York City, 166
agency
    aura, 78
    authorial, 46, 82
    euthanasia and relinquishing of, 74
    in *The Fruit of the Tree*, 5, 63, 64, 77–9
    market economy and, 178
    medical technology and, 78
    of nurses, 176
    in *The Reef*, 91
    in twentieth-century psychiatry, 174
Age of Innocence, The (Wharton), 153, 192
    Archer and Ellen's relationship, 153

Archer's fundamental misconception of his wife, 161
    authenticity as preoccupation of, 153, 158, 161
    Cesnola artifacts reflect Archer and Ellen's relationship, 158
    and controversy over Cesnola artifacts, 158–61
    cultural extinction as preoccupation of, 154
    Ellen Olenska as "dark heroine" of, 40
    inevitability of elite defeat in, 6
    innocence in, 161–2
    lovers' rendezvous in Metropolitan Museum, 6, 153–4
    May's pregnancy, 158, 161
    on New York as hieroglyphic world, 34, 153
    New York compared with ancient civilizations in, 155, 157
    opening sequence at Academy of Music, 161
    reader at two removes from the story, 155
    Wharton and May Welland compared, 1
    and Wharton's central dilemma, 34
Akeley, Carl, 5, 46, 47, 56
Alexander, Ruth M., 178
American Hostels for Refugees, 116, 146
American Humane Association, 74
American Indians. *See* Native Americans
American Language, The (Mencken), 27
Ammons, Elizabeth, 39, 53, 60, 167, 182
Anderson, Harriet, 69
Anderson, Margaret Steele, 180
Anderson, Thomas F., 127
anesthesia, 164
"Angel at the Grave, The" (Wharton), 3
antiquarianism, 53, 129
apathy, 11, 164
Appleton, William Sumner, 124, 126
architecture
    American versus French, 17
    historic preservation, 124, 126
    landscape architecture, 169
    ornament, 32, 170, 172
    overly restored, 156

214

on Parisian *salon*, 172
on race and artistic unity, 172
on real country, 120
on Wharton's motor-car, 172
Mound Builders, 23–4
Mount, the (Lenox, Massachusetts), 112, 119–21, 184, 187
Mrs. Dalloway (Woolf), 33
"Mrs. Lloyd" (Reynolds), 47, 50, 51
Munich, Adrienne Auslander, 183
"Muse's Tragedy, The" (Wharton), 3
museums
    Lily Bart as museum piece, 53, 56, 58
    National Gallery in London, 157
    Wharton on democratization of, 155, 173
    Wharton on turning old houses into, 173, 190
    see also Metropolitan Museum of Art
Mussolini, Benito, 163
Myers, John L., 154

National Gallery (London), 157
Native Americans
    American ambivalence about, 8, 168
    authenticity associated with, 19, 20
    break of continuity in, 23
    Cushing's fieldwork with, 20
    in *The Custom of the Country*, 17, 19, 20, 21, 26
    Ishi, 18
    as living relics, 20
    Mound Builders, 23–4
    playing Indian, 4, 19, 20, 21, 26
nativism, 54, 55, 56, 170
Nelson, Dana D., 19, 162, 167
Nemerov, Alex, 19
New England
    decline of, 123–5
    diversity of seventeenth-century, 185
    farms of, 124, 185
    Lenox, Massachusetts, 121, 130
    Newport, Rhode Island, 124
    New York's upper classes and, 149
    provincialism of, 124
    as tourist destination, 125–8, 135, 185
    villages of, 121–3
"New England" (Wharton), 130
New England Society (Chicago), 122
New England Society of Cincinnati, 150
Newfield, Christopher, 167
New Hampshire "Old Home Week," 126–8
New Negro, 170
Newport (Rhode Island), 124
New Woman, 87, 178
noblesse oblige, 150
Northern Securities Company, 68
Norton, Charles Eliot, 14, 43, 54, 74–5, 77, 177

Norton, Sara (Sally)
    father's death, 76
    Wharton's letters to, 68, 76, 92, 96, 100, 102, 113, 120, 122, 123, 167, 184
    Wharton visits summer home of, 186
novel, the, 29
nursing, 69, 176
Nutting, Wallace, 124, 170

"Old Home Week," 126–8, 138–9, 185
Old New York (Wharton), 191
Olmsted, Frederick Law, 120, 184
one-drop rule, 41
"On Mercy" (Seneca), 181
Oppenheim, John, 150
originality, 32–3, 35
Orvell, Miles, 9
Otis, Laura, 37
Our Country (Strong), 63
Outlaw, Lucius, 41, 171
overcrowding, 175

pain, social efficacy of, 92–3, 180
panic of 1907, 62–3
Paolo and Francesca (Phillips), 129
Paradise Lost (Milton), 61
Parkhurst, Charles H., 84
Parks, Leighton, 85
Parrington, Vernon L., 1
Pascoe, Peggy, 41
"Paste" (James), 50
Payelle, Georges, 146
Petchesky, Rosalind Pollack, 189
Pfeiffer, Kathleen, 182
philanthropy, 150–1, 190
Phillips, Forbes, 37
Phillips, Stephen, 129
photography, nineteenth-century uncertainty about, 9
Physician's Hand, The: Work Culture and Conflict in American Nursing (Melosh), 176
Pinkhof, H., 74
Pittenger, Mark, 94
Plessy v. Ferguson (1896), 170
"Portrait, The" (Wharton), 3
Portrait of a Lady, The (James), 103
Posnock, Ross, 101
Pound, Ezra, 1, 3
Powell, John Wesley, 24
pragmatism, 100
    in *The Reef*, 6, 99–106
    as tough-minded, 180
    Wharton on, 100–1, 105
"Pretext, The" (Wharton), 10
Price, Alan, 183

For EU product safety concerns, contact us at Calle de José Abascal, 56–1°, 28003 Madrid, Spain or eugpsr@cambridge.org.

www.ingramcontent.com/pod-product-compliance
Ingram Content Group UK Ltd.
Pitfield, Milton Keynes, MK11 3LW, UK
UKHW010042140625
459647UK00012BA/1553